# A PASSION FOR SERVICE:

## The Story Of

# ARAMARK

# A PASSION FOR SERVICE:
## The Story Of
# ARAMARK

## Jeffrey L. Rodengen

Edited by Stanimira Stefanova
Design and layout by Elijah Meyer and Sandy Cruz

Write Stuff Enterprises, Inc.
1001 South Andrews Avenue
Fort Lauderdale, FL 33316
**1-800-900-Book** (1-800-900-2665)
(954) 462-6657
www.writestuffbooks.com

The publisher has made every effort to identify and locate the source of the photographs included in this edition of *A Passion for Service: The Story of ARAMARK.* Grateful acknowledgment is made to those who have kindly granted permission for the use of their materials in this edition. If there are instances where proper credit was not given, the publisher will gladly make any necessary corrections in subsequent printings.

**Publisher's Cataloging in Publication Data**
*(Prepared by The Donohue Group, Inc.)*

Rodengen, Jeffrey L.
   A passion for service : the story of ARAMARK / Jeffrey L. Rodengen ; edited by Stanimira Stefanova ; design and layout by Elijah Meyer and Sandy Cruz ; [foreword by Donald M. Kendall].

   p. : ill. ; cm.

   Includes index.
   ISBN-13: 978-1-932022-20-9
   ISBN-10: 1-932022-20-1

   1. ARAMARK Corporation—History.  2. Food service management—United States—History—20th century.  3. Uniforms industry—United States—History—20th century.  4. Facility management—United States—History—20th century.
   I. Stefanova, Stanimira.  II. Meyer, Elijah.
   III. Cruz, Sandy.  IV. Kendall, Donald M.
   V. Title.  VI. Title: ARAMARK.

   TX911.3.M27 R63 2007        647.95/068
                               2006938184

Completely produced in the
United States of America

10 9 8 7 6 5 4 3 2 1

## Also by Jeffrey L. Rodengen

*The Legend of Chris-Craft*

*IRON FIST:*
*The Lives of Carl Kiekhaefer*

*Evinrude-Johnson and*
*The Legend of OMC*

*Serving the Silent Service:*
*The Legend of Electric Boat*

*The Legend of Dr Pepper/Seven-Up*

*The Legend of Honeywell*

*The Legend of Briggs & Stratton*

*The Legend of Ingersoll-Rand*

*The Legend of Stanley:*
*150 Years of The Stanley Works*

*The MicroAge Way*

*The Legend of Halliburton*

*The Legend of York International*

*The Legend of Nucor Corporation*

*The Legend of Goodyear:*
*The First 100 Years*

*The Legend of AMP*

*The Legend of Cessna*

*The Legend of VF Corporation*

*The Spirit of AMD*

*The Legend of Rowan*

*New Horizons:*
*The Story of Ashland Inc.*

*The History of American Standard*

*The Legend of Mercury Marine*

*The Legend of Federal-Mogul*

*Against the Odds:*
*Inter-Tel—The First 30 Years*

*The Legend of Pfizer*

*State of the Heart: The Practical Guide*
*to Your Heart and Heart Surgery*
*with Larry W. Stephenson, M.D.*

*The Legend of Worthington Industries*

*The Legend of IBP*

*The Legend of Trinity Industries, Inc.*

*The Legend of*
*Cornelius Vanderbilt Whitney*

*The Legend of Amdahl*

*The Legend of Litton Industries*

*The Legend of Gulfstream*

*The Legend of Bertram*
*with David A. Patten*

*The Legend of Ritchie Bros. Auctioneers*

*The Legend of ALLTEL*
*with David A. Patten*

*The Yes, you can do Invacare Corporation*
*with Anthony L. Wall*

*The Ship in the Balloon:*
*The Story of Boston Scientific and the*
*Development of Less-Invasive Medicine*

*The Legend of Day & Zimmermann*

*The Legend of Noble Drilling*

*Fifty Years of Innovation: Kulicke & Soffa*

*Biomet—From Warsaw to the World*
*with Richard F. Hubbard*

*NRA: An American Legend*

*The Heritage and Values of RPM, Inc.*

*The Marmon Group: The First Fifty Years*

*The Legend of Grainger*

*The Legend of The Titan Corporation*
*with Richard F. Hubbard*

*The Legend of Discount Tire Co.*
*with Richard F. Hubbard*

*The Legend of Polaris*
*with Richard F. Hubbard*

*The Legend of La-Z-Boy*
*with Richard F. Hubbard*

*The Legend of McCarthy*
*with Richard F. Hubbard*

*Intervoice: Twenty Years of Innovation*
*with Richard F. Hubbard*

*Jefferson-Pilot Financial:*
*A Century of Excellence*
*with Richard F. Hubbard*

*The Legend of HCA*

*The Legend of Werner Enterprises*
*with Richard F. Hubbard*

*The History of J. F. Shea Co.*
*with Richard F. Hubbard*

*True to Our Vision*
*with Richard F. Hubbard*

*The Legend of Albert Trostel & Sons*
*with Richard F. Hubbard*

*The Legend of Sovereign Bancorp*
*with Richard F. Hubbard*

*Innovation is the Best Medicine:*
*The extraordinary story of Datascope*
*with Richard F. Hubbard*

*The Legend of Guardian Industries*

*The Legend of*
*Universal Forest Products*

*Changing the World: Polytechnic*
*University—The First 150 Years*

*Nothing is Impossible: The Legend*
*of Joe Hardy and 84 Lumber*

*In it for the Long Haul:*
*The Story of CRST*

*The Story of Parsons Corporation*

*Cerner: From Vision to Value*

*New Horizons:*
*The Story of Federated Investors*

*Office Depot: Taking Care of Business—*
*The First 20 Years*

*The Legend of General Parts:*
*Proudly Serving a World in Motion*

*Bard: Power of the Past,*
*Force of the Future*

*Innovation & Integrity:*
*The Story of Hub Group*

*Amica: A Century of Service*
*1907–2007*

# TABLE OF CONTENTS

# FOREWORD

BY

## DONALD M. KENDALL

COFOUNDER, FORMER CHAIRMAN, AND CEO

### PEPSICO

SERVICE IS THE MOST important word in the ARAMARK vocabulary. It has long been true in nearly every industry that even if you can provide the best products and prices to your customers, it is ultimately the service that will keep them coming back. Service is more than a delivery date and a price point. These categories take good organizational skills, but don't require extraordinary abilities. The key to building and retaining a strong stable of customers is to exceed their expectations, anticipate their needs, understand their business, and consistently identify products and services that will allow them to efficiently succeed in their own operations. And, if you can provide that kind of service with passion, you will develop relationships that last for generations. That is just what ARAMARK has done.

I wish I could take some credit for the passion for service that ARAMARK Chairman and CEO Joe Neubauer exudes, which continually energizes his entire organization. Joe joined PepsiCo in 1971 as our treasurer when he was in his late twenties. Having earned an MBA from the University of Chicago, one of my favorite schools, Joe was already bursting with

passion when we hired him. In those days, PepsiCo was good at marketing, but our financial acumen was slightly lacking. Joe did an excellent job and had a wonderful ability with people. He was remarkable for his skills at encouraging, developing, and mentoring talent. He was also a great salesman because he always did his homework before presenting his arguments. We wanted him to gain some operating experience, so we gave Joe the challenge of our Wilson Sporting Goods business. He did a superb job, and even though we eventually divested Wilson to concentrate on our core markets, Joe contributed greatly to its success.

ARAMARK has consistently demonstrated the courage and confidence to acquire businesses that complement its wide customer base. It has a reputation as a fair and nurturing parent, allowing its divisions to grow and accelerate along well-defined strategic business plans. I know something about the challenges of being a pioneer. I established the first U.S./Soviet Trade and Economic Council to stimulate trade with the Soviet Union. PepsiCo was the first American soft drink company to enter that vast and enigmatic nation. We also brought Pepsi,

KFC, and Pizza Hut to China, long before trade with that country was common. As ARAMARK continues to grow, the diversification it has engineered and acquired will prove a substantial asset and an engine for growth in the decades to follow.

ARAMARK has recently been the beneficiary of one of the largest management buyouts in American history. It is a testament to the culture of shared responsibility and shared rewards that have allowed ARAMARK to attract and retain more than 240,000 talented employees and to service high profile customers within four major business categories in almost every corner of the globe. When I delivered a lecture to students at the Harvard School of Business, I told them that if you are excited to show up at work in the morning, and if you are truly passionate about the products and services you provide your customers, then you will be successful no matter what your field of business.

ARAMARK has always been and will remain successful because it is truly passionate about pleasing its customers and delivering innovative solutions to solve any challenges. It has an unlimited passion for service, and that is a formula for success in any enterprise.

# ACKNOWLEDGMENTS

MANY PEOPLE ASSISTED in the research, preparation, and publication of *A Passion for Service: The Story of ARAMARK.* The development of historical timelines and a large portion of the principal archival research was accomplished by research assistants Margaret O. Kirk and Susan Shelly. Their thorough and careful work made it possible to publish a great deal of interesting information on the origins and evolution of this unique company.

The research and writing of the book would have been impossible without the dedicated assistance of ARAMARK executives and employees. Principal among these is Justin Coffin, manager of internal communications, whose affable guidance made it possible for our research team to locate and identify records and individuals crucial to the ARAMARK legacy.

All of the people interviewed—whether current employees or retirees—were generous with their time and insights. Those who shared their memories and thoughts include Beth Arthur, John Babiarz, Mary Jo Becker, Harry Belinger, David Blackwood, Robert Callander, Bob Carpenter, Zelda Casanova, Bobbi Chaville, Ira Cohn, Tim Cost, Samuel Coxs, Jack Curtin, Ronald Davenport, Harold Davidson, Harold Dichter, Jack Donovan, Lee Driscoll, Steve Duffy, Owen Edmonston, Jamie Grant, Alan Griffith, Chris Gutek, Chris Hackem, Mike Hennessey, Jim Hodgson, Chris Holland, Bill Holmes, Donna Irvin, Hisato Ishida, Hiroshi Ito, Dan Jameson, Donald Kendall, Andrew Kerin, Rory Loberg, Laurel Lutz, John (Jack) J. Lynch, Andrew W. Main, Chris Malone, Lynn McKee, Drayton McLane, Frank Mendicino, Thomas Michel, Gerson and John Miller, Norman Miller, Gene Morris, Joseph Neubauer, John Orobono, Hirosuke Osada, Jane Pepper, Barrett Pickett, James E. Preston, Sean Rooney, David Roselle, Ravi Saligram, Martin Spector, Fred Sutherland, Joan Voli, Tom Vozzo, Jeff Wheatley, Marty Welch, Todd Wohler, and Richard Wyckoff.

Finally, special thanks are extended to the dedicated staff at Write Stuff Enterprises, Inc., who worked on the book. Thanks are due to Stanimira Stefanova, executive editor; Ann Gossy, Heather Lewin, and Elizabeth Fernandez, senior editors; Sandy Cruz, vice president/creative director; Elijah

Meyer and Ryan Milewicz, graphic designers; Roy Adelman, on-press supervisor; Abigail Hollister, proofreader; Mary Aaron, transcriptionist; Christine Michaud, indexer; Amy Major, executive assistant to Jeffrey L. Rodengen; Marianne Roberts, executive vice president, publisher, and chief financial officer; Steven Stahl, director of marketing; and Sherry Pawlirzyn–Hasso, bookkeeper.

Davre Davidson, who founded a small company that would one day become ARAMARK Corporation, is pictured here when he graduated from high school in California in 1929. Within two years, his father would die, and young Davre would step up to take over the family's already floundering clothing store.

## CHAPTER ONE

# KINDRED SPIRITS

## 1936–1949

*One had to be a committed optimist to consider opening a business in the depths of the Depression.*

—Davre Davidson, 80th birthday remarks,
October 1991

**D**AVRE JACOB DAVIDSON WAS just one of millions of Americans in 1936 reeling from the effects of the Great Depression. Although some economic recovery was under way, consumer confidence was low, and unemployment was running at about 17 percent. Many businesses that had remained open through the worst of the Depression were still in danger of failing.

Despite his best efforts following his father's untimely death in 1931, Davre was unable to keep his family's floundering clothing store afloat, according to Harold Davidson, Davre's son:

*It was a men's clothing store at Fifth and Beacon Streets in San Pedro, California. It just couldn't pay its bills. The Depression was full scale, and it was very, very difficult. So my father had to close the store in 1935 and went to work as a busboy in a Los Angeles hotel.*[1]

But Davre's legacy was not that of a busboy, and at age 25, he started a business that eventually would transform the service industry. With $400 of borrowed capital and a sense of optimism that the country's economic situation would somehow improve, Davre purchased 50 penny peanut-vending machines, which he installed in non-workplace locations, such as drugstores and bowling alleys. He described the beginnings of the business:

*I'll never forget the payments on that loan—$11.30 a week. This was launching a business on the proverbial shoestring.*[2]

Davre hoped to make $1 to $1.50 a week on each machine, which he calculated would provide enough money to buy more peanuts, make payments on his loan, and support himself.

At that time, he never imagined that D. J. Davidson, the one-man company he ran from the 1932 Dodge that served as both his office and warehouse, would provide the foundation for what would grow into the nation's premier professional services company. That dream would come much later.

### A Brief History of Vending

Davre Davidson entered the vending machine industry in the 1930s, more than 2,000 years after its birth.

---

Davre Davidson began his fledgling company, D. J. Davidson, in 1936. During the Great Depression, he installed peanut-vending machines in locations with high customer traffic—restaurants, bowling alleys, outside drugstores, and other public areas. Employees recall that Davidson kept a red vending machine with a glass globe on his desk, one of the company's early models.

Vending machines are believed to have been invented shortly before 215 B.C., the year Egyptian mathematician Hero produced a book titled, *Pneumatika*. In it, he described and illustrated a coin-activated machine that accepted 5 *drachmas* (equal in modern money to about 75 cents) to dispense holy water in Egyptian temples.[3]

An inserted coin would fall on a seesaw device, briefly raising a lid in the machine and dispensing holy water through a tube. Approximately 15 minutes after the distribution of the vending machine, the slug was invented for those who would risk plague and misfortune to get free holy water.[4]

Commercial, coin-operated machines—closer to the modern idea of vending—were first seen in 1615 in English inns and taverns, where patrons could deposit coins and receive a pinch of snuff or enough tobacco to fill a pipe.[5]

London in the early 1880s saw the arrival of machines designed to dispense postcards. Soon after, a British publisher and bookstore owner designed a vending machine for books.[6]

The first commercial vending machines in the United States are believed to have been introduced in the late 1880s in New York City by the Thomas Adams Gum Company. Those machines were located on elevated train platforms and stocked with a product called Tutti-Frutti gum. Cigars, stamps, peanuts, animated figures, and other products followed as the vending industry became more sophisticated.[7]

In Philadelphia, Horn & Hardart opened its first Automat eatery in 1902 to serve an affordable variety of cooked and prepared dishes. Customers would insert a few coins and twist a knob, and then a glass hatch would open based on the diner's selection. The Horn & Hardart self-service cafés quickly became a fixture of popular culture.[8]

In the early 1920s, the first automatic vending machines started dispensing sodas into cups, while the first cigarette vending machine appeared in 1926. When Davre entered the vending business in 1936, vending machines were fixtures in movie theaters, bowling alleys, amusement parks, and drugstores. Unfortunately, the technology of the machines had not been fully developed yet, and machines often malfunctioned. Coins deposited would dispense no products, soda cups would fill to overflowing, and frustrated patrons would sometimes kick, hit, and swear at the machines.

But the vending industry was working hard to gain respect. Davre bought his first vending

**1936**
Davre Davidson buys 50 penny peanut-vending machines and installs them in high-traffic areas such as pharmacies and bowling alleys.

**1939**
Davre marries Charlotte Sheffer, who would become a true partner in all aspects of his life. *(Photo courtesy of Celia Davidson Farkas.)*

**1937**
Davre receives a contract to install vending machines in the Douglas Aircraft Company's Santa Monica, California, plant. The machines are an immediate success and lead to contracts with additional factories.

**1939**
Davre's younger brother Henry joins the business, and the company's name is changed to Davidson Brothers.

machines in 1936, and that same year, the National Automatic Merchandising Association (NAMA) was founded in Chicago to give the industry a name and represent its interests. The membership of the national trade association of food and refreshment vending was, and still is, made up of service companies, equipment manufacturers, and suppliers of products and services to operating service companies. Through the years, NAMA has become a powerful voice for the vending industry, promoting it to legislators as well as to the general public.[9]

Vending machines did not become common in workplaces until World War II, when employers began to embrace the idea that employees could be more productive if they had quick access to snacks and beverages. Also, workers at that time became enthusiastic about the concept of a coffee break. Suddenly, the once-disparaged machines had become central to production, popular among workers, and indispensable to employers. As such, they could be seen as a sound basis for a business.

### Charlotte Sheffer: Davidson's Future Partner

As American business began to catch on to Davre's idea of vending machines in the work-

place, he would soon have a partner to help him meet the demand. Around the time Davre was buying his first vending machines, he met a dynamic young woman named Charlotte Sheffer, who had recently moved to California from Millville, New Jersey. While Davre was immediately captivated by the warm, witty, insightful woman—and she by him—he was determined to get his business started and earn some money before they married.

Vending machines were usually found in places where people gathered, but not where they worked. Davre, however, had heard about a Harvard University study conducted in the mid-1930s that concluded workers were more productive when they had access to foods that helped them maintain a high level of energy.

When he heard that the Douglas Aircraft Company's Santa Monica plant had opened an employee welfare department, he jumped at the chance to meet with the department head, J. L. Stevenson, and, using the study results, persuaded him to allow Davre to install some machines in the plant. "That was really his first big industrial break," said Harold Davidson, Davre's son.[10] Many years later, during a 1994 interview,

**1942**
Introduced by a mutual contact from Douglas Aircraft, Davre Davidson (left) meets William Fishman (right) from Chicago, and the two men establish an immediate rapport.

**1949**
The Davidson brothers' company is poised for growth as the decade nears an end. This was also true for the Automatic Sales Company, a Chicago-based firm co-owned by Fishman.

**1945**
Davidson Brothers grows to become one of the largest vending companies in Southern California.

# DAVRE DAVIDSON

**B**ORN IN 1911 IN PORTLAND, OREGON, Davre Jacob Davidson was the middle child of Abraham and Celia Davidson. His first name, pronounced "dave-ree," is a combination of the names of his maternal grandparents, David and Rebecca.

The family left Portland when Davre was 3 years old, eventually settling in Duluth, Minnesota. They lived there until Davre was 14 and then moved to California. Davre would live there for the rest of his life.

Education was very important in the Davidson home. Although Abraham had no formal education, Davre called his father "perhaps the best-read man I ever knew." His mother, a teacher, was one of just three women to graduate from the University of Utah in 1906.[1]

Davre's own education, however, was cut short. In 1931, having finished one year at Long Beach State, he intended to transfer to the University of Southern California in Los Angeles.

Just days before he was to go, his father, only 50 years old, suddenly died.

With an older sister, Eleanor, and a younger brother, Henry, who was still in high school, Davre took his father's place at the family's small clothing store in San Pedro. He ran the store for four years, until it was forced to close.

In 1936, Davre began his fledgling business. In 1939, he married Charlotte Sheffer, with whom he shared his life and work for almost 56 years. Charlotte raised their two children, Harold and Celia, and worked side-by-side with her husband. She provided unflagging support and encouragement and proved integral to the business by assisting Davre in all aspects of his endeavor. It was support Davre would need. He recalled:

*When I started the predecessor company of ARA in 1936, my aspirations were truly modest. I guess they were founded on the basis that I wanted to eat, because those were really rough days. After all, one had to be a committed optimist to consider opening a business in the depth of the Depression.*[2]

Davre possessed many special qualities—drive, energy, focus—that would enable him to remain successful during those tough Depression years when so many others were unable to move ahead. According to his son, one of Davre's most important qualities was vision. "My father was very intuitive," said Harold. "He could see the trends before other people could. He was a great visionary."[3]

Young Davre stands next to the 1932 Dodge that served as his first office and warehouse. He stored his inventory in the trunk and recorded transactions from the front seat. This photo has become an icon in the history of ARAMARK Corporation.

Davre recalled the Douglas Aircraft opportunity as a stroke of luck:

*Luck plays a good part in any business. I had the good fortune within the first year of my little peanut [vending] business of being permitted to put a few peanut machines in ... Douglas Aircraft Company.*[11]

Davre knew the workplace venture would be successful that first morning:

*I'll tell you when I knew I had a business. We used to put peanut machines out and go back and see them in a week. I put three sets of peanut machines in the ... Douglas Aircraft Company in the morning. And that afternoon, I got a call from a welfare manager who said the machines were empty. Then I knew I had a business.*[12]

Above: A photo of Charlotte Davidson (née Sheffer), taken around 1939. Charlotte met Davre after moving from New Jersey to California. The two were introduced through family members. *(Photo courtesy of Celia Davidson Farkas.)*

Right: Peanuts, gum, candy bars, and cigarettes made up Davre Davidson's inventory in 1939. By then, he had obtained contracts with the Vultee and Northrop aircraft plants in addition to Douglas, his original workplace account, and was about to launch his company on a period of expansion during World War II.

Apparently, the vending machines Davre had installed at the Douglas Aircraft Company seemed to intrigue people at the plant, including executives. In the book *Business Decisions That Changed Our Lives*, Davre recounts an episode in which a distinguished-looking individual wearing a yacht cap noticed that Davre was having some trouble with a new vending unit recently installed at the Douglas plant. The gentleman offered to help him repair the unit. Davre later learned that his assistant that day had been one of Douglas' senior executives.[13]

While his business was off to a good start, Davre still encountered issues as he attempted to expand his operations, not the least of which, he said, was a negative attitude among some managers:

*We had some interesting problems in those days, not the least of which was the acceptance of vending machines by management. At first, we had great difficulty in convincing management*

# CHARLOTTE DAVIDSON

FROM THE FIRST MOMENT THEY MET, Charlotte Sheffer Davidson was the inspiration for her husband Davre Davidson's work, and, in many ways, his life.

Charlotte, born the youngest of six children, lived in Millville, New Jersey, until the age of 20. She then moved to Los Angeles and took a job selling clothes in the basement of May Company. Through family, she met Davre Davidson, and the two quickly became a couple. They waited three years to marry, however, as Davre was determined to get his business up and running so he could support a wife and family.

Once they married, Charlotte became instrumental to the business. As her husband's first employee, she was also his sounding board, a constant source of valuable advice and encouragement, and his staunchest supporter. She kept the books, provided advice to her husband on handling various business activities, and offered support when he became discouraged. Charlotte was, in effect, Davre's first real business partner. She was there before Bill Fishman and even before Davre's brother Henry. Davre's son, Harold, described those early days:

*My mother and father lived in a one-bedroom apartment in Beverly Hills. My mother used to sack peanuts in the living room. My father used the trunk of his Dodge as his warehouse. He used to service machines out of his trunk. That's how they got started.*[1]

In addition to sacking peanuts, Davre and Charlotte recorded their company's sales at the kitchen table of their small apartment. They shared ideas and dreams, and celebrated together as the business grew and prospered.

While Charlotte tended to the couple's two children, Harold and Celia, she also found time to accompany her husband on many of his business trips, sometimes bringing the children. She was a very smart and highly effective businesswoman who played a key role in the creation of her husband's company.

Her important contributions in the early business were widely recognized and acknowledged. In fact, in 1994, when actors dramatized the history of the company at a series of meetings of ARAMARK managers, Charlotte's character played a major role in the production, which was called *Dreamers and Doers*.[2]

Warm, witty, and elegant, Charlotte Davidson helped inspire Davre Davidson to make his business a success. She enthusiastically jumped in during the early days to assist her husband Davre with work tasks, including sacking peanuts at the kitchen table. *(Photo courtesy of Celia Davidson Farkas.)*

The Douglas Aircraft Company was Davre Davidson's first workplace account and the one he credited with launching his business.

*that vending machines were in their interest. They would say, "No, these machines take up valuable space. They're a corridor hazard. They just take employees' time from their jobs, encourage loitering, and they're a big housekeeping problem." Based on the state of the vending art at that time, there was more than a bit of truth in the complaint about housekeeping problems.*[14]

In addition to these objections, the vending machines in those early days were prone to malfunction and required regular service. Davre described a machine one manufacturer claimed would not break down:

*One year a manufacturer came out with a multiple-flavor cold drink machine that was absolutely, positively guaranteed not to spill over or "run wild." When told this, one of our maintenance men said, "Fine, but when it does run wild, which flavor is it likely to pour?"*[15]

In addition to a high rate of breakdown, the early vending machines were also susceptible to tampering by workers in the plants, according to Davre:

*Vending machines were so vulnerable in those days that any mechanic could tear them apart or break into them. Bear in mind that most of our machines were in factories where everybody was a mechanic. ... We had machines broken into, and we would try to combat the problem with all types of protective devices, but they didn't work too well.*

*One day, in desperation and total frustration, I left 200 5-cent Hershey bars alongside one of our machines that had been repeatedly broken into and robbed. I came back the next day. All the candy bars were gone—and in the box was a $10 bill. The workers were telling me they weren't going to cheat me; they were just having a little fun with a machine. That experiment ... introduced the "Honor Snack" concept, which is in widespread use today.*[16]

**New Partners and a Growing Business**

After saving a few dollars, Davre began growing his business by adding other machines, including ones that dispensed candy and cigarettes. By 1939, his business had expanded enough that Davre was able to hire his first employee, his wife.

Charlotte and Davre married in May 1939 and would spend nearly 56 years as true partners. Davre would say that marrying Charlotte had been the secret to all his success.[17]

Meanwhile, Davre's younger brother, Henry, had recognized the potential of the business and joined as a partner. Renamed Davidson Brothers, the business was poised for significant growth.

Capitalizing on its success at the Douglas Aircraft plant, Davidson Brothers negotiated contracts to install machines at other aircraft plants, including Vultee, Northrop, and Lockheed. Employers were delighted to have the machines on site. Between 1939 and the beginning of America's involvement in World War II, Davre and Henry invested in additional machines and increased their inventories.

**The Davidsons' Secret to Success**

The Davidsons were known for being forthright and trustworthy—characteristics not always associated with those in the vending business. They also built their reputation by offering reliable and personalized service. Jim Hodgson, then head of the personnel department at the former Lockheed Aircraft Company (now Lockheed Martin) who became an ARAMARK Board member in 1977, explained Davre and Henry's belief that it was vital to supply the best service possible:

Henry Davidson, Davre's younger brother, was an integral part of the early business, joining as a partner in 1939. He rejoined the business after serving in World War II and remained involved until the 1960s, when he retired for health reasons. Davre was quick to praise his brother's role in growing the company, saying that Henry worked extremely well with customers and was a smart and intuitive individual.

*They were there to serve. That meant they didn't insist on putting equipment wherever they wanted. They worked with us to put it in the most strategic places that would be most accessible from an employee standpoint, and most out of the way from a production standpoint. I would say this concept of service—and it's all built around service, working with the customer served—was, right [at] the start, Davre Davidson's hallmark.*[18]

As their reputation for service and reliability spread, more contracts poured in, and the future looked bright for the young company.

World War II, however, brought changes to all sectors of the United States, including the vending industry and Davidson Brothers. While Henry left to serve his country, Davre, who did not qualify to serve in the Army for medical reasons, continued to run the business.

### Keeping Rosie at the Riveter

As the wartime economy brought more and more workers into America's mills and factories, the demand for on-site vending increased dramatically. The unemployment that had plagued the country throughout the Depression years ended and was replaced by worker shortages in many areas. Women and teenagers stepped up to take the places of the men who had gone to fight, working long hours to produce goods necessary to support America's war efforts.

While employers had previously balked at installing vending machines in their factories, they were now clamoring for the devices, aiming to keep workers satisfied and productive. Refreshment and rest periods were becoming a more accepted standard within the industry. At the same time, the faster pace of production required during World War II meant that vending machines represented the best option for workers to get snacks quickly during their busy workdays.[19]

While the increased demand for vending machines was good news for Davidson Brothers, the challenge was that these machines—and food to fill them—were in short supply. Rationing of goods such as coffee and sugar made it difficult to find enough product to fill the machines already in these workplaces. And, because all metal was conscripted for military purposes, no new vending machines could be manufactured.

While other vending companies failed, however, Davre used his keen business acumen to keep Davidson Brothers afloat.

### Hitting the Road

Traveling by train, Davre crisscrossed the country, visiting suppliers and persuading them to sell their product to Davidson Brothers. While on the road, he also purchased the machines of small vending companies that had gone out of business.

Although he couldn't always acquire the items he wanted to fill the machines, Davre developed relationships with suppliers to ensure the company always had attractive items to offer:

*Because the country was rationing commodities during the war, we sold whatever we could get our hands on—gum, candy, or cigarettes.*

*We would package raisins, cookies, pine nuts—anything to put into the machines to give workers something to eat and some way of breaking the monotony of the job. We really had little choice in what we sold. We sold what the market produced and the government allowed.*[20]

**On a Parallel Path**

While Davre worked to build and expand Davidson Brothers, a young man in Chicago was also making a name for himself in the vending industry. William S. Fishman arrived in vending on a different path from Davre's, but traveled a similar road as he established and built his company.

During his college years, Bill Fishman worked for his father-in-law's business—A. Silvian Tobacco

The staff of Davidson Brothers poses outside the company headquarters at 5109 West Pico Boulevard in Los Angeles in 1945. Davre stands at far left. At far right is John Lumpp, corporate secretary. By the end of World War II, Davidson Brothers was one of the largest vending operations on the West Coast.

# BILL FISHMAN

WILLIAM S. FISHMAN WAS BORN IN 1916 in Clinton, Indiana. His parents, both immigrants to the United States from Central Europe, named him Wolf Samuel Fishman, after his paternal grandfather. When Fishman entered school, however, his teachers doubted the boy who called himself "Wolf," so his mother decided to change his name to William. Although he never legally changed it, Fishman became known as William, or Bill, to everyone who knew him.

Fishman's family moved to Princeton, Indiana, where he went to high school. Later in life, Fishman would joke that his "Princeton background" enabled him to fit in with the Ivy League types he encountered upon moving to Philadelphia.

Fishman grew up working in his father's scrap materials and furniture businesses, doing office work until he was old enough to drive. He later made deliveries in the store's truck.

Bright and articulate, Fishman yearned to attend college. He was accepted at the University of Illinois, where he served as captain of the

Bill Fishman's newly organized company, Automatic Sales Company, serviced the Douglas Aircraft plant in Chicago. It was the firm's entrée into the vending industry. The machines at the Douglas plant sold Coca-Cola, orange drinks, and root beer. In addition to paying the bills and keeping the books for Automatic Sales, Fishman also ensured the company's vending machines were regularly serviced.

_____

debate team and played in the band. He finished in the top 1 percent of his class and earned the distinction of membership in the Phi Beta Kappa honor society. While participating in extracurricular activities and studying, Fishman paid for his education by working while in school.

The father of Fishman's future wife, Clara, owned the A. Silvian Tobacco Company, a large and profitable wholesale candy and tobacco distributorship in Chicago. Fishman and his future father-in-law worked out a deal in which Fishman sold Silvian products to shops on the University of Illinois campus. Fishman's business finesse

Company—selling tobacco and candy to campus shops, but his long-term goals focused on earning a master's degree and eventually becoming a college professor. When his father-in-law died unexpectedly the same year Fishman graduated from college, Fishman teamed up with another son-in-law to take over the company. He soon realized, however, that he was not interested in the wholesale business, so he began making plans to branch out into the vending industry.

Fishman purchased 200 candy machines and 100 cigarette machines but had difficulty finding customers. As a result, his 300 machines sat

unused for several years in the basement of the wholesale company.

### The Right Business at the Right Time

America's entry into World War II turned out to be a fortuitous twist of fate for Fishman, whose stored and previously unused vending machines suddenly became a very hot commodity. In 1942, Fishman received an offer to join the Illinois Vending Company from Harry Winston, who, with a minority partner, Seymour Genno, ran the business. Winston's firm had recently won a contract to

quickly became apparent, and he managed to put himself through school on his earnings.

He married Clara a week after their college graduation, planning to return to graduate school and eventually become a college professor. His plans changed, however, when his father-in-law died suddenly, leaving Fishman and another son-in-law to keep the business running. It was admittedly a learning experience for Fishman:

*I picked up whatever I know about business management by the process of making every mistake a human being could have made.*[1]

As he became more knowledgeable about the wholesale business, Fishman became disenchanted with it. He began thinking about diversifying and found himself drawn to the vending industry. To get started, Fishman purchased 200 candy machines and 100 cigarette machines. A shrewd deal-maker, he worked out a plan with his brother-in-law to swap his share of the wholesale business for his brother-in-law's interest in the vending business. So Fishman embarked on a career in the vending business, where he was to become a legendary success. "Bill Fishman knew people and knew how to deal with people," said Henry Davidson. "He was a very sharp individual, a very bright man."[2]

Ron Davenport, chairman of Sheridan Broadcasting in Pittsburgh and a former member of ARAMARK's Board of Directors, agreed with Davidson's assessment:

*Bill Fishman was very, very smart. He was an easy person to talk to, he was good with people, and he had good judgment of people.*[3]

A hard worker, Fishman possessed old-fashioned "moxie," as evidenced by the fact that he was willing to fly himself from one customer to another in his own plane:

*I covered the accounts by flying to them in my own single-engine airplane, a used Taylor Craft 45-horsepower aircraft that cost $750. My wife Clara never liked my flying days, but it was the only way to cover the territory.*[4]

Looking back on that time later in his life, Fishman marveled at his youthful fortitude:

*When I look back on that decision to move into vending ... I was 22 years old, with a family. I had a young son. It was a great risk to move out of one business into another. I don't know if I could do it again. But I did it then. The criteria for success had to do with being in the right place at the right time, and being motivated to work hard enough to be the best in that business.*[5]

Bill and Clara Fishman had three sons, Alan, Fred, and David. After Clara's death, Fishman married Selma Demchick Ellis.

provide vending services for the new Douglas Aircraft plant in Chicago but didn't have the necessary machines to do so. Fishman recognized the opportunity to move out of the wholesale business and jumped at the chance:

*About this same time [1938], a firm called the Illinois Vending Company won a contract with the new Douglas Aircraft plant in Chicago. They had a contract, but didn't have the vending machines or the candy and cigarette quotas. The War Production Board had imposed strict rationing and quota controls on commodities. Illinois*

*Vending knew we had the vending machines and quotas—and offered me an opportunity to join them. I decided to do it.*

*I negotiated an agreement with my brother-in-law to trade my financial interest in the wholesale business for his interest in the vending machines. ... That's how I got started in the vending business.*[21]

With Fishman as a new partner, Illinois Vending changed its name to the Automatic Sales Company. It installed the first cold-cup drink dispenser ever used in the Douglas Aircraft plant.

Fishman was responsible for servicing the machines, which, in the early days of vending, could be a full-time job.

### The Beginnings of a Lifelong Relationship

It was their mutual business dealings with Douglas Aircraft Company that brought Fishman and Davidson together in the middle of 1942. Each man had heard about the other from a Douglas Aircraft liaison. Fishman, whose company was just starting out with Douglas, was eager to learn how Davidson Brothers had become so successful with its Douglas account.

Fishman, based in Chicago, visited Davidson in Los Angeles and found him to be welcoming and cooperative. The two men, who were very different in many aspects of their personalities, discovered that, despite their differences, they had a lot in common. This included a similar spate of fairly unique business challenges, according to Davidson:

*Bill and I shared many of the same problems and challenges. I remember one day encountering a scene where four healthy, husky, and very irate longshoremen were hard at work, heaving one of my recalcitrant beverage machines off a pier and into the ocean. Bill told me about a similar occasion where three burly customers at a steel mill hurled one of his large beverage machines into an open hearth furnace.* [22]

These shared experiences meant a lot to both Davidson and Fishman. As a result, a friendship quickly

Workers during World War II embraced the notion of the coffee break and coffee machines, which became common sights in manufacturing facilities. The attitude toward vending machines in the workplace changed dramatically during the war, as employers realized workers were more productive when they had access to nourishing snacks and drinks.

developed between the two men, a bond that would endure for the rest of their lives.

### The Concept of Service

Sharing an almost instinctual commitment to service, Davidson and Fishman each recognized that their companies' primary focus was to provide the best service possible to all customers. While other people ran vending machine businesses, they were running service companies. Long before there was talk of a service sector or service economy, they understood that their primary business was not providing machines and product, but rather service with a capital "S."

Fishman and Davidson, joined by Henry Davidson when he returned from the war, remained in close contact, sharing the daily trials, tribulations, and triumphs of running their businesses. They would learn from each other and address issues that affected both companies.

While the Automatic Sales Company in Chicago was still a modest operation, Davidson Brothers had grown tremendously during World War II, along with the vending industry itself. As Davre Davidson recalled, "By the time the war was over, we had one of the largest vending companies in Southern California." [23]

There were, however, still challenges to meet in the years immediately following the war. Aircraft producers, including Douglas, cut back their workforces, and some, including Kaiser–Frazier, an automobile and aircraft manufacturer that was one of Automatic Sales Company's largest clients, shut down their plants completely.

Many years later, Fishman related how Davidson came to his aid immediately after the closing of the Kaiser–Frazier plant:

*I'll never forget the day Kaiser–Frazier closed. ... They shut down the auto line the same day they shut down the aircraft line. The auto line was practically shut down anyhow. And there I was, and we were operating with a negative net worth. I know how to do that from experience, but when your cash flow gets cut off and today's money isn't coming in so that you can write a check to meet bills that were due last week, you got a cash flow squeeze. I was pretty unhappy, I guess.*

*I drove back to Chicago, walked into my office the next day, and here was a check from Davre for $25,000 with a little note saying, "Bill, I know you must need cash. Here's $25,000. It might help you with some of your bills. You don't have to bother sending me a note unless you want to, and when you can, you pay it back." That was the kind of relationship we had.*[24]

The Davidson brothers and Fishman continued operating their separate businesses in the last years of the 1940s, with each company expanding and growing. They broke into new product lines as Americans began demanding a greater variety of goods. While products in vending machines had been limited, consumers now could buy coffee, milk, ice cream, and fresh foods, in addition to packaged snacks.

The Davidsons and Fishman found some of these product lines profitable, while others, such as ice cream, were distinct setbacks. Still, both companies moved ahead—separate, but connected—as their owners shared ideas, strategies, advice, and a strong friendship.

With a new decade on the horizon and an environment of optimism and excitement in the United States, Davidson Brothers and Automatic Sales Company were poised for even further growth and expansion.

Innovations made it possible to vend soup and other hot foods during the 1950s. Employees embraced these heartier options, such as Spanish rice, split pea soup, chicken noodle soup, and chowder for 15 cents a can. Egg noodles with beef, as well as beans and franks, sold here for 25 cents a can.

## CHAPTER TWO

# A DECADE
# OF OPPORTUNITY

## 1950 – 1959

*Davre had this concept that there weren't any really impressive American corporations that emphasize solely service.*

—James D. Hodgson, Board member,
1977–1993

WEARY FROM THE GREAT Depression and the trials of World War II, Americans greeted the 1950s with optimism and excitement. Entrepreneurial spirit was high as the economy shifted from wartime to peacetime, and production and consumer demand for items such as cars, televisions, and washing machines were on the rise. Businesses and individuals responded with innovation, in some cases finding new uses for materials that had been developed during the war. In other cases, they capitalized on a changing American society.

Energetic, innovative, and expansionist, Davre Davidson and William Fishman were symbolic of the 1950s, a time when business visionaries all across the country were boldly making their own marks on society.

In Massachusetts, after World War II ended, a young inventor named Earl Tupper was exploring the area of plastic consumer goods. Using polyethylene slag from DuPont, Tupper tried to create plastic that was easier to mold and handle. After a great deal of trial and error, he created a method to transform the black, foul-smelling slag into a more resilient, solid, grease-free plastic that was also clean and translucent. At the same time, he developed an airtight seal, modeled on the lid of a paint can.

After World War II, another entrepreneur, Laurence Marshall, was witnessing the probable demise of his company, Raytheon, which developed and tested radar systems for the U.S. military. Marshall knew there would be small demand for his products and services when the wartime contracts ended. So he consulted with some of his top employees, asking them to design an innovative product to save the company. As a result, they created an oven that could cook with microwave radiation. The company licensed the new technology to Tappan, which introduced the first home microwave oven in 1955.[1]

### The Golden Era of the 1950s

Thousands of servicemen had returned home as the 1950s began. They were eager to resume lives that had been disrupted by World War II. Young couples married; purchased homes in new, suburban settings; and began raising families.

Americans were buying automobiles at record rates, and radios—previously the dominant means of mass communication—were quickly being replaced

The Davidson Brothers logo appeared on promotional items for current and prospective clients. Davre and Henry Davidson had established reputations as being fair and honest, major factors in their continued business growth.

with black-and-white television sets. TV sales jumped to more than 10 million a year, up substantially from the end of the 1940s.[2]

According to government statistics, the nation's gross national product rose from about $200 billion in 1940 to $300 billion in 1950. By 1960, it escalated to more than $500 billion. Additionally, the employment rate was high, giving people more expendable income. And with war production no longer necessary, Americans once again had access to goods that had been rationed or unavailable in the past.

Both Davidson and Fishman benefited tremendously from the rise in production, as the demand for factory vending services skyrocketed to keep up with the dramatic upsurge in the manufacturing of new consumer products.

### The New Service Sector

The 1950s also saw a dramatic increase in the number of service jobs, a home turf for Davidson and Fishman. For the first time in U.S. history, more people were working to provide services than produce goods. White-collar jobs also were increasing, and by 1956, white-collar workers had surpassed blue-collar employees.

Indeed, by the end of the decade, the service industry was firmly established as a major component of the country's economy. As a result, Davidson's and Fishman's service-oriented firms were both poised for significant long-term growth.

With growing demand for products and services, the vending industry was changing quickly. Basic machines that dispensed just one or two products were being replaced with machines that offered a variety of choices, including hot and cold foods and drinks. Customers demanded more options, which greatly benefited Davidson's and Fishman's individual firms, both of which expanded with new accounts and increased sales.

### Fishman's Territory and Business Scope Expand

By the mid-1950s, Seymour Genno, the minority partner with Fishman and Harry Winston, had sold his interest in the Automatic Sales Company, and the firm had been renamed Automatic Merchandising Company (AMCO). The company had expanded greatly, establishing branches in several towns in Ohio, Michigan, and Illinois. This was due in no small measure to Fishman's incredible work habits, according to Gerson Miller, a longtime busi-

**1950s**
Davidson Brothers and Fishman's Automatic Sales Company establish themselves as industry leaders in their geographical areas.

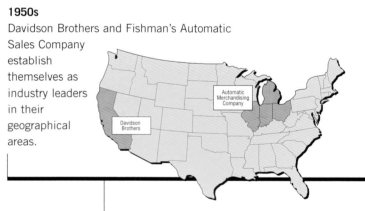

**1955**
Davidson Brothers is recognized as the largest independent vending company in the United States.

**1955**
One of Bill Fishman's partners sells his interest in the Automatic Sales Company. It is renamed Automatic Merchandising Company.

**1956**
Fishman and the Automatic Merchandising Company lead other vending companies to form a cooperative purchasing group, Federated Vendors, to compete with the industry giant, Automatic Canteen Company of America, for purchasing power with suppliers.

Vending in American workplaces gained popularity following World War II, when employees could get cold drinks in addition to coffee, cigarettes, candy bars, and snacks.

ness colleague of Fishman's and later the chairman of North American Corporation:

*Bill was constantly working, 24 hours a day. He would work beyond that if there were more hours in the day. … That was always the way he was existing and living his life.*

*Now, one of his men had a vending company that Bill had been involved with. I think he bought it out, and he put this man to work for him, a very nice, young fellow from Chicago by the name of Frank Kulp. One evening, I think it was around 2 or 3 A.M., Frank had some papers that he wanted to leave for Bill. He was flying in from St. Louis and*

*figured he'd leave the papers at Bill's office so Bill could see them first thing in the morning. So he quietly went up to the office [and went inside]. All of a sudden, a person rises up from the sofa at the office. It was Bill Fishman, and it scared the hell out of [Frank]. [Bill] was still there working. That's just the way he was.*[3]

Fishman had purchased his first airplane in 1939 so he could visit his mother, who was ill and lived 300 miles away. He now used his airplane to visit customers and the company's various operations. He enjoyed flying so much that he even used the airplane for short trips.

While Fishman continued to hone his business skills, he also remained mindful of always providing the best possible service to every customer. He credited his older partner, Harry Winston, with instilling

**1957**
Davre (shown here) and Henry Davidson begin to weigh the advantages of bringing their company to the public equity markets.

**1959**
Davre and Henry Davidson, working with their advisors, incorporate Davidson Automatic Merchandising Co., Inc.

**1959**
Davidson Automatic Merchandising Co., Inc., acquires Automatic Merchandising Company, making the longtime partnership of Fishman and Davidson Brothers official. The company is soon renamed Automatic Retailers of America, called ARA.

# AMERICA ON THE MOVE IN THE 1950s

DAVRE DAVIDSON AND BILL FISHMAN both possessed the rare gift of business acumen and foresight. Before almost anyone else in the United States, they intuitively understood that the nation was rapidly evolving into a service-based economy, a fundamental transformation from previous years.

They understood that various key trends and developments would most likely bring service work to center stage, and that the idiom of service was certain to dominate the contemporary world in the upcoming years. Both men were determined to capitalize on this new situation.

**Some Key Trends and Developments**

Automobiles became increasingly important during the 1950s as society became more and more mobile. Suburban housing developments made cars necessary for traveling to work, the grocery store, and the brand-new shopping malls that were emerging on the landscape. And, with increased leisure time and more money to spend than before, Americans took to the roadways, pumping money into an expanding economy.

**A Need for New Services**

With increased mobility, additional financial resources, and a growing population, the demand for all types of new services in the United States increased like never before. Along with the demand for services came a demand for workers. More time spent in the car resulted in more visits to restaurants and roadside attractions. Service stations, where it became routine to wash windshields and check fluid levels and tire pressure in addition to pumping gas, needed additional workers.

Travelers stayed in motels and hotels, expecting and demanding dependable service from staff members. Increased attendance at sporting events required additional workers to supply fans with pretzels, popcorn, and other refreshments.

Indeed, from east to west and north to south, Americans were now demanding a vast array of new services to further a rich, new way of life that was quickly becoming the envy of the world. Davidson and Fishman, each in his own way, were fully determined to meet this new demand.

Like many other Americans in the 1950s, Davre and Charlotte Davidson were constantly on the move, shown here on a business trip to Hawaii. Charlotte often accompanied her husband, sometimes bringing their children, Harold and Celia. (*Photo courtesy of Celia Davidson Farkas.*)

Fishman, who would formally join forces with the Davidsons in 1959, used this single-engine airplane to service his accounts in the late 1940s and 1950s. Fishman loved to fly, often using the airplane to reach locations that were within driving distance. He claimed that piloting the airplane was a soothing and therapeutic experience.

in him the notion of selling service and not products, citing a sales call early in his career on which he accompanied Winston.

As Winston and his customer talked about fishing, their families, and other matters, Fishman recalled that he became increasingly restless. Unable to maintain patience, he interrupted the conversation to talk about the vending machines their company offered. When the meeting ended, Winston strongly admonished Fishman:

*You want to talk about vending machines, but that's not what we're selling. We're selling service. We're selling personality. We're selling integrity. We're selling the buyer's confidence in our company and in our people. What I was doing was building credibility in the mind of that customer about our ability to serve his people better.*[4]

Fishman took Winston's advice to heart and never forgot the lesson.

As Automatic Merchandising Company grew, Fishman, who was ever the visionary, started thinking about branching out into food service:

*I began to think about expanding AMCO to include food service. I saw a market demand for both food and vending services and thought it would be logical for one company to provide both services to a customer.*[5]

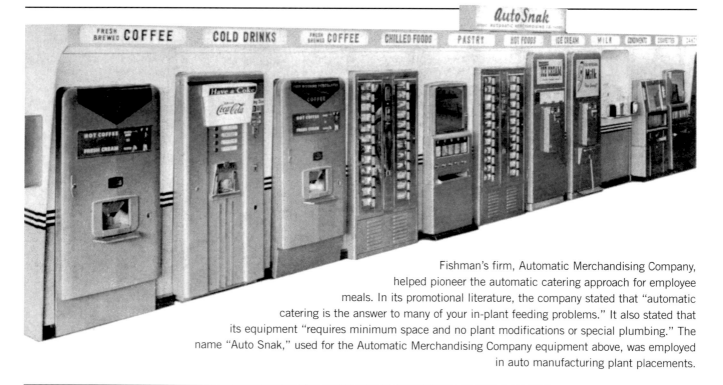

Fishman's firm, Automatic Merchandising Company, helped pioneer the automatic catering approach for employee meals. In its promotional literature, the company stated that "automatic catering is the answer to many of your in-plant feeding problems." It also stated that its equipment "requires minimum space and no plant modifications or special plumbing." The name "Auto Snak," used for the Automatic Merchandising Company equipment above, was employed in auto manufacturing plant placements.

Fishman's company received such an opportunity in 1956, when the Detroit plant of Budd Manufacturing asked it to take over its food service operations. At the same time, Fishman's firm had an opportunity to also handle food service operations for another plant run by Chrysler at Eight Mile and Outer Drive Streets:

*I don't know if [the two separate plants] talked to each other, or if it was just a coincidence, but simultaneously they decided to discontinue the old food carts that the catering people, as they were called then, pushed through the plants. Somebody had read about vending machines serving food.*[6]

It was the perfect opportunity for Fishman and his firm to expand operations. However, it came at no small cost—the company had to purchase $100,000 worth of new machines capable of vending sandwiches and other food items, which was a sizable investment at the time. "[The $100,000 price] was a lot of money for us," said Fishman. "As a matter of fact, it was a lot of money during those years for anybody."[7]

But always the bold opportunist, Fishman, along with his more prudent partner Harry Winston, took

the plunge and invested in the new equipment. Automatic Merchandising Company was now serving meals from vending machines; it had entered what Fishman called the personal food service business:

*That was our first entry into personal food service. ... In the beginning, we were vending sandwiches. ... We put refrigerator compressors in the sandwich machines and ... converted them to cold sandwich machines.*[8]

The cold sandwiches caught on right away, but soon workers began to ask for other food items, including soup. According to Fishman:

*Now we had broth [coming] out of the instant coffee machines. That wasn't difficult, you know, chicken broth and powder. But they wanted heavy soup like chili and stew. So finally, Ed Higgins [formerly a Kaiser–Frazier manual food service cafeteria manager] and I one night decided to take some Pure-Pak® milk cartons, the ones with the tent top, and pack soup in them.*[9]

Over the years, incremental improvements led to the food vending business as it is today.

### An Industry Leader

While Fishman was becoming more involved in food service, Davidson Brothers was also establishing itself as an industry leader. By 1955, it was the largest independent vending company in the United States. "My brother Henry and I worked hard," recalled Davre. "Our people worked hard, and our company grew and grew."[10]

With the help of Henry's intuition and gift of persuasion, Davidson Brothers was acquiring one vending company after the next. Davre, who was more conservative with regard to acquisitions, recalled how Henry managed to deal with his own hesitation about acquiring companies.

For example, if Henry was ready to finalize a deal to purchase a company, he would ask Davre if he would be interested in buying the business

Henry had already decided they should buy. When Davre told his brother that he *was* interested in that particular business, Henry would then say he believed it was a poor acquisition.

Davre would then insist that acquiring the business would be a smart investment. He could astutely judge the worth of a business because of his facility with numbers, according to his son, Harold:

*My father was very good with numbers. These were days before calculators, but he didn't need a calculator to know what he was looking at.*[11]

Davre valued his brother's common sense in the acquisition process and also credited Henry with playing a large part in building the business through the excellent rapport he established with customers. According to Davre, Henry possessed a keen understanding of customers' needs. Company Board member Jim Hodgson, however, cited another reason for the success of Davidson Brothers— Davre's remarkable vision. He recalled:

*Davre was a man with little education, starting just about at the bottom of any ladder you could*

By 1955, vending machines were dispensing sandwiches, milk, and traditional items such as candy bars and peanuts. Some companies offered employees lunch wagon or cafeteria services and used vending machines as supplemental food sources.

From his earliest days in business, Fishman always exhibited an abiding and deep-felt commitment to community betterment, as evidenced in his company's annual work on behalf of the United Way. Fishman (left) poses with Chicago television personality Dorsey Connors (center); company executive Frank Sandera (right); and two unidentified children in a photo that was used to promote a vending industry campaign for the United Way in the late 1950s. The machine shown, which dispensed Coca-Cola for 5 cents a cup, was one of the first of its kind used in the vending industry by Automatic Merchandising Company of Chicago.

*imagine and building on a concept. Davre had this concept that there weren't any really impressive American corporations that emphasize solely service, and he proceeded to build an organization doing just that. I would say you could call him a pioneer in the multiservice industry.*[12]

As the company expanded, Davre and Henry searched for ways to protect their investment and secure their futures. Davre, with a wife and two children, was particularly interested in stability. So the Davidsons decided that selling the company might be their best choice. They received several offers over the next several years, none of which was appealing. So in 1957, the Davidsons started investigating the advantages of turning Davidson Brothers into a publicly held corporation with stock shares available through the equities market.

### Formation of Federated Vendors

As large as Davidson Brothers and Automatic Merchandising Company had grown, neither business was a match for the Chicago-based Automatic Canteen Company of America, which had gone public in the 1940s and had more capital to spend on its operations, along with substantial buying power with suppliers.

Fishman, who always relished a challenge, brainstormed ways that smaller companies could compete with Canteen. He soon struck on the idea of forming a cooperative purchasing group, which would give smaller companies a welcome advantage. Fishman joined his company with a dozen or so others to form Federated Vendors and became its president. The group, which hired a full-time purchasing agent, enjoyed strong purchasing power and could negotiate attractive volume-driven deals on equipment and merchandise at greatly reduced prices.

Finally, smaller companies were able to compete with the industry leader, but it was clear that joining forces would be a necessary next step, as smaller vending companies fought to survive. Corporate consolidation was clearly on the horizon.

### Weighing Their Options

Meanwhile, out on the West Coast, the Davidson brothers were weighing their options. Having received no satisfactory offers for their company, they discussed various scenarios, such as going public or merging with another firm, with their advisors: Herman Minter, their company's auditor, and Aaron Clark, a financial consultant.

Instead, Davre and Henry, along with other investors, incorporated Davidson Automatic Merchandising Co., Inc., which acquired the stock of Davidson Brothers and its affiliated companies. Davre felt strongly that the company had been formed at the right time, and indeed, he was right. Soon after the formation of Davidson Automatic Merchandising Co., Inc., the Davidsons and Fishman began discussing the next step. It was time for Davidson Automatic Merchandising to acquire Automatic Merchandising Company.

Timing for the Davidson brothers and Fishman partnership also seemed perfect, considering that Fishman's partner, Harry Winston, was in ill health and planning to leave the business. Also, both the Davidsons and Fishman believed they had taken their companies as far as possible on their own. Merging their companies would give them a broader client base, making each company less vulnerable to industry fluctuations.

Davre later recalled that the acquisition provided them with an integrated corporate structure and, eventually, access to additional capital for expanding the business. It solved the problem of estate planning, as Davidson and Fishman both approached their fifties. It also gave them a more varied range of clients and allowed each to concentrate on his individual talents, all while sharing the combined workload.

In September 1959, Davidson Automatic Merchandising Co., Inc., officially acquired Automatic Merchandising Company. Davre served as president of the company and remained in Los Angeles to head up that area of operations. Fishman stayed in Chicago, serving as head of the Midwest operation.

### Launching the Dream

When the Davidsons' new company acquired Fishman's company in 1959, the principals began to re-examine their role in the service industry. Although their previous companies had some experience with personal food service through subcontracting catering jobs, and Fishman's company had won the Budd Manufacturing contract, the primary focus of both companies had always been vending. Now, they began to look at personal food service as an extension of vending services, according to Davre:

*Many of our clients operated cafeterias for their employees, but vending was almost always separate and something to subcontract. However, we began to realize the services should be complementary, and they are.*[13]

With that realization in the forefront, coupled with its firm commitment to service, the Davidson Automatic Merchandising Co., Inc.—soon to become Automatic Retailers of America, or ARA—actively launched its dream of becoming a publicly held, multifaceted service corporation.

In the summer of 1966, the company that was then known as ARA packed and distributed thousands of lunches each day as part of its service to Project Step Up, a cultural enrichment program for children in Washington, D.C. All these lunches could require as much as 15,000 bananas, 30,000 slices of bread, and 1,750 pounds of ham. Piled high, the baskets of plums above contain only a portion of the total amount of plums (three to a lunch bag) used in a day. The company moved to diversify its customer base during the 1960s to include new programs funded by the federal government.

CHAPTER THREE

# DARING AND GROWTH

## 1960–1969

*The Slater acquisition actually moved us into the service management industry. It created a launching pad from which our company was able to diversify, to grow, to really take off … that one acquisition.*

—Bill Fishman, as quoted in
"From Penny Peanuts to Industry Leader"

THE CAREFUL PLANS OF DAVRE and Henry Davidson and Bill Fishman to take the company public were achieved in February 1960, when they sold 120,000 shares of common stock to the public in an over-the-counter offering. The company, with combined annual revenues of more than $24 million, had been renamed Automatic Retailers of America (ARA), and its initial public offering had resulted in sales of approximately $1.8 million in stock. Three years later, the Davidsons, Fishman, and other ARA officials would travel to New York City to witness the company's initial appearance on the New York Stock Exchange. Henry, who suffered from health problems, would retire from the company in 1963.

Although they were now officially co-executives, Davre remained in Los Angeles and Fishman in Chicago. At that time, the Los Angeles business employed about 1,500 people, while the Chicago–Detroit operation had about 600 employees. The men remained in close contact, however, conferring on day-to-day operations, as well as long-term goals and plans.[1]

### Building a National Company

The motivation for taking ARA public was to secure its future with access to capital for growth. Soon after the initial public offering, Davidson and

Fishman started building their regional firm into a national company.

The Davidsons and Fishman were well known and very well liked within the vending industry. "There was an exceptional, fundamental decency about Davre Davidson," said retired Board member Jim Hodgson.[2] Gerson Miller, chairman of North American Corporation had similar thoughts on Fishman: "He had a very engaging manner and was very warm and passionate in all his relationships."[3]

Fishman, especially, had many contacts as a result of serving as president of the National Automatic Merchandising Association (NAMA) from 1957 until 1959. The men saw an opportunity to acquire companies and expand their business by approaching owners of small vending operations who were contemplating retirement.

They traveled around the country, meeting with the owners of highly regarded, well-managed, independent companies that had considered selling their businesses. Generally, Davre Davidson and Fishman were very well received. Harold Davidson discussed his father's role during a typical acquisition:

---

Technicians employed by Automatic Retailers of America wore uniform shirts that bore the new ARA logo patch on the sleeve.

**1960**
ARA debuts as a publicly held
company with an over-the-
counter offering listed on the
Philadelphia–Baltimore–
Washington and Pacific Coast
stock exchanges.

**1963**
ARA is listed on the New York
Stock Exchange.

SLATER

**1961**
ARA stuns the food service industry when
it acquires a much larger food service
company, Slater System, Inc., for $14.5
million in cash. It moves its headquarters
to Slater's Philadelphia offices.

**1966**
The company forms a new division called
ARASERV to meet the needs of the
leisure and recreation markets.

Opposite: Officials celebrate the listing of ARA on the New York Stock Exchange on June 7, 1963. Davre Davidson is at center, Henry Davidson is at far left, and Bill Fishman is second from left.

Right: ARA Chairman and CEO Davre Davidson. Those who knew him said his smile, the tilt of his head, and his kindly eyes were Davidson's trademark characteristics.

*My dad was personally involved in just about all of the acquisitions. He would go out and meet with a company, sit down, and review their books and their operation. He was very proud of the fact that he could sit across the table from someone and be able to tell them pretty much what their company was worth.*

*He would always do that in the context of not trying to shortchange the other person, but to pay fair value for what he and Bill Fishman were buying. I think there are a couple of occasions where he may have told someone that the business was*

*worth a million dollars more than what that individual was asking, simply to preserve his integrity in terms of what he himself believed in. His acquisitions were always something that he was most proud of in his career.*[4]

Martin Spector, who served as executive vice president and general counsel of the company for almost two decades, described that acquisition period:

*Most of the acquisitions were small operations. They would buy the companies of entrepreneurs whose sons wanted to be doctors and lawyers, and who didn't have any ready "out" for their businesses. These were usually stock, not cash acquisitions, so the owners became stockholders of Automatic Retailers of America.*[5]

Davidson and Fishman had no specific formula for acquiring companies. They simply decided on a case-by-case basis which companies

**1967**

ARA becomes an international company by acquiring an interest in Canadian manual and automated food service company Versafood Services Ltd.

**1968**

ARA manages the food service at the Summer Olympic Games in Mexico City, organizes Environmental Services, and forms ARA Offshore, which provides services for the crews on oil rigs in the Gulf of Mexico. District News joins ARA to form the beginning of the magazine and book division.

**1967**

ARA continues to diversify with the acquisition of Air La Carte, a company that specialized in preparing and delivering airplane passenger meals.

**1969**

Automatic Retailers of America becomes ARA Services.

ARA acquires Ground Services, a company that provides airport services for airlines.

Above: John Slater (seated on left) was featured with Boy Scouts on NBC's *Tonight Show* on July 10, 1957. He is sitting next to Al Collins, who hosted the show prior to Jack Paar and Johnny Carson. *(Photo by: NBC Universal Photo Bank.)*

Below left: This commissary on Irving Street in Philadelphia was one of several Slater locations where food was prepared and dispatched to customers around the city in the 1930s and 1940s.

Below right: Slater's sales volume had grown dramatically over the years, making it an attractive acquisition target. Food service sales had climbed from around $10 million in 1950 to more than $50 million by 1959.

would be a good match. They did, however, always consider whether they liked the people who owned the business.

"We didn't have a rule book," Fishman said. "We did have to like the people, though. An acquisition is about the closest thing to a marriage there is in the business world."[6]

The 1960s were a period of monumental acquisitions. These would lead the company into new areas of service and new businesses. This entrepreneurial approach continued long after the 1960s ended, requiring an assumption of risk as well as an ability to evaluate the situations that worked and the ones that didn't. Industries were entered and sometimes exited as the company defined its own path.

While Fishman and Davidson carefully examined the companies they considered acquiring, they also did so very efficiently, according to Lee F. Driscoll, Jr., a former Slater System employee. Driscoll would become general counsel and eventually vice chairman and a Board member of ARA. "They made maybe 100 acquisitions in the space of 18 months," he said.[7]

Once they had acquired a company and provided it with capital for further growth, Davidson and Fishman left local management in place, while stressing the need for quality service. The new acquisitions operated independently, therefore fostering both entrepreneurial behavior and goodwill. Davidson spoke of the strategy he and Fishman employed:

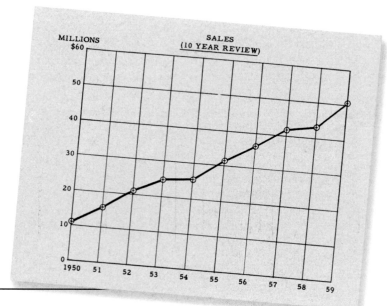

Ever entrepreneurial, Slater System saw an opportunity to provide coffee service to factories and other institutions that did not have installed brewing equipment. Large quantities of coffee were made every morning at a commissary and delivered in stainless steel urns to customer locations. The empty containers were picked up by the route drivers and returned for the next day's refill.

*We were trying to combine the advantages of the small companies—the local recognition and acceptance in the community—with the corporate assets of ARA. Our ability to do this was a major factor in our success.*[8]

The company's first annual report, issued at the end of 1960, stated that there were operations in 19 states, with sales and other income totaling $37,440,105.[9]

### Looking Ahead

While the Davidsons and Fishman were busy acquiring vending companies and growing ARA, they also kept an eye on the natural relationship between the vending and food service industries. Fishman recalled that there was mounting pressure from customers for companies to provide both automatic and manual food services:

*We began to see the probability of those two industries becoming one. They really always were one. The food service was using contractors like ourselves for vending needs. We were serving the same clients, and the clients were beginning to express a preference for dealing with one service company, not two. And we would go out on our solicitation and sell vending, and we'd be asked if we could also provide the food service.*[10]

Fishman was eager to acquire several food service companies, but Davidson was more conservative. Finally, Davidson agreed to have Fishman acquire two small companies in the Midwest:

*I nagged Davre, aggravated him long enough to where he said, "OK, Bill. You can make those two acquisitions." I think he was hoping that would put an end to my aggravating.*[11]

When it became evident that the companies would not be lucrative, however, Fishman and Davidson discussed a possible change in direction. When Davidson asked Fishman about his plans for the failing food service companies, Fishman played his trump card:

*I said, "Well Davre, you know, you can't be half pregnant. We're in the food service business, but we really don't have a big enough business or the right management. We have to acquire a big company."*[12]

The stage had been set for Automatic Retailers of America to move into food service in a fundamental way. No one, however, fully realized the giant leap that ARA would make next.

### The Slater Acquisition

Slater System, with headquarters in Philadelphia, was the premier food service business in the country in 1961, but its founder and owner, John H. Slater, was ready for a new adventure. In a 1976 speech at the University of Pennsylvania, Slater spoke of his relationship with his company:

*The business was no longer compatible with my personality or with my inclinations. It had outgrown me.*[13]

Left: ARA executive committee members meet to review plans in the Lamplighter Room of ARA headquarters in Philadelphia in 1964. The room was a model of a "vendeteria," a dining concept introduced in the 1960s. From left are officers Ralph Globus, James Hutton, Bill Fishman, Davre Davidson, Harvey Stephens, and Herman Minter.

Below: Looking for an instantly recognizable graphic image to symbolize the merger of Automatic Retailers of America and Slater System, ARA designed a new logo based on the Slater System logo, which was so familiar in the food service industry. As the scope and dimensions of the company's services continued to broaden during the 1960s, the company became known as ARA Services. The shareholders formally approved that name in 1969.

Opposite: In addition to managing food service on customers' premises, Slater System from time to time took on "off-premise catering" business that included large events requiring heroic effort. In the 1940s, the company chartered a Colonial Airlines plane to transport food and beverages prepared at a Maryland location to a large event in Indiana.

Tuned into the industry buzz, Fishman heard that a competitor was considering the purchase of Slater's company. However, negotiations were not progressing well, so Fishman decided to visit Philadelphia and talk to Slater to learn more about the situation. Slater decided that he preferred to turn his company over to ARA.

Fishman recommended to Davidson that they acquire Slater System. This time, Davidson was easily persuaded. The company had an excellent reputation, and its sales had grown tremendously over the years. Davre's son, Harold, recalled hearing his father speak about the possibility of acquiring Slater:

*I remember my dad saying there was a company in Philadelphia that was a perfect fit with Automatic Retailers of America. It was a perfect fit because ARA was 98 percent vending and 2 percent food service. Slater was 98 percent food service and only about 2 percent vending. So, it was a very logical move to blend the two companies.*[14]

### A Big Step Forward

According to Driscoll, a Slater purchase would enable ARA to become a truly national company—a status it had not yet achieved, despite its numerous small acquisitions across the country:

*With its acquisitions, ARA had become a national company, but it was only little operations where local guys still ran [businesses]. [ARA] wasn't very little anymore. It might have been doing $10 million a year, we'll say. But there was no centralization. They hadn't reached the next stage.*

*Slater, on the other hand, was a multistate company. It had, in Philadelphia, a general counsel, me, and it had financial people. It had accounting and purchasing people. It had personnel departments*

as well. It was relatively small, but it had a national status. We were … an integrated business.[15]

A Slater purchase would provide another valuable advantage to ARA—the inside track on additional vending business, according to Driscoll:

*When manual food service companies were asked to provide the [cafeteria] service, let's say, at Boeing, they always subcontracted the vending, when it was required, to small, local vending companies. So, when I was at Slater, and we would bid on the food service business at a company like Boeing, it would include both the manual food service, that is the cafeteria,* and it would also include the vending. We would always subcontract the vending.[16]

John Slater agreed to sell his company to ARA for $14.5 million in "cash on the barrelhead," according to Driscoll. Slater did not accept an offer of ARA stock as payment. Once again, Davidson turned to financial consultant and friend Aaron Clark to structure the financing. Working with the Metropolitan Life Insurance Company, ARA borrowed enough funds to purchase Slater System.

The Slater acquisition provided ARA not only with a national presence, but also stable management and business systems along with an experi-

enced staff. Recognizing the importance of retaining key people, Davidson and Fishman created a fund that would reward employees who agreed to stay with the company. Those who agreed to remain for three years after the acquisition received sizeable bonuses. Driscoll recalled the technique Davidson and Fishman used to persuade Slater employees to commit:

*ARA was very sophisticated in the way they handled that. They wanted John Slater to ensure the continuity and the staying on ... of his key people, and he wouldn't do anything to guarantee that. So ARA came up with ... a block of money, which was a stay bonus. If you stayed, you received a bonus, and I remember I got $4,000 out of it.*[17]

With a committed senior staff, ARA set about combining the two companies. It continued to use the Slater name for some accounts and retained the

# DAM COMPANY

ONCE THE DAVIDSON BROTHERS AND Fishman joined forces in 1959, they began to solidify their plan to take the company public and offer its stock on the New York Stock Exchange. A glitch in the plan, however, was the translation of the company name into a symbol for the stock exchange.

Nobody thought that the current acronym—DAM—would be appropriate as a symbol. As the men considered the predicament, it became clear that they would have to change the name of the company.

After much consideration, they chose Automatic Retailers of America, soon to be known as ARA because their core business was then vending, or "automated retail" through machines, and they aspired to become a national company.

look of the Slater branding as it worked to combine two very different corporate cultures.

While Slater had all the formal business mechanisms in place, ARA operated in a more entrepreneurial fashion, full of energy and enthusiasm. The combination of those traits eventually resulted in a strong company.

Slater's manual food service business, coupled with ARA's vending interests, combined to position the company as a diversified service provider and as a service management company. Looking back, Fishman recalled the importance of the acquisition:

*The Slater acquisition actually moved us into service management. That one acquisition brought us even more talent, reputation, and size in the food services business. It created a launching pad from which our company was able to diversify, to grow, to really take off.*[18]

### Joining Forces

The acquisition of Slater System doubled the size of ARA, creating challenges along with unparalleled opportunity. After the acquisition, ARA's client list included 175 schools and colleges, 600 business and industrial accounts, 100 government installations, and 125 hospitals across nearly every state.

Despite Davidson's and Fishman's good intentions to reassure Slater personnel, tension became apparent as employees realized that they had been acquired by a Slater subcontractor. John Farquharson, a former Slater employee who became the longtime president of ARA's food services group, recalled how well Fishman handled the general reaction of the junior Slater employees at the time of the acquisition:

*When I heard that we had been acquired, the first thing that I did, along with several other assistant manager trainees, was get my résumé out. We all thought we would be fired. And then my first contact with the organization and the changes was Bill himself. Everyone was impressed that the president of the organization would come out and visit us. We all calmed down, and it has been a good relationship since then.*[19]

Recognizing the importance of keeping the Slater management team and system intact, Fishman elected to move to Philadelphia and oversee the day-to-day operations of the business.

Fishman later said that he moved to Philadelphia to preserve ARA's greatest acquired asset:

*I went back to Davre and Henry and said, "Look fellows, if we try to move, we're going to lose the biggest asset we bought. And that's their experience, their personnel, their organization, and their structure." And, so I said, "I'll move to Philadelphia. That's where we'll go."* [20]

There was another reason for Fishman's move, according to Harold Davidson:

*At the time, ARA primarily was doing vending and automated food service, which was not very labor-intensive. On the other hand, Slater was an employee and food service company—a manual food service operation where they would go in and do schools, hospital food service, college dorms, and all the rest. This type of operation required more managerial attention. Consequently, the headquarters needed to be in Philadelphia. So, Bill Fishman volunteered to move from where he was living in Elgin, Illinois, to Philadelphia.* [21]

According to Harold, it was unlikely that the Davidsons would also move from California to Philadelphia. "My mother was from the New Jersey–Philadelphia area, but she didn't want to leave Southern California, where all of her family now lived," he said. [22]

Harold described how his father and Fishman ran their company, with one man on the East Coast and the other on the West:

*They were a terrific combination and had a very healthy respect for each other. It was a great combination. Bill was running the day-to-day operations in Philadelphia, and they were on the phone all the time. I can remember the calls. My dad would get up at 5 A.M. Los Angeles time to get ahold of Bill at 8 A.M. Philadelphia time before certain things would get done in the day, and to cover things he had thought of during the night. They were separated by thousands of miles but still were very, very close.* [23]

IN 1963, ARA HELD ITS FIRST MANAGE-ment conference in Atlantic City, where 300 ARA executives and frontline managers met to learn from one another and set the standard for the service industry of the future. President Davre Davidson paid tribute to the 14,623 employees throughout the country: [1]

*That 23rd person is very important as we see ARA. Although service is our product, people are the life of our business. ARA's people are its greatest asset.* [2]

Executive Vice President Bill Fishman stressed service in his remarks, stating that providing excellent service to ARA clients and customers was the company's primary objective:

*We have to make people happy, to make them smile ... to help them perform their daily tasks.* [3]

The first annual ARA Management Conference was just that: a conference, a working meeting. It included "information trading post stations" from 8:30 P.M. to 10 P.M. on subjects such as accounting, equipment, food standards, labor relations, recruiting, public relations, commissary operations, sales, and vending.

Hotel officials were impressed by the large amounts of time ARA attendees spent in working sessions. Even the hotel doormen noticed. "When we have conventions here," one said, "the delegates are out on the town." [4]

# SLATER SYSTEM

SLATER SYSTEM TRACED ITS ROOTS TO 1926, when its founder, John H. Slater, assumed responsibility for food service at the fraternity houses of the University of Pennsylvania in Philadelphia. Slater entered the food service business for the most prosaic of reasons, according to Joan Voli, a long-term ARAMARK employee who originally worked for John Slater in the 1950s at his company's Philadelphia headquarters. "John Slater went to the University of Pennsylvania, but he didn't like the food there. That's why he started the business," she said.[1]

In 1946, patrons could buy eggs served any style for 20 cents, orange juice for 10 cents, and two doughnuts for 5 cents in this Slater cafeteria. By the time ARA acquired Slater System in 1961, it was the largest food service company in the country.

A brilliant entrepreneur and salesman, Slater persuaded the officers at the Delta Kappa Epsilon House, a fraternity where he resided, to permit him to take over the management of the fraternity's dining room in return for free board. This worked out well for the enterprising but moneyless Slater, who was attending Penn on a track scholarship. Before long, he and Mary Hunt, a woman whom Slater had hired as the house cook, formed a partnership to manage food service operations for all 12 fraternities at the university.

Track star John Slater was off and running—but this time in business. Indeed, a nascent business had been born—small, unprepossessing, and confined in its early days to a handful of Penn campus houses and some fraternity brothers. Slater's new firm would eventually become the country's largest manual food service business.

Above: The headquarters of Slater System at 25ᵗʰ and Lombard Streets in Philadelphia. *(Photo courtesy of Philadelphia Magazine.)*

Right: John Slater (left), president of Slater System, accepts a "Hall of Fame" plaque from Philadelphia Mayor Richardson Dilworth in 1959. It was awarded to him on behalf of his company for its contributions to the city.

From its humble beginnings, Slater System moved into other colleges, then hospitals, and then into industrial and factory accounts. Slater possessed all the qualities necessary to achieve business success, including a strong entrepreneurial drive, high energy, and a dynamic personality—but his timing was terrible. Like many other businessmen, Slater struggled to keep his young business afloat during the Great Depression. But the company rebounded when World War II began. Factories everywhere dramatically increased production, and their workers' hours, to meet the vital wartime demands. People needed to be fed during their long hours and multiple shifts on the job, and Slater System was there, ready, willing, and able to serve them. It was the perfect combination for business success, as John Slater and his burgeoning firm quickly expanded to meet the growing demand.

**More Than $50 Million in Sales**

By 1950, Slater System sales reached $10 million, and that amount doubled by 1952. Between 1950 and 1960, sales rose to more than $50 million, as the company served more than 1.2 million meals a day to businesses, factories, hospitals, and schools in 42 states.[2]

By the early 1960s, after more than 30 years in business, John Slater decided to sell his company. He had accomplished something truly remarkable during his three decades in business: taking a tiny two-person operation feeding a few fraternity brothers and turning it into a $50 million food service juggernaut. In 1961, Slater sold his business to Automatic Retailers of America for $14.5 million.

# PROJECT CAFETERIA FREEMAN

ARA'S SUCCESS AT PROVIDING FOOD SERvice during the 1968 Summer Olympic Games to athletes from many different countries and with many different tastes can be attributed to an unusual project in which the company had participated several years earlier.

In 1965, ARA was requested to participate in a pilot program designed to make America's abundant food resources available to hungry people in other parts of the world. ARA agreed to establish a school cafeteria lunch program in an Alliance for Progress community outside Bogotá, Colombia. Named for President John Kennedy, who visited there, the community was called Ciudad Kennedy.

Working to combat the poverty and malnutrition in the village, the Founders' Club of the Academy of Food Marketing at St. Joseph's University in Philadelphia sponsored the program. It was also supported by the Colombian government and U.S. government agencies in collaboration with CARE, a humanitarian organization fighting global poverty.[1]

ARA employees traveled to Colombia, where they developed recipes and menus using local ingredients and Food for Peace commodities, which appealed to local children. ARA also designed the cafeteria, selected equipment and oversaw its installation, trained local workers to serve as kitchen staff, and managed the operation, which served 2,400 children.

ARA faced many challenges during its years at Ciudad Kennedy. At first, the cafeteria staff served portions that were too large for the children, causing many to become ill. Children also needed to learn proper hygiene, such as washing their hands before meals. In addition, dining table legs had to be shortened because children in Colombia were shorter than American children of the same age.

Despite these obstacles, however, the cafeteria was fully operational and ran smoothly for many years. ARA eventually turned the operation over to the Colombian government.

---

Left and center: The cafeteria was named for U.S. Secretary of Agriculture Orville Freeman. Here, children are lined up awaiting lunch.

Right: Children at Ciudad Kennedy help to clean up after lunch.

Above: ARA received national attention in 1967 when it provided refreshments for a "country fair" on the White House lawn. ARA served popcorn, ice cream, candied apples, and cotton candy at the event. *(Photo courtesy AP/WIDE WORLD PHOTOS.)*

Right: First Lady "Lady Bird" Johnson accepts some popcorn from Jim Petersen, president of the ARASERV division. The First Lady threw the party for 700 children and grandchildren of members of Congress, the Supreme Court, the Cabinet, and government department heads.

With Fishman on the scene in Philadelphia, managing and introducing new methods, the former Slater firm began to take on a new status locally.

As Slater and ARA personnel began their partnership, they introduced a centralized accounting service and established an internal auditing department. In 1963, a new computerized data processing system was installed. Fishman himself began to receive some valuable local recognition. Driscoll discussed these changes:

*It took a little while, but the company began to get recognized in Philadelphia. Before that, it was considered to be just a little food service business up at 25th and Lombard. ... My office was in a converted elevator shaft. It really wasn't a very fancy place.*

*Everybody was cheek by jowl, but we put on a little addition. It wasn't long after that when Bill Fishman was asked to join the Board of the orchestra, which was a big plum in Philadelphia. Then, a little later, he was asked to join the Board of Fidelity Bank. So he was seen as a significant businessman in Philadelphia, and I think he enjoyed that.[24]*

### Customized Service and Quality

The acquisition of John Slater's company meant new opportunities for Davidson and Fishman to enlarge their ideas on customized service.

Between 1961 and 1965, the company developed various combinations of vending and manual food service methods designed to provide more choices and convenience for customers. It hired more dietitians, equipment engineers, packaging experts, food preparation specialists, facilities designers, and other support staff to further improve food service for individual clients.

It opened an experimental commissary in Chicago to improve packaging techniques and devise new methods for preserving food. It studied customers' dining area color preferences. The company also purchased an equipment center in Wilkes-Barre, Pennsylvania, to improve vending machine design and repair capability.

The 1962 annual report noted the corporation's extraordinary commitment to customized service:

*Giving clients personalized service is an integral part of ARA's corporate way of life. Each school, busi-*

Building upon the expertise of Slater System, ARA hired more dietitians and food preparation specialists to develop processes to take quality customer service to new levels.

*ness, corporation, hospital, government installation, and public location has its own individual requirements for service. These needs were met in a variety of ways, whether at campus snack facilities or in college dining halls, in Army or Navy [Post Exchanges], at executive dining rooms, or in industrial plants, at hospital staff or patient dining facilities, or at airline terminals and a wide variety of other public locations.*[25]

As the decade progressed, people were dining out in record numbers, travel continued to increase, and the pursuit of leisure activities was an American pastime. Soon, Davidson and Fishman recognized

# NOTABLE STADIUMS AND ARENAS

ARA, UNDER ITS SPECIALIZED MARKETing and operations division known as ARASERV, began operations at the Atlanta Stadium in 1966, and quickly established itself as an industry leader. Today, ARAMARK serves about 165 stadiums and arenas in North America and Europe, providing food service in restaurants, suites, and club box seats, as well as general concessions. It also runs retail stands where novelty items and team merchandise is sold, and manages cleaning services.

Sean Rooney, former president of Stadiums & Arenas, ARAMARK Sports and Entertainment Services, said company managers develop a sense of ownership of the stadiums and arenas they serve, which causes them to care deeply about the success of the total operation:

*I think it all comes from the people and the management team we have, and really, the entrepreneurial spirit that's conveyed by Joe Neubauer, our chairman. He instilled a mindset that the stadiums we run are like our businesses. So, when I ran the Spectrum [a Philadelphia sports facility] way back when, it's like I had ownership in it. We owned it. I really think that philosophy and culture have made us one of the industry leaders, because we care about it. We*

emerging opportunities in the leisure and travel markets and responded decisively.

## A Period of Remarkable Diversification

In 1966, ARA established ARASERV, a specialized division created to meet the needs of the leisure and recreation markets. The division began operations at Atlanta–Fulton County Stadium, which had opened the previous year.

ARASERV attracted the attention of major league ballpark and stadium managers, and soon was providing services at arenas, convention centers, state parks, racetracks, and other leisure facilities.

In 1967, ARA acquired Air La Carte, a company that specialized in preparing and delivering airplane

ARA Founder Davre Davidson samples a new sauce in a test kitchen in ARA's Philadelphia headquarters in 1965. Davidson, who remained in Los Angeles after the Slater System acquisition, was not a stranger in Philadelphia. He kept in close contact with his partner, Bill Fishman, who had relocated to the East Coast.

*care about the customer, our clients, and our fans. We look to see how we can serve them better, and that's because of this ownership feeling that has transpired over the years.*[1]

Listed below are some notable stadiums and arenas ARAMARK has served over the years.

- The Astrodome Complex, Houston
- Turner Field, Atlanta
- Paul Brown Stadium, Cincinnati
- Trans World Dome, St. Louis
- Cashman Complex, Las Vegas
- Mile High Stadium, Denver
- San Jose Arena, San Jose, California
- Oriole Park at Camden Yards, Baltimore
- Alamodome, San Antonio
- Coors Field, Denver
- The Spectrum, Philadelphia
- Reliant Stadium, Houston
- Arrowhead Pond, Anaheim, California

- Wrigley Field, Chicago
- Minute Maid Park, Houston
- Pyramid Arena, Memphis
- Shea Stadium, New York
- Wachovia Center, Philadelphia
- GM Place, Vancouver, British Columbia
- Angel Field, Anaheim, California
- Citizens Bank Park, Philadelphia
- PNC Park at North Shore, Pittsburgh
- RFK Stadium, Washington, D.C.
- Silver Cross Field, Joliet, Illinois
- U.S. Steel Yard, Gary, Indiana
- Victory Field, Indianapolis

ARAMARK has provided services to Super Bowl events, Major League Baseball's All-Star Games, rodeos and livestock shows, PGA national golf tournaments, minor league sporting events, and much more. Its goal is to create the ultimate fan experience, while helping clients to run a cost-effective facility.

# THE OLYMPIC GAMES

AT ITS FIRST OLYMPIC GAMES IN 1968 IN Mexico City, ARA served 10,000 athletes, coaches, and officials from 117 countries. At the 2004 Summer Games in Athens, Greece, the company now known as ARAMARK needed to offer even more choices to suit the tastes and nutritional needs of participants, as it served more than 10,500 athletes, media members, officials, and trainers from a record 201 countries.

Lunch and dinner at the 1968 Games featured various soups; three entrées (one was always beef); four vegetables; five salads; six desserts; and assorted cheeses, beverages, and fruits. In contrast, ARAMARK served the 2004 Olympians an international menu that catered to the nutritional requirements of every sport and all cultural and religious preferences.[1]

For the 2004 Games, chefs in Philadelphia spent six months creating menu plans and testing recipes for hundreds of different meals from various international cuisines. Their efforts resulted in an eclectic selection of foods that was served from numerous stations within the Olympic Village's huge dining hall. Delicious offerings from Central and South America, North Africa, Asia, and coun-

tries such as Spain, Italy, and Greece were featured. Culinary options included Greek *moussaka*, *spanakopita*, and *pastitchio*; Korean *kimchi*; Japanese *miso*; curry pastes; Chinese noodle dishes; Brazilian fish stew; and Moroccan chicken with lemon and olives.

In 2004, ARAMARK served about 2 million meals at the Athens Olympic Games, which included 500,000 pounds of meat and seafood, 76,000 pounds of salad greens, 20,000 pounds of rice, 19,500 pounds of olives, 177,000 pounds of potatoes, 640,000 bananas, and almost 2 tons of garlic.[2]

Above: Olympic athletes eat astonishing amounts of fruit. At the 1968 Summer Olympic Games in Mexico City, ARA recruited and trained a local operating staff of 1,250 to prepare and serve 1.25 million meals.

Left: One of the six dining areas in the Olympic Village in Mexico City. Depending on their training schedules, athletes ate at all different times of the day and night. Dining areas remained open almost constantly to accommodate them.

Olympic athletes from Ghana proceed through a serving line during the 1968 Olympic Games in Mexico City. Athletes competing in the Games could have as much food as they wanted, with selections familiar to them.

Every food item included a card that listed its nutritional value, calories, protein, carbohydrates, fat, and sodium in several languages.

When it comes to serving the Olympic Games, ARAMARK keeps things running smoothly, despite inevitable challenges. In Athens, for example, there were construction delays, major security concerns, and a blackout just one month before the games were set to begin.

Once menus are selected, a supply chain must be established; shipping arrangements made; cooking and dining areas designed, set up, and decorated; and local workers located, hired, and trained. Issues of every sort must be considered—transportation, security, sanitation, nutrition, storage, and finances—all necessary to make it possible to serve more than 10,000 athletes and others.

ARAMARK sent 85 executives and chefs, assisted by more than 1,000 students from Greek and U.S. culinary schools, to manage and staff the kitchens in Athens.

Here is a list of all the Olympic Games the company has served:

1968: Summer Olympic Games in Mexico City, Mexico
1976: Summer Olympic Games in Montreal, Canada
1980: Winter Olympic Games in Lake Placid, New York
1984: Winter Olympic Games in Sarajevo, Yugoslavia
1984: Summer Olympic Games in Los Angeles, California
1988: Winter Olympic Games in Calgary, Canada
1988: Summer Olympic Games in Seoul, Korea
1992: Summer Olympic Games in Barcelona, Spain
1994: Winter Olympic Games in Lillehammer, Norway
1996: Centennial Olympic Games in Atlanta, Georgia
1998: Winter Olympic Games in Nagano, Japan
2000: Summer Olympic Games in Sydney, Australia
2004: Summer Olympic Games in Athens, Greece

passenger meals. The following year, ARA procured another in-flight food service company, Mack Brothers Ltd. ARA now provided food and beverages for major international and domestic airlines.

Through its new Aero division, the company also managed concessions and bookshops in airports. In 1969, ARA acquired Ground Services, Inc., and formed a division to handle baggage, cargo loading, and ground transfer for passengers. Providing a range of services to one client group—in this case, airports—was and continues to be a fundamental company strategy.

In addition to expanding its services to one client group, ARA also grew across country lines. In 1967, ARA acquired an interest in the premier Canadian manual and automated food service company, Versafood Services Ltd.

The following year, ARA continued to expand its food service into new markets by forming Davre's, an upscale, fine-dining division. The 95$^{th}$, the division's first restaurant, was impressively located at the top of the John Hancock Center in

Chicago. In 1969, ARA also acquired J. L. Richardson, a company that provided food service to offshore oil rigs in the Gulf of Mexico, taking ARA far beyond its original institutional client base.

ARA continued to diversify throughout the decade as the company moved further into new service areas outside of the food service industry. ARA acquired Sigma Marketing Systems and other similar companies that specialized in mass-marketing merchandise programs and the development of promotional ideas for retailers.

Recognizing the similarity between the wholesale periodicals business and its already well-understood vending business that distributed product from central warehouses, ARA purchased District

---

ARA asserted its international presence when it was awarded the food service contract for the 1968 Summer Olympic Games in Mexico City. The 1968 Games were the first Olympic Games ever to be served by a food service management company.

With athletes and trainers from 117 countries around the world, some language barriers were likely at the Olympic Games. In 1968, in Mexico City, international symbols were used to direct athletes and others to the dining hall, restroom, healthcare facilities, and other areas they needed to find.

News, a company that delivered newspapers, magazines, and books to retailers. This acquisition became the foundation for ARA's magazine and book division, which would grow to become one of the largest distributors of periodicals in the country.

Expanding even further into new service areas, ARA entered the business of building and grounds maintenance in 1968 with the formation of a new division called Environmental Services. Initially, this division served only hospitals, but it soon grew to include schools, nursing homes, offices, and hotels.

### More Notable Achievements

ARA's first appearance at the Olympic Games was in 1968, when the company served 1.25 million meals to 10,000 athletes, media members, officials, and trainers at the Summer Games in Mexico City. ARA's unflappable spirit prevailed over the daunting task of providing round-the-clock food service for people from 117 countries, and the food service at the Olympic Games was hailed as an outstanding success.

By this time, ARA had won a contract from NASA to provide food services at the Kennedy Space Center in Cape Canaveral, Florida. Operating cafeterias, mobile snack bars, and food-vending areas for scientists and technicians working in the 88,000-acre complex, the company was proud to have served a historic meal to the *Apollo 11* astronauts—their final meal before blasting off on their first trip to the moon in 1969.

ARASERV continued to grow rapidly, adding ski resorts, indoor arenas, and cultural centers to its client list. In 1967, ARASERV received national attention when it provided refreshments during a "country fair" event on the lawn of the White House.

In a forward-thinking endeavor, the ARA Hospital Food Management division designed a community-sponsored senior citizen nutrition program to bring attention to seniors' health and nutritional issues. Federal specifications would later be based on ARA's program.

### New Name for a Diversified Services Company

To better reflect the increasing number and wide variety of services ARA managed, the company decided to change its name from Automatic Retailers of America to ARA Services. The shareholders formally approved the name change in 1969.

By the end of the 1960s, the company's revenues had reached $596 million. ARA experienced astonishing growth and diversification through the 1960s. After its numerous acquisitions and expansions, the company was proud of its diversity and flexibility, which was virtually unmatched in the industry. It had been a remarkable decade for ARA, and the future looked full of opportunity.

ARATEX workers hang uniform shirts after they have been cleaned. The ARATEX division was formed after ARA Services purchased the domestic rental service division of the venerable, Ohio-based Work Wear Corporation.

## CHAPTER FOUR

# INVENTING AN INDUSTRY

## 1970–1978

*ARA Services is a unique company in that its product is service, or more specifically, the management of service.*

—Bill Fishman, CEO, ARA Services,
from his 1977 address to
The Newcomen Society in North America

THE RAPID GROWTH AND EXpansion of ARA Services extended into the 1970s, as Chairman and CEO Davre Davidson and President Bill Fishman continued to understand and act on trends.

The management systems that the company had developed while in food service were quickly applied to a wide variety of other services, from building maintenance to transportation. And, in every business entered, ARA continued to customize services, tailoring them to meet the specific needs of each client. Always, in every separate area of business, ARA continued to deliver exceptional service, the company's hallmark. "Davre Davidson always had the attitude that we were serving in somebody else's house, wherever we were, wherever we had a contract," said Harry Belinger, a former ARA vice president of public affairs, who joined the company in 1976.[1]

As a result of Davidson's and Fishman's belief in services, ARA's service capabilities and its client base expanded dramatically, despite a stagnant national economy, rising inflation, some major national strikes, and social unrest in cities and college campuses. Davidson and Fishman were determined to continue expanding ARA Services. "Bill Fishman told me very early on that his goal was to double the size of the company," said Belinger.[2]

Inflation and the economy would continue to worsen, however. In 1974, the company celebrated yearly sales that exceeded $1 billion for the first time, but in 1975, earnings declined by 10 percent.[3]

Not easily daunted, and always quick to learn from the past, Davidson and Fishman rallied the company, which in 1976 again posted record gains.[4]

In the 1970s, ARA would complete several acquisitions that moved the company into different service areas. Some of those ventures proved to be profitable and remained in place for years to come. In other cases, when officials determined that an acquired business was no longer a good fit, it was divested.

Davidson and Fishman developed a singular expertise in the business of acquisitions. This was particularly true for Fishman, the bolder of the two who was always pushing for expansion. It became clear during night classes at the University of Pennsylvania, which Fishman attended in his pursuit of a Master's degree in Business Administration. Gerson Miller, the chairman of North American Corporation and a longtime business colleague of Fishman's, related the story:

---

The management of healthcare was an integral part of services provided to seniors at ARA-operated living centers. By 1978, ARA managed the largest nursing home operation in the United States.

An ARA guide directs riders on a trail in the Shenandoah National Park in Virginia. The park, for which ARASERV managed lodging, recreation, food services, grounds, and camping stores, was the company's first national park account.

*I remember one time Bill was telling me that he [hired] a lot of [people with] MBAs from the University of Pennsylvania. The dean of the school asked Bill, "As long as you're hiring so many, why don't you become an MBA, too?" He said, "OK, I'll try."*

*One of the classes he was involved in was mergers and acquisitions. His professor would start telling him what the parameters were for doing business, for mergers, and for making acquisitions, and Bill would take issue with the man. Finally, the professor asked him, "Mr. Fishman, how many [acquisitions] have you been involved with if you're speaking like this, with so much experience?"*

*"Give or take 500," Bill replied.*[5]

During the period of acquisitions, it became increasingly apparent that ARA excelled at contract management in a variety of services.

By the time Davre Davidson stepped down as chairman in 1977, ARA was providing services that ranged from transporting schoolchildren to caring for elderly residents in geriatric facilities. It had become a diversified service management company,

**1970**
Despite a challenging economy, ARA Services sets records with revenues of $648.4 million and profits of $18.6 million. The company now has 35,000 employees.

**1973**
ARA enters elder care management when it acquires National Living Centers and Geriatrics, Inc.

**1972**
ARA acquires Educational and Recreational Services, Inc., forming a division that manages bus transportation for school districts.

The company breaks into the European market with the acquisition of Eurovend NV, giving it food service capabilities in the United Kingdom, France, Germany, and Belgium.

**1974**
Company sales exceed $1 billion for the first time.

having virtually created a new category within the rapidly growing service sector of the economy.

**Expanding and Diversifying the Core Business**

While ARA Services was moving quickly into other areas, the company remained focused on its core businesses of vending and manual food service, meeting consumers' needs through innovation.

To meet the demands of a changing market, vending machines had come a long way from the old-style peanut and snack machines of the 1940s and 1950s. Customers not only demanded a greater variety of items from their vending machines, but also a surrounding area where they could sit and enjoy their purchases.

Food service, too, continued to change, and ARA Services proved to be an innovative leader in the field. With a long and solid background in food service for schools, colleges, hospitals, and businesses, ARA had expanded its operations to include airlines, oil rigs, and subsidized school lunch programs. It had created a rapidly growing coffee service unit and a fine dining division. The company began to consider exporting its food service model overseas.

An ARA serviceman stocks vending machines that are located in a newer, brighter setting designed to attract more customers.

**1975**
Bill Fishman is appointed CEO, a step in the planned succession of Davre Davidson.

**1976**
A joint venture with Mitsui & Co. Ltd. positions ARA Services in Japan.

**1977**
Davidson is named Founder–Chairman after stepping down as Chairman of the Board. He continues to serve as a director, while Fishman replaces him as Chairman.

ARA acquires a division of Work Wear and forms ARATEX.

**1978**
A new health services division is formed to manage medical services in hospitals and prisons.

Above: An ARA Ground Services employee repairs a piece of airline equipment. ARA handled a range of flight-related services, from in-air meals to equipment maintenance.

Below left: ARA had a notable airport presence during the 1970s. Here, an employee services an airplane interior.

Below right: The acquisition of J. L. Richardson put ARA in the business of providing food and housekeeping services on drilling rigs and oil-producing platforms located from two to 180 miles offshore in the Gulf of Mexico. ARA employees were taken to the rigs on helicopters or boats, normally working seven-days-on, seven-days-off schedules.

The Aero division provided in-flight meals at major airports in cities such as New York, Boston, Los Angeles, Minneapolis, Miami, Mexico City, and Philadelphia.

A coffee service business called Coffee System, created a few years earlier by ARA, continued to grow. By the mid-1970s, the company provided more than 60,000 coffee brewers in thousands of locations across the country. By the end of the decade, the business boasted 116,000 locations. Serving offices and shops with 10 to 100 employees, this innovative system provided coffee-making equipment and ground coffee, which employees prepared themselves in automatic brewers.

Although each account was relatively small, the number of locations across the country made the coffee business very profitable. During an interview in 1978, Fishman commented on the company's ability to make big profits from small transactions:

*That is one of our talents—managing high-volume businesses with very small transactions. The average account may be $35 in gross revenues— that's sales, not profit. But multiply by 95,000 customers, and it adds up.*[6]

Davre's, the fine dining division, expanded to many fine dining locations in prestigious corporate buildings and civic centers.

Service to oil rigs soon expanded from the Gulf of Mexico to those in the North Sea, as well.

**Feeding the Nation's Schoolchildren**

In the early 1970s, ARA formed a new division called Community and School Food Service. The division initially managed contracts under the National School Lunch Program for schools that lacked food preparation facilities. Piloted in the Detroit Public Schools, ARA developed a portable, nutritious lunch package called the Astro-Pack. The division rapidly expanded to provide the management of on-site food service in public schools, as well.

While ARA Services focused on providing superior food services for its customers, it learned a great deal about its clients' needs for other services. At the end of the 1960s, the company had formed a building services group, which during the 1970s, managed maintenance and cleaning services primarily for healthcare institutions, many of which were already ARA food service clients. The group expanded greatly over the years and is a core ARAMARK division today.

**Acquisitions Broaden Scope of Businesses**

ARA Services became widely recognized following the 1968 Olympic Games in Mexico City for its ability to handle huge events under challenging circumstances. This resulted in increased opportunities for the company and heightened the can-do, entrepreneurial attitude among company employees and management. Davidson reflected on that attitude in a message to employees in 1977:

Above: Coffee service is profitable only if the coffee is good. Taste testing makes certain the product meets rigorous standards.

Below left: A wine steward assists diners in the Carnelian Room in the Bank of America building in San Francisco, one of the fine dining establishments operated by Davre's. Although ARAMARK no longer operates ARA's fine dining division, the Carnelian Room, residence of the Bankers Club, is open to the public for dinner and Sunday brunch.

Below right: ARA was the first food service company to participate in the National School Lunch Program, designing prepackaged Astro-Packs that could be prepared off-site, then transported into schools that did not have cafeterias or food preparation areas.

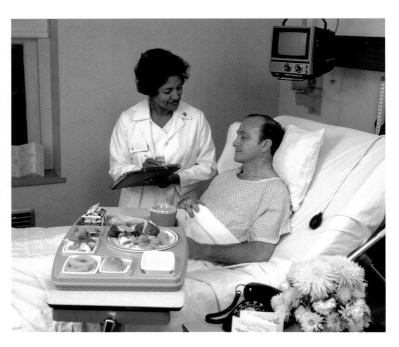

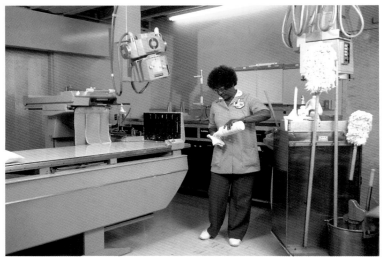

Left: Making sure hospital patients are served nutritious, good-tasting meals has always been an important part of ARA's food service business. Here, an ARA registered dietitian discusses nutritional concerns with a patient who has been put on a special diet.

Above right: ARA management's strong entrepreneurial instincts spurred the company to branch out into numerous new areas, offering new services to existing and prospective clients. Already providing food service to hospitals, schools, colleges, businesses, and industries, the company moved into building services, such as indoor cleaning and building and grounds maintenance. Here, an ARA employee cleans a testing facility in a hospital.

*It is generally the entrepreneurial spirit that is willing to experiment and explore new opportunities. This involves some risk, but, without risk, there are few rewards. This entrepreneurial spirit has enabled ARA to consistently expand its service management horizons. Most of these ventures have been successful. We have made some mistakes, but these were recognized within a short time, and we did not sustain any serious setbacks. Because of this venturesome spirit, however, we have been able to build important, new service activities through acquisition and through internal development, which have contributed significantly to the overall success of the company.*[7]

Confident of its ability to transfer its finely tuned management skills to additional service areas, ARA's entrepreneurial spirit spurred the company to acquire additional companies as diverse as school bus transportation services and construction management. By the mid-1970s, the company had acquired:

- National Living Centers and Geriatrics, Inc., which specialized in managing extended-care facilities for elderly people, many of whom were recovering from surgery or illness. By 1978, ARA managed the largest nursing home operation in the United States.

- Carl A. Morse and Diesel Construction, which specialized in building consultation and construction management, with an emphasis on "creative construction" that set it apart from other companies in the field. One of the division's most notable jobs was its work on the construction of the Sears Tower in Chicago.
- Educational and Recreational Services, Inc., which provided transportation services for school districts, private industry, and government agencies. Starting with 1,600 yellow school buses in 1972, the division doubled its business by the middle of the 1970s, and by 1979 it was transporting more than half a million students to and from school each day.

ARA quickly exited some additional service ventures it entered, including a management consulting business and a municipal fleet maintenance business, because they did not prove viable long-term investments. For the same reason, ARA divested the Morse Diesel Company after only a few years.

Rather than using cash-only transactions, ARA often made acquisitions through stock-for-stock transactions. This manner of transaction offered company owners the opportunity to reap the benefits of their lives' work without onerous capital gains taxes. Previous owners of companies acquired by ARA became holders of ARA stock and, in nearly every case, continued to manage their original businesses as division presidents of ARA Services, which benefited both ARA and the original business owners. Davidson and Fishman continued to act on their strong conviction that when the business is service, the expertise of those who understand the business is the most valuable asset to be acquired.

ARA Services continued to grow in the early 1970s through the expansion of previously acquired businesses. For example, Sigma Marketing Systems began to offer purchase incentive programs to

Left: Sigma Marketing developed promotional ideas to build customer traffic and encourage repeat shopping for its clients, including banks, grocery stores, gas stations, and retail outlets. Sigma also imported gifts, such as this fine china, to be sold in specialty shops.

Below left: Students pose with their bus driver on one of ARA's contracted school buses. By 1979, the company's transportation services group was transporting more than 550,000 students to and from school every day, as well as providing tour bus services in some areas.

Below right: ARA Services entered the European market with the acquisition of Eurovend NV, providing it with markets in Belgium, the United Kingdom, and Germany, where this cafeteria is located. The operation grew into ARA Europe and expanded services into Spain.

supermarket chains, oil companies, and banks. Sigma also operated specialty gift sections in retail venues such as department stores, where one of its signature items was imported fine china.

The periodicals distribution group also increased its client base to include train stations, airports, supermarkets, drugstore chains, military installations, and U.S. Navy ships. The Aero division

augmented its operations by moving into restaurants and cafeterias, in addition to gift shops and bookstores in 12 major airports. Ground Services expanded its bag-handling operation to include passenger screening at airports, as well as aircraft maintenance and interior cleaning services.

As ARA Services continued to expand and diversify, Bill Fishman worked hard to maintain the family-type atmosphere that had been characteristic of the firm since its earliest days. "Everybody knew everyone," said Joan Voli, who has been with the company for more than 50 years. "My daughter also works for ARAMARK, and my father worked for ARAMARK for 20-some years. I also had an uncle and a nephew who worked for ARAMARK. We're just an ARAMARK family."[8] Fishman explained:

*We were successful at maintaining a family-type atmosphere. Of course, it never works 100 percent, [but] I never stopped trying to achieve this. I constantly tried to be out in the field and … meet the people who performed the service, tell them about the company, listen to their criticisms and questions, and give them a voice, give them an audience … and that was the way I managed the company.*[9]

**Overseas Expansion**

ARA Services had entered the international market in 1967 with the purchase of an interest in Versafood Services in Canada. Early in the 1970s, Fishman began pushing Davidson to explore overseas markets. Davidson, however, argued that ARA

# FROM WORK WEAR TO ARATEX

WHEN ARA SERVICES ACQUIRED THE domestic rental service division of Work Wear Corporation in 1977, it gained a company with a long and interesting history dating back to 1890.

During that time, when all laundry, whether for private customers or commercial concerns, was washed by hand and delivered in horse-drawn wagons, Red Star Laundry opened in San Jose, California. The company's most famous employee was a Stanford University campus worker and young engineering student: Herbert Hoover, who later became the 31st president of the United States.[1]

In 1914, Samuel Rosenthal started a work clothing manufacturing business, the Cleveland Overall Company, which would eventually become Work Wear. Rosenthal revolutionized the industrial garment industry with his idea to rent work clothing to businesses and industries, pick

Below: ARATEX President Joe Kirshbaum helped make it the premier uniform rental and textile firm in the country.

Opposite: Red Star Laundry became a part of ARATEX when the company acquired the uniform rental business and Work Wear in 1977. This photo of Red Star's early days was taken circa 1920 in San Jose, California. Horse-pulled buggies were used to pick up and deliver laundry to clients.

it up, launder, repair, and return it to the workers. He convinced laundries to adopt the idea, and then began selling the clothing manufactured at Cleveland Overall Company to industrial plants, such as Red Star, for their new work clothing rental operations. As selling work clothing to laundries for rental proved far more profitable than selling the garments to traditional retailers, Work Wear grew into a giant in the work clothing manufacturing business.

should continue focusing on opportunities in the United States. He reasoned that diverting attention from domestic operations would allow competitors to get the upper hand. Davidson's tendency to prefer a prudent approach was characteristic of his overall personality, while Fishman's was just the opposite, according to Martin Spector, a former general counsel of the company:

*Dave ... was extraordinarily conservative. Bill Fishman, on the other hand, was aggressive. He would just make the leap. The two of them were a perfect balance.*[10]

Never one to be easily dissuaded, Fishman continued his push to go international, and, in 1972,

ARA broke into the European market with the acquisition of Eurovend NV. The acquisition provided the company with food service capabilities in the United Kingdom, France, Germany, and Belgium. As the operation grew, it was renamed ARA Europe and expanded to include a variety of food and refreshment services.

ARA Europe employed nearly 5,000 people and managed food service for its clients and customers at more than 6,000 at-work market locations in five Western European countries. Corporate headquarters was located near London's Heathrow Airport.[11]

In 1976, a joint venture with Mitsui & Co. Ltd. positioned ARA Services in Japan. AIM Services, as the joint venture was named, brought professional food service management methods to Japanese

As his company grew, Rosenthal and his son, Leighton, began buying laundries to which they had been selling garments.

To expand his customer base, Rosenthal also set up launderers in business. Harry Kirshbaum, who in 1935 founded the Kovakar Company in Chicago, approached Rosenthal with a request for a loan so he could move his business to California. (Rosenthal was known to extend liberal credit terms to launderers who were potential customers.)

With the loan from Rosenthal, Kirshbaum moved to California and expanded his business. In 1945, he purchased Red Star, which remained a Work Wear customer until 1967, when it merged with Work Wear.

Kirshbaum's sons, Joseph and Ira, had taken over the operation of the business from their father soon after World War II. When Red Star merged with Work Wear, Joe and Ira assumed responsibility for the Work Wear rental operations, with Joe at the helm as president and Ira as vice president. By then, Red Star had become Red Star Industrial Service with 12 plants, and the Kirshbaums were giants in the uniform rental business.

Work Wear, which both manufactured and rented work clothing, also developed a network of industries including linen supply companies. Its computerized operations set Work Wear apart from other laundry and uniform services companies.

In the 1970s, the U.S. Department of Justice ordered Work Wear to split its manufacturing and rental divisions and divest one of them.

Fishman, recognizing an opportunity for ARA, moved to buy Work Wear's rental business, with the understanding that the Kirshbaum brothers would continue to run it.

As a respected leader in the textile maintenance industry, Joe Kirshbaum was named president of the new ARATEX division in 1977. In addition, he later assumed responsibility for the magazine and book division as well as the transportation division. He remained with the company until his death in 1989.

businesses. ARA's facilities planning department also designed the preparation and service areas of a six-restaurant complex in Mitsui's headquarters in Tokyo. ARA-trained AIM managers directed the work of more than 200 employees and operated six restaurants, a coffee shop, and a building-wide coffee service. The restaurants included three cafeterias that offered Japanese, Chinese, or Western menus, a "Noodle Shop," a waitress-service dining room featuring Japanese specialties, and a popular "Snack Shop," where customers could purchase hamburgers and pizza, as well as Japanese-style fast-food items.[12]

Although Davidson had not shared Fishman's initial enthusiasm for international expansion, he later acknowledged its importance. In remarks at his 80th birthday celebration in 1991, Davidson discussed the significance of international business and recognized Fishman as the catalyst:

> *The company has continued to develop, expanding market potential in other countries. And for this, we can thank Bill. Today, international business accounts for more than 15 percent of total revenues. The percentage is increasing and should continue to increase in the coming years.*[13]

### Passing the Baton

In 1975, Bill Fishman was named CEO, an important first step and a smooth transition that started the process of management succession. In 1977, Davidson stepped down as Chairman of the

Above: The newly formed ARATEX division managed rental and leasing options—including cleaning and delivery services—for workforce uniforms.

Below left: In accordance with Bill Fishman's wishes to expand its international presence, ARA Services entered a joint venture with the Japanese firm Mitsui & Co. Ltd. in 1976. The joint venture, called AIM Services Ltd., managed institutional food services for clients in Japan and other countries in the Far East.

Board of ARA Services. He was 66. The Board elected Fishman as Chairman, and Marvin Heaps, who had been executive vice president of operations, took Fishman's place as company president and chief operating officer. Davidson received the title of Founder–Chairman and remained a member of the company's Board of Directors until he died.

In a farewell message to ARA employees, Davidson expressed his confidence regarding the transition:

> *I am optimistic about the future of the company. The American economy is increasingly service-oriented, more so than any other industrialized nation. It seems certain that this trend will continue at least through the end of the century. This increasing demand for services presents important new opportunities for ARA Services. We have the people, the technical expertise, the systems, and the financial strength to satisfy the*

*steadily expanding demand for quality services at reasonable cost.*[14]

### Continuing Forward

Just as Davidson had anticipated and planned for, business at ARA Services continued to grow after his retirement. ARA made a landmark acquisition in 1977, when it purchased the domestic rental service division of Work Wear Corporation, a well-established, Ohio-based international uniform service company.

An ARA division called ARATEX was formed, and the company quickly began to expand the scope of its uniform and textile services. Soon, the division served 200,000 clients in 36 states, delivering uniforms and providing related services to hospitals, schools, colleges, and many kinds of businesses.

# THE 1970s ECONOMY AND ARA SERVICES

THE DECADE OF THE 1970s WAS ECOnomically challenging to the nation. Inflation was high. So were energy prices, federal budget deficits, and foreign competition. There was a deepening trade deficit, an unpopular war during the first half of the decade, and rising unemployment. The stock market plunged, along with consumer confidence.

And yet, ARA Services not only survived this decade, but also prospered. The company's 1970 annual report stated that records had been established in service revenues and profits, despite a general economic slowdown, severe inflation, and other economic hardships.

By 1975, when "stagflation" had become a household word, the company was really feeling the pinch of the weak economy, experiencing its first decline in net income in its history. Revenue growth, however, continued to increase.

The decline in net income was addressed in the 1975 annual report:

*Widespread economic dislocations and inflationary pressures throughout the world had a severe impact on some of the markets we serve. Inflation of food and fuel prices, the decline of general economic activity and stresses on consumer budgets created difficult challenges for our service management business.*[1]

In response to economic conditions, aggressive programs were introduced to reduce operating costs. Client contracts were renegotiated when necessary to accommodate swiftly changing operating conditions. ARA continued to expand its service lines, giving it a buffer to more significant downturns in certain areas of the economy. The 1979 annual report described the situation as follows:

*The mix of our business protects us to a considerable degree from downswings in the economy, with healthcare, school transportation operations, and services to governmental clients being especially recession resistant.*[2]

ARA Services, which had identified service management as an industry well before most other individuals and companies even understood the concept of the term, understood that despite economic conditions, people would continue to require services. As a result, it moved confidently and profitably ahead during a decade with economic problems that seriously challenged many businesses in the United States.

In the last year of the decade, ARA surpassed the $2 billion mark in revenues, and its net income exceeded $52 million. The company employed more than 100,000 people.

Above: Fishman thanks an employee who assisted with food service at the 1976 Summer Olympic Games in Montreal. Fishman was genuinely appreciative of outstanding efforts.

Below: A luncheon honoring Davre Davidson (seated on the left) was held after his retirement on July 16, 1977. Gathered here to honor him are (standing from left): Henry Davidson, Davre's brother and former partner; Herman Minter, who served as a director and ARA treasurer and chief financial officer; Aaron Clark, Davidson's longtime friend and advisor; Felix Juda, a director; and Douglas Moore, a former vice president. Bill Fishman is seated on the right.

Fishman, who had pushed for the acquisition, said that ARA's expertise in managing central warehousing and distribution, route delivery systems, inventory controls, quality controls, and vehicle operation and maintenance made the acquisition a logical one for ARA. He predicted that the newly formed ARATEX division would provide a profitable growth opportunity.[15] In retrospect, Fishman's prediction turned out to be correct. The ARATEX division continued to grow, eventually becoming ARAMARK Uniform and Career Apparel.

The late 1970s also ushered in the formation of a health services management division: Physicians Placement Group, later named Spectrum Emergency Care, specialized in the staffing and administration of hospital emergency facilities, counseling programs for employees, and trauma physician recruitment. The division expanded to manage healthcare services in correctional facilities, including in-house clinics and drug and alcohol rehabilitation for inmates. The ARA division managed physician staffing for more than 1,500 hospitals, clinics, dispensaries, mental health facilities, and other healthcare institutions, as well as other prisons.

**ARA SERVICES, INC.**
INDEPENDENCE SQUARE, WEST · PHILADELPHIA, PA. 19106 · (215) WA 3-7700

December 1, 1971

WILLIAM S. FISHMAN
President

Mr. Ara Parseghian
Head Football Coach
University of Notre Dame

Dear Mr. Parseghian:

Perhaps I should have taken the liberty of addressing you as Ara, for that's our corporate name (all caps). Often the press calls us Ara instead of ARA. Our PR staff receives almost as many news clippings about Ara (you) as about Araserv (our recreation division which provides food and refreshments at such places as the Astrodome, Atlanta Stadium and the Cotton Bowl).

Anyway, I see by last night's paper (clipping attached) that there's a chance Ara will come to Philadelphia. A decade ago, the other ARA came to town and we've been happy about it ever since (clipping attached). We recommend the move highly. Since establishing corporate headquarters here, our annual sales have zoomed from $100 million to $750 million, the size of our team from 8,000 to 40,000. We've made our goals each year and think you can do the same with the Eagles.

I'm a midwesterner myself, grew up in Indiana and was graduated from the U. of Illinois. I'm sure there's comfortable room for two Aras in Philadelphia. Should you decide to relocate in the City of Brotherly Love, you're assured of built-in rapport with our ARA. We've grown and flourished here, like the city very much and are confident you'll feel the same.

Next time you're in the city, please drop in to see me at our new corporate headquarters on Independence Square at 6th and Walnut sts. Meanwhile, I'm sending some materials under separate cover to better acquaint you with ARA.

Cordially,

*Bill Fishman*

William S. Fishman
President

---

**University of Notre Dame**
Notre Dame, Indiana 46556

Ara Parseghian
Head Football Coach

December 27, 1971

Mr. William S. Fishman
President
ARA Services, Inc.
Independence Square, West
Philadelphia, Pennsylvania 19106

Dear Mr. Fishman:

First of all, may I say I was indeed pleased to receive your letter. On more than one occasion I have pointed with pride to your insignia on trucks and various other advertisements indicating to those within hearing I was incorporated nationally. Unfortunately, no one doing business with you has seen fit to send to my office any of the checks that have shown up in your profit and loss statement. All I get are letters of complaint from our Notre Dame alumni and subway alumni. Seriously, I do appreciate your writing and by this time I'm sure you are aware the Philadelphia Eagle rumor was just exactly that - a rumor. There was not one fabric of truth to the story, but I was indeed honored some people would consider me a capable candidate. I have many friends in the Philadelphia area and have always enjoyed my brief visits to the city.

May I say I was impressed with the tremendous growth and accomplishments of your organization and I feel a small measure of pride in knowing you grew up as a Hoosier and graduated from a midwestern Big 10 school.

A few years ago several capable young insurance executives put together a corporation calling it Ara Parseghian & Associates. You have offered me an invitation to see your corporate headquarters and the next time I'm in Philadelphia and I would certainly welcome the opportunity to do so. I can't think of anything better than Ara getting together with ARA. APA is involved in a multitude of insurance services and, frankly, I'm not sure where we might be of service to you, but certainly would like to explore the possibility of getting together in some way. It would make a great story and maybe even surpass the rumor that I was going to the Eagles! I really think it is a natural and will look forward to any suggestion you might like to offer.

I wish you the happiest of holiday seasons and may the New Year bring you continued health, happiness, and success!

Sincerely,

ARA PARSEGHIAN

Cotton Bowl Champions 1971
"The Fighting Irish" National Football Champions
1964 Hall of Fame MacArthur Bowl
1966 Associated Press · United Press International · Football Writers Award
Co-Champions Hall of Fame MacArthur Bowl

---

When the news media reported that famed Notre Dame football coach Ara Parseghian might be leaving the college ranks to coach the NFL's Philadelphia Eagles, Bill Fishman quickly wrote Parseghian to invite him to visit ARA headquarters when he was in town. "I'm sure there's comfortable room for two 'Aras' in Philadelphia," he stated. Parseghian wrote back that the Eagles story was just a rumor. He also wrote that he would look forward to dropping by ARA's corporate offices when he was in town. "I have pointed with pride to your insignia on trucks and various other advertisements indicating to those within hearing I was incorporated nationally," Parseghian replied.

# DEVELOPING A NEW INDUSTRY: SERVICE MANAGEMENT

FROM ITS EARLIEST DAYS, ARAMARK'S predecessor companies always focused on providing quality service to customers. That customer orientation was and remains the foundation of the service management industry.

On January 20, 1977, Bill Fishman, president and CEO of ARA Services, delivered an address on service to The Newcomen Society in North America at the Franklin Institute. Titled "Developing a New Industry: Service Management," the address focused on ARA's philosophy on professional services management. Some key excerpts from this well-received address, which was also provided in print format to some 17,000 business leaders, appear below. Fishman's words aptly describe the service management philosophy that ARAMARK has been developing, refining, and practicing since its earliest days:

*Each and every one of us uses the word "service" many times in the course of any given day. The word means different things to different people. ... In preparing for this speech, I turned to the latest edition of* Webster's New Collegiate Dictionary *to get the formal definition. There was almost a full page devoted to service but nothing on service management.*

*Service management is an important industry that we at ARA identified many years ago and have been working on developing almost exclusively. It might sound somewhat ridiculous to talk about identifying an industry, but some of the most serious, even disastrous, mistakes have been made by businessmen who failed to do just that.*

*Harvard business professor Theodore Levitt in a recent reprint of his now classical article on "Marketing Myopia" in the* Harvard Business Review *cited two excellent examples of failing to properly identify the industry: railroads and movies.*

*Levitt contends the railroads ... let others take away their customers because they considered themselves to be in the railroad business, not the transportation business. They were product-oriented, not customer-oriented.*

*The same thing happened with Hollywood with the advent of television, according to Levitt. He noted that Hollywood incorrectly defined its industry as the "Movies"—rather than entertainment. This led Hollywood initially to scorn and reject TV, when it should have recognized and welcomed it as an opportunity to expand its industry—the entertainment industry. They, too, were product-oriented, not customer-oriented.*

*We at ARA have been customer-oriented from the very beginning. It is reflected in the way we operate, the way we've structured our company, the way we've identified our markets. ... Our success [has been] based on the fact that we developed a system for professionally providing a service, a direct service to people.*[1]

BILL FISHMAN

More than 100 physicians were under contract on a full-time basis, and 1,200 physicians were under contract part time.[16]

ARA's beginnings in the 1930s were in vending. In the 1960s, it became a full-service food company and expanded into a diversified service firm. Having successfully added new service lines in the 1970s, ARA further developed management systems, mastered the transfer of expertise across service lines, and improved its ability to recruit, train, and motivate service employees.

In the words of Bill Fishman at the end of the decade:

> We inventoried our resources. ... The conclusion was that we had evolved into a unique service management company.
>
> Service management is the professional application of basic and specialized business skills used to manage a wide range of direct personal services more efficiently, more effectively, more economically.
>
> There is great promise for the service management industry. More and more firms and institutions forced to cope with increasing economic pressures are re-examining some of the services they provide to see what can be contracted to professional managers ... who will have to deliver more efficiently, more economically, or be replaced.
>
> We at ARA have proven we can do this, and we stand ready to meet new challenges.[17]

Above left: An employee maneuvers a medicine cart between rows of prison cells. ARA began providing healthcare services to prisons in the late 1970s under a subsidiary called Correctional Medical Systems. By the end of the decade, it was providing medical services in 19 prisons.

Above right: Emergency personnel work to transport a critically ill patient by helicopter. ARA Services, under its Spectrum Emergency Care (formerly Physicians Placement Group) segment, provided physician staffing for hospital emergency rooms in 41 states. *(Photo by LYONS STUDIOS, INC.)*

In the coming years, the company would continue to draw the map of its future as it walked the path. Being on the cusp of a new industry called for some trial and error as it discovered what would fit this new model. It also required a healthy dose of vision and no small amount of guts.

An employee of the ARA Services magazine and book division unloads magazines for reading rooms on a U.S. Navy ship. The Navy was a customer of this wholesale periodicals distribution business.

## CHAPTER FIVE

# A NEW LEADER

## 1979–1983

*He knew exactly what was going on, what he wanted to do, and how he was going to do it, and yet the guy had only been there a couple of months at that time.*

—Harry Belinger, former vice president of public affairs, speaking about Joe Neubauer's early days with ARA Services

CONFIDENT AS HE WAS IN THE strength of the company, Bill Fishman recognized that the tremendous expansion and diversification in the past two decades had created some challenges that required attention. Management systems demanded further strengthening to create an infrastructure capable of supporting such a diverse collection of service divisions. Now in his sixties, Fishman knew it was time to make decisions regarding the company's future leadership.

More immediately, however, he recognized a pressing need to take the company to a higher level of professional management. While Fishman and Davre Davidson were brilliant entrepreneurs, ARA had grown to the point where it required people with more advanced knowledge of business practices. Financial systems needed improvement, the organizational structure required expert analysis, and there was work to be done in the public affairs area.

Realizing the need to fill key positions with the best people available, Fishman searched outside the company for those with the experience and vision to shore up the financial systems and institute a better management structure. Fishman believed it was time to take a more proactive approach to communicating to the public what ARA was all about. The time had arrived for the company to bring in new people capable of preparing the company for continued growth.

### Joe Neubauer

Using the many contacts he had made over the years, Fishman sought a professional who could bring the company's financial systems up to date. He received word about a young man, Joe Neubauer, who was a senior vice president at Wilson Sporting Goods, a subsidiary of PepsiCo. Acting on recommendations and his own instincts, Fishman interviewed Neubauer twice, and offered him a job after the second interview. Once again, Fishman's instincts would prove reliable.

Neubauer was intrigued by the idea of working for a company headquartered in Philadelphia, with executive offices in Los Angeles, and mergers and acquisitions work coming out of Chicago. Plus, as Neubauer recalled, he believed ARA Services could easily become far more profitable:

*I looked at some of the numbers. I remember my mother was living in Germany at the time, and during the summer that we started talking about [joining ARA Services], I actually was in Germany.*

This new logo, introduced in 1981, signaled a change in corporate attitude and accompanied an ambitious public relations and advertising program that told the world about ARA Services.

*I took the [papers] with me to read, and at the time, the company was doing $2.5 billion worth of business and had very thin margins. I said, "Boy, if we just improve the margins by ¼ percent or ½ percent, they can make a lot of money." I was a naive kid at the time. I thought well, you know, that's not difficult to do. You can do that. Everybody can do that.*[1]

Neubauer joined ARA Services in February 1979 as executive vice president of finance and development, treasurer, and chief financial officer. He was also elected to the Board of Directors.

Neubauer recalled his first day at ARA and how Fishman welcomed him:

*I remember coming in here the first day, and Fishman showing me to my office. He handed me a set of keys, gave me a list of banks, and told me if I had any problems to give him a call. That was my introduction to the company.*[2]

Fishman's brief interaction with Neubauer on his first day with the company, however, belied the support and encouragement he would continually offer to the man who would eventually succeed him.

Bill Fishman, who had replaced Davre Davidson as Chairman of the Board of ARA Services in 1977, planned carefully to ensure the company would remain in good hands when he eventually stepped down.

"He was a great mentor," Neubauer said. "He was a great supporter. He believed that everything is possible if you put the right people in the right places."[3]

Neubauer also worked with Davidson, who had been named Founder–Chairman when he stepped down as Chairman of the Board in 1977. Still living in Los Angeles, Davidson, who was passionate about the financial aspects of the business, remained active in the company through his participation in Board meetings. He and Neubauer often talked at length on the telephone prior to meetings. Neubauer described the conversations:

**1979**
Joe Neubauer joins ARA Services as executive vice president of finance and development, treasurer, and chief financial officer. He is also elected to the Board of Directors.

**1980**
Acquisition of Smith's Transfer Corporation takes the company into freight transfer as a new service line.

**1980**
ARA continues to expand its scope of services when it acquires National Child Care Centers, Inc., including the company's more than 60 early childhood learning centers.

**1981**
Neubauer is elected president and chief operating officer.

A new corporate identity program is introduced with a new logo and a plan to make the company more visible to the public.

*He would call before every Board meeting, and he would run me through the drill. He knew relationships, and he understood the economics of the business, and after two or two-and-a-half hours, he would say, "OK, you've listened to the old man. Now what do you want to do?" I'd tell him, and he would support 100 percent what I wanted to do.*

*It was as if he was saying, "I'm trying to give you the perspective of where these things are coming from, and trying to make sure you've thought about most of them, but at the end of it, I'm in your corner. I'll support you." He never interfered once.[4]*

It is unknown whether Fishman and Davidson recognized the degree to which Neubauer would affect ARA. However, Fishman, who had identified and hired him, had extremely high expectations of the young chief financial officer. Neubauer would not let them down.

### The Beginning of the Neubauer Era

Once hired, Neubauer immediately started reorganizing the company's financial systems. He developed financial performance improvement programs by introducing concepts such as return on net assets (RONA) and earnings before interest and taxes (EBIT) to analyze financial results and measure the profitability of business units. Neubauer introduced a new way of looking at the business:

*I was the first CFO who was not an accountant, and that was a big change. I looked at things in terms of what the numbers tell you about the business, not what the numbers are.[5]*

Several managers at the time recalled that Neubauer, while fostering the entrepreneurial spirit that had characterized the company throughout its history, brought a new dimension and a more disciplined approach to the business.

Chris Hackem, president of ARAMARK Higher Education, joined ARA in 1977. She personally witnessed this transformation from its first days:

*The company was always very entrepreneurial. But programmatically, and from a process standpoint, we've become significantly better in terms of being able to harness the power, the best practices of divisions across business units in the organization.[6]*

**1982**
ARA becomes a charter member of the Coalition of Service Industries (CSI), an organization that promotes understanding of the importance of the service sector of the American economy.

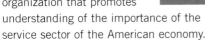

**1983**
Neubauer is named CEO. Fishman remains as Chairman of the Board.

**1982**
ARA provides a grant to the Wharton School of the University of Pennsylvania to create the Fishman–Davidson Center. Its purpose is to support research on issues in the service sector. *(Photo courtesy of University of Pennsylvania.)*

**1983**
ARA acquires Solon Automated Services, a leading manager of laundry equipment services for apartment buildings, college dormitories, and military bases.

# JOE NEUBAUER

JOE NEUBAUER WAS BORN IN 1941 IN what is today Tel Aviv, Israel, three years after his parents had fled Nazi Germany. Life in his war-torn homeland, which during the early years of his life was still called Palestine, presented many difficulties.

Still, Neubauer was a happy child, attending a parochial school, playing soccer, and spending time with his friends, older sister, parents, and the grandmother who lived with his family. Education was important in his household, and Neubauer met his parents' expectations by excelling in school.

His parents wanted to afford him the best opportunities available. His father, in particular, insisted that he finish school in the United States. When Neubauer was 14, his parents sent him by ship to live with his aunt and uncle in Danvers, Massachusetts.

Neubauer recalled his arrival in New York Harbor in February 1956:

*I was alone but very excited about this new country. It was all very mysterious and strange. We docked outside New York Harbor at night, and I could see the Statue of Liberty in the distance. Then, we steamed past it in the morning to the docks. It was wintertime, and it was cold.*

*I had no warm clothes with me. But I was determined to make it.* [1]

Neubauer's aunt and uncle cared for him, with the understanding that he would help out in their small store after school and on weekends. Knowing very little English, Neubauer enrolled in the local high school as the first and only foreign student to attend there.

Neubauer flourished in his new land, encouraged by his aunt and uncle, his high school principal, a dedicated English teacher, and others who saw great possibilities in him. He mastered not only the language, but also the culture of America. Neubauer recalled:

*I had never seen American football before. I mean, here was a teenage kid who didn't know anything about American customs, holidays, cars, girls, or clothes. I had to learn it all from scratch.* [2]

Left: Joe Neubauer took his schooling seriously, even as a young boy growing up in Israel.

Above right: Neubauer participates in a safety drill on the boat that brought him to the United States. Although he traveled alone, he was excited by the prospect of living in a new country and was determined to be successful.

Upon graduation from high school, Neubauer enrolled at Tufts University in Boston, where he majored in chemical engineering. He worked part time in the chemical engineering lab and paid for his membership in a campus fraternity by working as a waiter in the dining room. He eventually worked his way up to food steward, which he said provided excellent preparation for ARA.

While at Tufts, Neubauer encountered an economics professor who encouraged him to consider economics, which he did. With his mentor's help, Neubauer won a scholarship to the University of Chicago Business School, placing him among some of the world's most influential economists. Neubauer recollected:

*Those were the halcyon days at the University of Chicago. You could just feel the academic fervor all around you. My basic economic principles were developed there and helped shape the way I think today.*[3]

After earning a Master's of Business Administration from the University of Chicago, Neubauer landed a job with Chase Manhattan Bank soon after graduation. At 27, he became the youngest vice president in the bank's history.

He left Chase Manhattan in 1971 to join PepsiCo, where he became the youngest treasurer of a FORTUNE® 500 company, and then vice president. Seeking to gain all the hands-on operating experience possible, however, Neubauer surprised his peers when he left his corporate job to join Wilson Sporting Goods, a division of PepsiCo. He explained:

*Many of my friends on Wall Street didn't understand why I would go from a corporate job to a division job. My philosophy is that while you're young, you have to get as much experience as you can. You have to build your pyramid base very wide.*[4]

Much of Neubauer's great success stemmed from his personal ambition, hard work, and ability to overcome obstacles. However, he gives enormous credit to those who helped him along the way:

*People invested in me all through my life and all through my career. That's why I feel so strongly about investing in people and giving back. As an immigrant kid who came to this country with nothing, I recognize it's the only country in the world where ability, character, determination, and hard work pay off. How could I not give back?*[5]

Neubauer credits many people, including his aunt and uncle, high school principal, a special English teacher, and a college economics professor, with helping him succeed academically. Graduating from Tufts University and the University of Chicago Business School, Neubauer fulfilled his parents' dream of attaining an education in the United States.

Neubauer carefully analyzed the business lines to determine if they met the company's long-term profit expectations. He scrutinized growth objectives with a sharper view on profit margins and return on investment.[7]

As chief financial officer, Neubauer significantly improved the financial operations and assumed an increasingly important role in ARA Services. Harry Belinger, former vice president of public affairs who retired in 1995, recalled a financial review Neubauer presented at a managers meeting early on in Neubauer's tenure at ARA:

*He knew exactly what was going on, what he wanted to do, and how he was going to do it, and yet the guy had only been there a couple of months at that time. Maybe a couple of weeks. You suddenly got a sense of a guy who really had control. It wasn't until that meeting when I realized what a smart move Bill Fishman had made.*[8]

Neubauer was always appreciative of Fishman's and Davidson's complete confidence in him, the executive decisions he made, and the actions he took. In an interview, Neubauer described their shared attitude toward him:

*As we built the company, and we started both adding and subtracting from the business, and we talked about the vending business—the original vending business—Davidson said to me, "You do whatever you think is right. Just because I started the business doesn't mean you have to continue it." It was really amazing.*[9]

### Campbell Hired for Management and Public Affairs

While Neubauer worked to improve the company's financial organization, Fishman sought to bring a greater degree of professionalism to the areas of human resources and public affairs. To that end, in December 1980, Fishman hired Alan K. Campbell as the executive vice president of management and public affairs.

Campbell, known as Scotty, served as director of the U.S. Office of Personnel Management and earlier as chairman of the U.S. Civil Service Commission under President Jimmy Carter. He also had been dean of the Maxwell School of Citizenship and Public Affairs at Syracuse University. Retired Board member and general counsel Lee Driscoll described Campbell:

*Campbell was very, very good and very, very sophisticated. He'd been running human resources groups, including in the federal government, for a long time. He ran a whole civil service system and was responsible for training and wages, and salary grades and wage grades.*[10]

Campbell's new role at ARA, according to a statement in the company's 1980 annual report, was to further develop the company's most impor-

Neubauer joined ARA in March 1979 as executive vice president of finance and development, treasurer, chief financial officer, and a member of the Board of Directors. He was elected president in April 1981 and CEO in February 1983. As *Nation's Restaurant News* reported, Neubauer "possessed exactly the right mix of leadership and discipline, as well as financial savvy, to make this work." Prior to ARAMARK, Neubauer held senior positions with PepsiCo, Wilson Sporting Goods (a PepsiCo division), and Chase Manhattan Bank.

While new financial programs were introduced, efforts were also under way to provide training, assistance, and support for frontline managers, such as this manager in the food service division. Frontline managers have always been considered crucial to the company's success.

tant asset: its more than 120,000 employees. Retired Board member Jim Hodgson discussed Campbell's role regarding ARA Services employees:

*Bill Fishman hired an absolutely outstanding personnel man by the name of Scotty Campbell. He came out of government and was responsible for building up a workforce of ultimately well over 100,000 people in many, many countries and across many continents. Campbell was a solid anchor. He made sure all decisions that could have an impact on the future of the company took into account the importance of human resources.*[11]

First, Campbell decentralized the corporate personnel function to the company's individual lines of business. That move essentially provided each division with its own personnel department rather than having all personnel decisions controlled at the corporate level.

Campbell also led the formation of the company's Executive Corps, a group of 75 executives who created a forum to share experiences and work together to move the company forward.[12]

Recognizing the vital role of the company's frontline managers, Campbell also worked to provide support for that level of employee, instituting training programs and promoting their recognition. This fully supported Neubauer's philosophy of providing a viable methodology for ARA Services managers to improve their business and leadership skills. Driscoll noted:

*After Joe took over, the company went through a series of major leaps forward in terms of the quality of people, the quality of training, the quality of incentives, and so on. It was all about leadership; Joe was very good at that.*[13]

While overseeing the human resources organization of ARA, Campbell also began improving its

public affairs program. Although it was, by then, a $3 billion company, most of the world did not recognize the ARA Services name. Of those people who were familiar with it, many did not know what services the company provided.

Up to this point, the company had regarded itself as a guest in its clients' houses, and ARA rarely identified itself by name in customer locations. But this would soon change.

To improve ARA's brand-name recognition, Campbell commissioned the creation of a new corporate logo, which successfully unified the identity of the various units that had been operating under different names and logos. The introduction of the new logo was accompanied by a clear plan for its appearance on trucks, uniforms, and signage to maximize visibility even in client locations.

Launching the largest public relations campaign in its history, ARA explained its mission to the media. Many executives spoke at conferences, and Fishman served as an especially effective ARA ambassador. He conveyed the message that ARA had become an important and powerful force in the growing service sector for the economy. Advertising campaigns were launched to reach prospective customers with a clear message about what ARA could offer them.

### Neubauer Named ARA President

In 1981, the president and chief operating officer of ARA, Marvin Heaps, resigned from his position, and Neubauer was appointed to succeed Heaps as the new president and chief operating officer.

Any speculation about who would then take over as CEO when Fishman eventually stepped down ended during a 40th birthday party for Neubauer later in 1981. Neubauer remembered:

*People had brought all sorts of gag gifts to the party, and someone asked Fishman what he had brought. Fishman said, "I didn't bring a present. I think I'm going to give Joe the company." So, he obviously had thought about this for quite a while.*[14]

"[The Neubauer transition] went down like chicken soup," said retired general counsel Martin Spector. "There was no problem at all. Joe was groomed from the time he came over as chief financial officer to be the [president]. He was ready and willing, and the company needed him."[15]

Neubauer's appointment as president of a major corporation at such a young age attracted attention from the business world and the media. He discussed his age and his new job in an article in *Focus*, a Philadelphia business newsweekly:

*I cannot make apologies for my chronological age. It is what it is, and there is very little one can do about one's birth date. One can do an awful lot with one's ability, however, and one's relationship with peers, subordinates, and superiors. And, I've been able to achieve very high levels of responsibilities at a very young age. In fact, my first boss told me that I was born old, and that has been true ever since.*

Neubauer said, in the same article, that his job as president involved recruiting and hiring excellent employees, and motivating them to succeed:

*I have a reputation for attracting top-grade talent. I will be judged here by the way I am able to motivate people. I get a great deal of pleasure from seeing the young people I have brought into the company perform and succeed. I will not be judged in my current position on how I do my job singularly, because the job outgrew the singular person a long time ago. I will be judged by the kind of talent I am able to bring in and motivate to perform.*

From his first days on the job, Neubauer emphasized the importance of all ARA Services employees working as a team to achieve shared goals, according to Lynn McKee, ARAMARK's executive vice president for human resources. Under Neubauer's management, she said, egos were always put aside:

*Joe uses the term "humble confidence," and I think it's a good term. It's very characteristic of the people here. Whether you're a Harvard MBA or you graduated from one of the local schools, you can't tell the difference here. There is not a lot of arrogance and egotistical behavior. What you do have is*

As president, Neubauer immediately demonstrated his ability to understand and enjoy the company's varied business operations.

*a group of people who are truly concerned about what impact their actions will have on the culture of the organization.*[16]

ARA Services had an established entrepreneurial culture, marked by truly visionary leadership. Neubauer contributed strongly to this culture, according to Ron Davenport, who served on ARAMARK's Board from 1980 to 2007:

*There's a high quality of leadership [among] Joe Neubauer and [his] cadre of associates. ... I think being a winner is having a winning attitude and honesty and integrity. Excellence, you see.*[17]

While Neubauer moved capably into his role as president of ARA Services, the troubled national and worldwide economies negatively affected ARA and many other companies.

"We were struggling with some issues at the time," Neubauer said. "It was clear that the company was not doing all that well. It was 1981—the beginning of the inflationary era."[18]

Management's letter to its shareholders, published in the 1981 annual report, also addressed the difficult economic conditions of the time:

*We must still deal effectively and immediately with the present day economic environment. It is, of course, very cloudy. Current double-edged inflationary and recessionary factors have placed continuing pressure on both expenses and operating margins of companies throughout the world.*

*ARA has not been immune to these global pressures. While our sales increased modestly, thus reemphasizing the growing demand for services, income and earnings per share before extraordinary items for the fiscal year declined 29 percent and 25 percent respectively, from 1980 results.*[19]

**Looking for Common Systems**

As president, Neubauer endeavored to create common systems among the historically diversified and decentralized divisions of the company. He aimed to find a middle ground between the entrepreneurial spirit that ARA always embraced and the professional business systems necessary to manage the company profitably.

Neubauer achieved his goals, and, more than 20 years later, Martin Spector, who served as executive vice president and general counsel at the time, recalled some of the changes that were implemented under Neubauer's leadership:

*I don't think that Bill Fishman, who was brilliant for his day, could have managed a really professionally run company, and I think he realized that. That's why he brought in Joe. ... After Joe came in, we started bringing in much more professional people ... all sorts of really highly qualified people.*[20]

While he was developing a culture of professionalism, however, Neubauer was able to maintain the entrepreneurial energy of the company:

*Joe did not let that professionalism quell the entrepreneurial spirit of the company. He really believes that decisions are made right down at the line. But, unlike the old days, each company now knows how much money it has to invest, and it has to come up with a business plan, a strategic plan, and a capital plan, and it has to live within those plans.*[21]

Next, Neubauer turned his attention to the company's portfolio of service businesses. He needed to decide which services met EBIT and RONA targets and therefore should be developed, and which lines should be divested. He also evaluated opportunities to enter new service areas that would be good matches for ARA.

**Focusing on Core Competencies**

The great flow of acquisitions that brought ARA into new services in the 1960s and 1970s slowed dramatically in the early 1980s, as ARA management worked hard to identify the company's core competencies. Neubauer understood that ARA needed to take a more focused approach to its operations, according to Fred Sutherland, ARAMARK executive vice president and chief financial officer:

*I came down as assistant treasurer in 1980. ARA Services really seemed to be involved in a lot of different activities at the time, a lot of interesting activities. There seemed to be a lot of breadth and scope to the company. I found that intriguing. When I got here, I found it was a little bit like the Wild West in that it was, in many ways, a core food service company to which a lot of other service companies had been added and which were managed by a corporate holding company.*

*There was a special connection between the corporate folks and the food company folks because they were all at Sixth and Walnut [in Philadelphia]. [But] there was clearly separation. There were all these, what were called, unconverted companies, which ranged from a school bus company to a trucking company to an emergency staffing company to a company that maintained condominium appliances in Florida, to a nursing home company, to a magazine and book distribution company, and on and on.*[22]

Taking note of the steady increase in two-worker and single-parent households, combined with the higher birthrate trend, ARA saw the oppor-

Above right: After acquiring National Child Care Centers in 1980, ARA quickly became one of the nation's premier service providers, furnishing child care for children ranging from newborn to pre-teens. The company featured more than 100 centers in 12 states, benefiting more than 20,000 children daily.

Below: A child care specialist works one-on-one with a student in an ARA-run child learning center. A steady increase in the number of two-worker and single-parent households created a demand for child care services.

tunity to capitalize on the rapidly expanding child care market. Because of ARA's experience with the management of "people care" in its senior living centers division, the company developed competence in this service area. As a result, it made good business sense to expand in the people care industry. In 1980, ARA entered the early childhood care and education business with the acquisition of National Child Care Centers.

ARA also attempted a foray into the trucking business, despite its lack of applicable freight transfer experience. The company decided to purchase Smith's Transfer Corporation, along with additional trucking companies. Unfortunately, the trucking industry was undergoing deregulation at this time, which eliminated automatic rate increases. Forced to cover rising fuel costs and other expenses in a recessionary environment, the division was unable to operate profitably.

Unable to successfully apply its existing expertise to stem the trucking division's losses, ARA determined that the business should be operated by those who had more experience in that industry. As a result, ARA sold various segments of its trucking business.

Hodgson described the problems Smith's Transfer presented to ARA Services:

*The company made so many smart moves. But the trucking company acquisition was ill-advised, not because it didn't look right at the time, but because of what was happening, sub-surface, within the trucking industry: deregulation. There was no way you could win. I had dealt with the truckers union as a secretary of labor, and I knew those difficulties would be manifest, but there were a lot of difficulties beyond merely the price of labor.* [23]

ARA ended its aggressive movement into new service areas after the purchase of Solon Automated Services, a company that provided management services for laundry equipment in sites such as apartment buildings and campus dormitories. ARA then changed strategy to focus on selecting the service divisions with the best profitability potential and then to build those divisions through investment in additional acquisitions. For example, ARA expanded its ARATEX division, which had become a national leader in the garment and textile rental service business, by purchasing Chicago-based Means Services,

Inc. The company added value to ARATEX by providing a broad client base and a range of services that greatly enhanced the capabilities of the division.

### America's Leading Service Management Company

Following a carefully planned management succession strategy, ARA's Board of Directors made the expected announcement in 1983, appointing Neubauer CEO and retaining Fishman as Chairman of the Board.

With the continuing support of Fishman and the advice and counsel of Campbell, Neubauer, as the new CEO, led the company into an era of proactive communication.

The new promotional effort would help define ARA in the public eye as the premier service management company in the country. It would also

In 1980, the acquisition of Smith's Transfer Corporation marked the beginning of ARA's involvement in the trucking industry. Unfortunately, ARA entered the business shortly before it was deregulated, which negatively affected profits for carriers across the board. Shortly thereafter, ARA divested the trucking firm. (Photograph © H. Mark Weidman.)

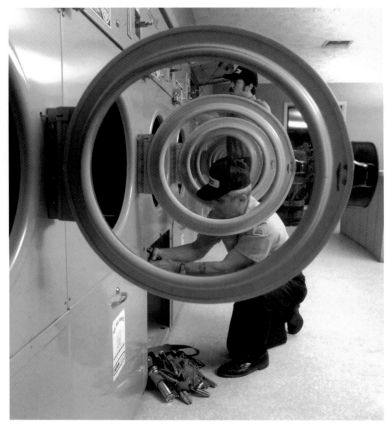

*ent. You have to tailor the service—the menu, the hours, the kind of service—to the needs of the ultimate customer.* [24]

It was ARA's belief that, along with other companies in the service sector, it should promote the importance of service industries to the vitality of the American economy during its transition from a manufacturing-based economy.

By 1981, seven out of every 10 workers in the United States were employed by service companies, producing more than 50 percent of the nation's economic output. In the annual report's management letter to shareholders, ARA claimed its leadership role in the service industry was a result of its history of innovation. According to Neubauer:

*ARA has been at the forefront in developing innovative concepts, determining new techniques, establishing broader dimensions in the development of service delivery systems, creating unique approaches to solving new problems, and exploiting expanding opportunities. We are proud of our leadership role in stepping forth where other companies have never gone before.*

*We believe we are on the cutting edge of change, and that puts a tremendous responsibility upon us in rising to meet the challenges of a changing society.* [25]

Neubauer, when speaking of the future of the service industry, echoed the sentiments of Davidson and Fishman:

*Services offer almost unlimited growth opportunities because the demand for services will never be filled. Unlike the need for manufactured goods, which is finite, research, technology, and innovation will continue to open new doors for the delivery of services and provide even more employment opportunities within the service industry.*

establish ARA as a service industry leader with its work to raise public awareness and understanding of the economy's service sector.

Of course, service had been the hallmark of ARA since its earliest days. Davidson and Fishman had recognized from the start that their company's primary product was not the food sold at baseball stadiums or the souvenirs in gift shops, but the service that it managed for the clients. The company was instrumental in defining service management as a new industry and in bringing recognition to the growing service sector of the American economy.

Fishman was particularly articulate when speaking about service management and was recognized as an authority. He spoke of this topic in a 1978 *Forbes* article.

*We're in the service management business. We do not think of ourselves as a vending company or a school bus company, or even as a food service company. We are in the business of anticipating and managing services which meet basic needs and expectations. … Every client we have is differ-*

*The service sector represents hope for the future. ARA uses this tag line in its advertising: "The world will never outgrow its need for service." I happen to firmly believe in this statement. It applies not only to the services ARA provides, but also to the vast and steadily increasing services provided by a growing legion of American companies.*[26]

Attention to the company's position in the service sector continued to increase during the Neubauer years. Along this line, ARA served as an active member of the Coalition of Service Industries (CSI), which it helped create. Members included banking and financial services, transportation firms, advertising agencies, communications firms, and engineering and construction companies. Neubauer served as a director of the coalition.

The company also established the Fishman–Davidson Center for the Study of the Service Sector with a grant to the Wharton School at the University of Pennsylvania with the mission to research fundamental issues and problems in the service sector in an effort to obtain data for better policy decisions.

## A Bright Future

ARA Services continued to make strides in becoming a more recognized and better-understood company. These efforts would position it to take its place among major American corporations. In less than 25 years, ARA had grown from a small food service company into a more than $3 billion corporation that daily provided more services to more people than any other company in the world.

But for ARA Services, under the capable direction of Joe Neubauer, the company was really just beginning to triumph. Indeed, it was particularly well placed to capitalize on several important trends, including the growing recognition by businesses that contracting with outside experts such as ARA could increase efficiency and reduce costs.

As it moved into the mid-1980s, there was no question that ARA's future lay bright and beckoning before it. As Neubauer said, "The world will never outgrow its need for service"—and ARA was the No. 1 service company in the world.

ARA commissioned a series of illustrations by artist Robert Ziering for its national advertising campaign, including the one above, which captured the Olympic Games' universal symbol—the torch runners.

## CHAPTER SIX

# A MONUMENTAL YEAR

## 1984

*After we defeated Siegel, we went down to Goldman Sachs for a meeting. We asked them what our chances were of remaining independent. They told us now that we were on the radar screen, sooner or later, someone else with much more financial depth and know-how would come along and take us over.*

—Martin Spector,
retired executive vice president
and general counsel

WHEN JOE NEUBAUER AC-cepted the position of Chairman of the Board of ARA Services on April 6, 1984, he had no way of foreseeing the portentous events that would soon begin unfolding before him.

In keeping with plans for an orderly management succession, Bill Fishman stepped down as chairman, recommending Neubauer as his successor. Alan K. Campbell, known as Scotty, was named vice chairman. In a management information bulletin released the same day, Neubauer paid tribute to the man he succeeded:

> *I personally wish to thank Bill for his help, guidance, and support since I came to ARA. Bill Fishman's leadership qualities are well known to the outside world. But those of us in the company who have had the pleasure of working with Bill know that his single greatest quality is that of a warm, caring, compassionate human being whose first concern has always been for the welfare of others. This is a quality that I, as an individual, and we as a company, will do well to try to emulate.*[1]

Neubauer's first days as chairman proved challenging, as ARA Services continued to struggle with a national economy that was still recovering from a lengthy recession and high interest rates. The company's poorly performing trucking operations had also proved a substantial encumbrance. Just months after Neubauer was named chairman in addition to his role as president, the company's transportation sector had reported a drop in operating results for the quarter, citing intense competition within the trucking industry and the sale of its school bus operations in a portion of the country.[2] The overall economy also hurt ARA's trucking division, which "was severely affected [in the previous year] by the recession," according to *Barron's*.[3]

More than 20 years later, Neubauer explained that ARA's trucking business had posed a serious threat to the company's well-being in the mid-1980s. "We bought [the] trucking company right at the beginning of deregulation," he said. "It almost killed the company."[4]

Retired Board member Jim Hodgson agreed that deregulation had turned ARA's trucking company acquisition into an uphill fight:

---

"So extensive is the ARA Services empire that its much-trumpeted contract to feed and transport the 12,000 athletes at the Summer Olympics in Los Angeles—a Herculean task by most standards—will hardly cause a ripple in the company's revenues," reported *The Philadelphia Inquirer's* business section.

*The trucking company was a very ill-advised matter, not because it didn't look right at the time, but because of what was happening sub-surface to the trucking industry in this country—deregulation.*[5]

### The Olympic Games

In addition to these difficulties, ARA Services was gearing up for two Olympic Games in the same year. It was the company's first attempt at such an endeavor, but before serving at the 1984 Winter Games in Sarajevo or the Summer Games in Los Angeles, ARA would have to attend an event in Caracas, Venezuela.

Led by John Scanlan, vice president of special projects for the Leisure Services Group, with James Hutton, one of ARA's original Olympic food service architects, beginning with the Games in Mexico City, ARA provided service management expertise at the IX Pan American Games in August 1983.

Working with 800 Venezuelans who had been recruited and hired to assist ARA personnel, ARA Services served up to 17,000 meals a day to athletes and 75,000 meals a day to employees of the Pan American Games.[6] According to Neubauer, manag-

ing food services for the momentous sporting event was a true test for the company:

*[This] was even more demanding than we had anticipated, since the Pan American Village was not completed when the athletes arrived, nor were other services available. Despite these problems, our dining halls were in operation and meals were being served when the athletes arrived. We were delighted that* The New York Times, *in an article which described all the difficulties, pointed out "only the cafeteria food service has met wide approval."*[7]

Next came the 1984 Winter Olympic Games in Sarajevo. The company served as consultant to the United Agriculture Trade and Industry in the former Yugoslavia, helping to provide professional food services to athletes, staff, and spectators. Additionally, ARA served 10 restaurants in the city's Press Village, which lodged some 8,000 press representatives.[8]

Supervised by Scanlan, ARA's Olympic work in Sarajevo proved to be an exceptionally challenging task. At the time, Yugoslavia was still a communist country, and as such, it insisted that all food items served at the Winter Games be purchased from

---

**February 8–19**
ARA Services serves as consultant to a former Yugoslavian firm to help it provide food service for athletes, press, staff, and spectators at the 1984 Winter Olympic Games in Sarajevo.

**July 11**
Joe Neubauer meets former ARA executive William M. Siegel for lunch at the Sherry–Netherland Hotel in New York City. Siegel informs Neubauer of his plans to take over ARA Services.

**July 16**
ARA's Board of Directors unanimously rejects Siegel's offer for the company.

**July 31**
Siegel, unable to secure the required additional financial backing, withdraws his offer.

**April 6**
Neubauer is appointed ARA's Chairman of the Board.

ARA services
Proud To Serve Again
Los Angeles 1984 Olympics

**July 28–August 12**
ARA Services provides food, laundry, and transportation services at the 1984 Summer Games in Los Angeles. The Olympic event provides the company with unprecedented positive publicity.

John Scanlan (center), vice president of special projects for ARA's Leisure Services Group, played the key role in organizing all of ARA Services' activities at the Winter Olympic Games in Sarajevo.

**A High-Profile and Multifaceted Event**

cooperative farms and similar socialist-style suppliers. Securing the necessary food items became an enormous task for ARA, as the company was responsible for supplying a wide variety of meal choices and an enormous amount of food on a daily basis to athletes from all around the world.

The language gap also proved to be a problem, according to Bill Grant, associate director of facilities planning for ARA's international sector and designer of the Olympic Village food service facilities. "We used mostly Yugoslavian equipment, and sometimes there were a few misunderstandings," he explained. "Once we asked for char-broilers, and we got charcoal grills."[9]

Despite these issues, ARA Services was able to serve everyone at the Winter Games as planned and according to schedule. These challenging events, however, paled in comparison to the 1984 Summer Games that took place in late July and early August in Los Angeles.

Led by Scotty Campbell, ARA Services had commissioned an unprecedented Olympic-themed advertising campaign in preparation for the Los Angeles event, hoping to attract attention of both the media and the public. ARA managed all food and refreshments at these Olympic Games, includ-

**September 10**
At a special meeting of the Board of Directors, Neubauer proposes that a management group purchase the company for $1 billion. Neubauer promises his group will secure the money and close the transaction within 100 days.

**October 4**
Members of the Board's Special Committee meet with management to discuss the Trust House Forte dealings, agree to the proposal price of the shares, and provide tentative approval to management's buyout proposal.

ARA Services' 25th anniversary is celebrated at a gala party, during which Neubauer informs managers that the Board has tentatively approved the buyout plan.

**September 28**
ARA managers learn that Trust House Forte, a large and powerful British company, is interested in buying 100 percent of ARA Services. After several days of meetings, ARA declines to cooperate in the 100 percent acquisition but invites Trust House Forte to assume a minority position in the company by investing in the buyout. The British firm declines the offer and agrees not to pursue the acquisition of ARA.

**December 19**
The management buyout closes one day prior to the 100-day deadline, followed by a celebration at The Palace Hotel in Philadelphia.

Right: As the Olympic torch was carried on its 12,000-mile, 82-day run from New York City to Los Angeles, ARA provided bus caravans complete with food, refreshment, and laundry services for the Olympic torch relay participants and support staff, using a special mobile kitchen and a network of laundry pickup points.

Below: Torch relay support workers board an ARA bus.

ing concessions for the public and transportation for the athletes, both of which provided the perfect opportunity for ARA Services to showcase its expertise to the world.

In addition to serving at the Games, ARA personnel also provided services for the highly publicized motor caravan that escorted Olympic Torch athletes running across the country. The company provided all laundry and linen services to workers and runners traveling with the caravan, while ARA chefs worked in extremely tight quarters to provide breakfast, lunch, dinner, and snacks to caravan personnel and torch bearers. A trailer housed a diner-type eating area that seated 30 people. The *Los Angeles Times* described the challenges ARA Services met to successfully serve the runners and their support staff:

*The logistics of this event are staggering. Consider that during an 82-day torch relay, virtually every meal for anywhere between 125 and 200 people will be served at a different location. A typical day reads something like Doyle, California, for breakfast, Borderline, Nevada, for lunch, and Washoe Lake, Nevada, for dinner. …*

*To handle the crush of official and unofficial guests, ARA has two teams of six chefs and two alternate supervisors. Each chef works a two-week tour before being replaced. The work has been unusually demanding. …*

*The menu is first class and features baked lobster tail, swordfish steak with caper sauce, filet mignon, and medallions of veal as just some of the two entrées offered at each meal. …*

*The dining car reflects the high morale of the relay team with electricity in the air and laughter abounding throughout the 90-minute meal services. The esprit de corps extends to the kitchen, where providing quality and quantity quickly is the objective.*[10]

As part of its efforts to promote its role in the Olympic Games in Los Angeles, ARA Services also sponsored Olympic preview dinners, at which guests could sample the remarkable variety of foods that would be provided to athletes from around the world. In recognition of the great—indeed, "Olympian"—challenge it had accepted for itself, ARA declared the period between the Pan American Games and the Summer Games as the company's "Year of the Olympics." This was detailed in an *ARA Management Review*:

*This is ARA's Year of the Olympics. We won despite near impossible odds with food service for athletes at the Pan American Games in Venezuela; we're going for the gold in food service for athletes, the press, and the public at the Winter Olympics in Sarajevo, Yugoslavia; and we plan to set records in both food service and transportation services for athletes at the 1984 Summer Olympics in Los Angeles.*[11]

### A Large Logistical Effort

The Olympic Games in Los Angeles were reported as the single largest sporting event in history.[12] Watched on television by 2.5 billion spectators—half the world's population—it was crucial that all events, including food service, ran according to plan. ARA Services faced a particularly daunting task of

---

The 1984 Summer Olympic Games in Los Angeles began with colorful opening ceremonies—a Hollywood-produced extravaganza that featured 8,000 athletes, 9,000 performers, and a card trick by the 90,000 spectators, which transformed the stands into flags of all nations.

providing food services to 12,000 Olympic athletes and support staff from 150 different countries, all with different tastes and widely varying nutritional requirements. Nevertheless, the company handled the undertaking exceptionally well.[13]

With some 3,000 ARA employees serving up to 60,000 meals daily, typical Olympic meals included four hot entrées, five hot vegetables, 14 salads, 14 fruits, two soups, 26 bread items, a large selection of domestic and imported cheeses, and 21 beverages. Meals in the five-day menu cycles usually included a beef, poultry, and fish entrée, along with vegetarian and lamb or pork main dishes. ARA served national foods that included *kimchi*, pickled raw vegetables (Korea); *couscous*, a semolina dish (North Africa); *dalo*, a root vegetable (Fiji); New Zealand kiwi fruit; and Chinese beef with green peppers.[14]

To handle the Olympic Games' gargantuan food requirements, ARA's shopping list took on a *Ripley's Believe It or Not* quality, according to an article in *Focus*, Philadelphia's business newsweekly. It featured "470,000 pounds of meat—the equivalent of 1,000 Grade A steers—and 42,500 gallons of milk—enough to fill 6,800,000 eight-ounce cartons. Also included were 250 tons of fresh fruit—some 500,000 pounds—and 103,500 loaves of bread."[15]

ARA served the athletes at nine different locations in three Olympic Villages: the University of Southern California; the University of California, Los Angeles; and Santa Barbara. The company also prepared some 20,000 box lunches for athletes at 24 competition sites and served as general manager of public food and refreshment concessions at Olympic venues. In addition, ARA Coffee System supplied some 3,500 crew members for ABC network television.[16]

Making arrangements for all these food items and preparing and serving them on time to the right groups represented a huge undertaking, according to Ira Cohn, current president of ARAMARK's Business and Industry Group:

*[The Olympics] are the biggest logistics event in comprehensive food service. There are armies and wars, but they have pre-prepared food, not fresh food. So it's different; but for a complete and total*

*menu, [the Olympics] is the largest logistical effort in food service.*[17]

According to Peter Ueberroth, president of the Los Angeles Olympic Organizing Committee and later *Time* magazine's "Man of the Year," ARA Services was the right company for the challenge:

*ARA Services is providing invaluable expertise to our planning efforts. They are the premier food and transportation service managers in the world, and they are just the organization to tackle this monumental responsibility.*[18]

**Transportation Challenges**

Considering the already heavily congested Los Angeles area, many observers predicted that the Olympic Games, to be staged in venues across five counties in Southern California, would result in traffic nightmares. A July 1984 *SportsNow* article described the situation:

> *People familiar with Los Angeles are predicting an Olympic-sized headache for anybody trying to get around on the area's streets and highways during the Summer Olympic Games. Preventing a freeway free-for-all on the world's most heavily traveled traffic routes will probably present one of the greatest challenges of the Games.*[19]

As the Games' transportation provider, ARA Services was confident of its ability to successfully

Opposite and below: The University of Southern California's Olympic Village for the Summer Games in Los Angeles. The University of California at Los Angeles and the University of California at Santa Barbara comprised the other two sites. ARA Services served up to 60,000 meals a day to athletes at nine different locations at the three Olympic Village sites.

channel athletes on time and according to schedule in 500 buses over a 2,200-square-mile area. Dozens of the world's busiest highways connected the various Olympic Villages around Los Angeles with 60 different training and competition sites, often as much as 90 miles apart. During the Games, ARA estimated that its fleet of buses, provided from its ARA transportation division, would travel more than 2.5 million miles—the equivalent of nearly 900 trips across the United States.[20] With no margin for error, the right athlete would need to arrive at the right event at the right time, every time. "We can't afford to have any athlete disqualified because they're late showing up for the competition," said Robert Franco, part of ARA's transportation team for the Games.[21] To meet this goal, ARA assembled more than 1,300 drivers, mechanics, and supervisors.[22]

Drivers were trained and road tested; routes and alternate routes were carefully plotted, color-coded and placed on computerized mapping systems; and bus stop locations were carefully determined. So, instead of the logistical nightmare that

everyone—except ARA—was expecting. Olympic athletes were transported efficiently and without a single incident.

**Thousands of Positive Stories**

With the 1984 Summer Olympic Games in Los Angeles as ARA Services' fifth Olympic event, ARA had become a veteran at serving the Olympic Games. In fact, its experience had started back in 1968 with the Olympic Games in Mexico City, when ARA became the first professional services management company to design and manage food service for an Olympics event.

Press coverage of ARA's Olympic role was unprecedented, with reports lauding the company and the amazing abilities it exhibited in many diverse areas. These stories appeared in national news magazines, industry publications, and newspapers from *The New York Times* to the *Los Angeles Times* and many others. In total, there were more than 5,600 newspaper and

magazine articles published about the company's role at the Olympic Games in Los Angeles, along with hundreds of radio and television news stories.[23]

ARA Services had, indeed, proven to the world that it was far more than just a food service management company. A 1984 article in *The Philadelphia Inquirer* discussed this point by describing ARA's vast array of services:

*Every day, in one way or another, ARA Services does something for 10 million people. More than half of those people eat the Philadelphia-based service giant's food—from hot dogs at Atlanta's Fulton County Stadium to sandwiches on North Sea oil-drilling platforms to steamed shrimp on airline flights to the Far East.*

*An additional 16,500 people, inmates in prisons across the country, receive medical and dental care from ARA. And the company's 116,000 employees*

Above and left: A bus control tower in the Olympic Village was instrumental in successfully channeling Olympic athletes on time and according to schedule in 500 buses over a 2,200-square-mile area. Dozens of the world's busiest highways connected the various Olympic villages around Los Angeles with 60 different training and competition sites, often as much as 90 miles apart.

*also transport 400,000 students each school day, distribute magazines to 25,000 newsstands, and operate the 2,810-acre Sugarbush Valley Ski Resort in Vermont.*

*So extensive is the ARA Services empire that its much-trumpeted contract to feed and transport the 12,000 athletes at the 1984 Summer Olympics in Los Angeles—a Herculean task by most standards—will hardly cause a ripple in the company's revenues.*[24]

### A Momentous Lunch

Just months after he had been named Chairman of ARA Services, and weeks before the commencement of the Olympic Games in Los Angeles, Joe Neubauer attended an important lunch meeting in New York City that would forever change his life and the future of ARA Services.

Already in the city for an Olympic Games preview dinner at Hunter College in Manhattan, Neubauer met with William M. Siegel, a former ARA executive who had served as president of the ARA Food Services Company and was a past director and a past member of the company's management

Above and below: ARA Services' buses are lined up and ready to transport athletes at the 1984 Summer Olympic Games. During the Games, ARA estimated that its fleet of buses, provided from its transportation division, traveled more than 2.5 million miles—the equivalent of nearly 900 trips across the United States—transporting the Olympic athletes efficiently and without incident.

committee. A number of ARA employees, including Neubauer, had remained in close touch with Siegel after he had left the company in 1980.

"Bill Siegel was a very energetic person, a very smart person," said Neubauer. "He had been [with ARA] for a long time and knew a great deal about the company and the industry."[25]

So, Neubauer thought little of it when Siegel invited him to lunch at the Sherry–Netherland Hotel on July 11, 1984. Expecting to meet Siegel in the hotel's dining room, Neubauer was surprised to learn they would be dining instead in Siegel's suite. Still, the lunch began routinely enough, with the two men speaking about their families and discussing the significant events in their lives.

Neubauer soon realized that he was faced with an absolute defining moment in his career when

Siegel informed him that, with the backing of some investors from Texas, he was planning to take over ARA Services:

*He said, "You know, some associates of mine and I are going to buy the company. We'd like to buy 90 percent of the company, and we're prepared to give you 5 percent and another 5 percent to the other senior managers of the company."*[26]

Investors Charlie Thomas and Red McCombs backed Siegel in his plan. Thomas owned the Houston Rockets, and McCombs owned the Denver Nuggets of the National Basketball Association.[27] Siegel was also backed with buyout money from Drexel Burnham, the large and aggressive Wall Street investment banking firm prominent in numerous deals of the day.[28]

Siegel explained to Neubauer that he would name himself chairman of the company, while Neubauer would serve as CEO. Parts of the company would be sold off, but after that, Neubauer could continue to run the company without interference.

Joe Neubauer and a Los Angeles County official discuss the best ways to implement security measures at the 1984 Summer Olympic Games in Los Angeles. With thousands of people attending, safety remained a priority.

# 1984 SUMMER OLYMPIC GAMES

THE 1984 SUMMER GAMES IN LOS Angeles—the first Olympic event funded through corporate sponsorships—provided a unique opportunity for ARA Services to showcase its expertise to the world, even though it had already served the world's greatest athletes at four previous Olympic Games. The company also traded its services for promotional rights, which launched the largest advertising campaign in its history.

Serving as "the official food and transportation provider" of the events, ARA was one of 30 corporate sponsors that contributed an aggregate total of more than $500 million in cash and services to fund the games. Peter Ueberroth, a Los Angeles entrepreneur who directed the 1984 event, had envisioned and implemented the corporate sponsorships that supported the Games.

Knowing that the City of Los Angeles had refused to use any municipal money for the event, Ueberroth looked to corporate America (or to foreign corporations, if they were willing to outbid American firms) to finance the Summer Games. He presented bidders with everything from TV time to the rights to sponsor athletes' watches.

Recognizing that TV rights would bring in the most revenue, Ueberroth shocked even his own advisors when he commanded an astronomical $225 million bid for broadcast rights from the ABC television network. His staff members had predicted that the network would not pay more than $150 million for the rights.[1]

The high price, however, paid off for ABC, as it had purchased the rights to declare starting times for major events. Viewed by 180 million Americans, the prime-time Olympic events beat every other television event in history.[2]

So, despite the predicted nightmare scenarios of terrorism and massive traffic jams that threatened to drive down ticket sales and

Joe Neubauer and Peter V. Ueberroth, president of the organizing committee for the 1984 Los Angeles Summer Olympic Games, sign the agreement that established ARA Services as a sponsor. For the Olympics, Ueberroth created a financially successful competition that reversed a trend of heavy deficit spending by host cities and resulted in a surplus that financed youth sports in Los Angeles for many years.

lessen the impact of the event, the 1984 Summer Games generated a profit of $215 million, placing Ueberroth in the national spotlight. *Time* magazine even awarded him its 1984 "Man of the Year" designation.[3]

ARA Services, highly praised for its efficiency in both the food and transportation services for 12,000 international athletes, coaches, and staff, also received a major share of recognition, with thousands of articles published and hundreds of radio and television reports airing about its professionalism, expertise, and diverse capabilities.

Obviously excited about his plan, Siegel urged Neubauer to meet immediately with one of his associates who would help fund the takeover. Neubauer, however, refused to meet with this individual:

*I said, "I don't need to see him. I'm not interested in doing this." He said, "Well, do you understand this is not voluntary? We're going to do this whether you like it or not." I said, "My suggestion is that you not do it at all." But he said, "Well, we're going to do it anyhow." That's how he left it.*[29]

Shaken, Neubauer left the hotel and immediately convened the company's lawyers and investment bankers to discuss what had just occurred:

*I was stunned. I mean, I was shocked. I didn't realize what I was getting into at the time. I walked out of there and called our general counsel, Marty Spector, and the next phone call was for Larry Lederman [the lead attorney at Wachtell, Lipton, Rosen and Katz, the law firm that represented the company during the takeover attempt and subsequent buyout]. Then I called Pieter Fisher, who was a partner at Goldman Sachs.*[30]

ARA employees from all of the company's service sectors pose in front of the Los Angeles Memorial Coliseum in Exposition Park, center of the 1984 Summer Olympic events.

Acting on his own instincts and the advice of the experts he consulted, Neubauer called Siegel early the next morning to reiterate that ARA had no intention of agreeing to his proposal. Hours later, as he said he would, Siegel announced to the press his hostile takeover attempt of ARA Services. ARA's stock prices jumped as shares were heavily traded, and arbitrageurs, hoping to make a financial killing, began buying up stock from long-time investors. Events had been set into motion, and the company was facing a new and serious challenge.

**Confronting a Series of Hurdles**

As news of the takeover plan spread throughout the company and among the business community, tensions were high and speculation rampant. "[The Board] was very worried," said Hodgson. "None of them had ever been through a hostile takeover before."[31] Employees wondered if they would be able to keep their jobs; many began updating their résumés. Customers, suppliers, and prospective clients conjectured openly about the future of the company. Indeed, the entire ARA community was understandably nervous in the days following Siegel's proposal to Neubauer.

Hoping to calm the suddenly troubled waters, ARA released its own press announcement, stating that it was not interested in Siegel's proposal. At the same time, management worked with its advisors to develop a strategy to deal with the takeover attempt.

In this regard, the company's key executives debated and discussed legal and financial matters at an off-site location. As much intelligence as possible was gathered concerning Siegel's financial capacities and his partners. Developing an effective strategy to counter Siegel's takeover attempt became an all-consuming activity for ARA's top executives and their financial and legal advisors.

According to Neubauer, while ARA's management team worked at a feverish pace to counter the hostile takeover plan, they made sure to play their own cards very close to their vest so Siegel would not realize any advantage from their activities:

*Part of Larry Lederman's advice to us was, "You're inside the house. The lights are on. Pull down the shades so they don't know what you're doing inside the house. All they can do is to try to figure out what's going on from the outside, but as long as you guys don't talk, you'll be fine." I think we did a very good job of that.*[32]

The company's Board members, who were ultimately asked to vote on Siegel's proposal, also remained busy around the clock, and after gathering outside opinions and performing an evaluation of the offer, the Board of Directors unanimously rejected it. *Nation's Restaurant*

*News* described ARA's reaction in a feature article about the company:

*Virtually all ARA executives labeled the bid "hostile," and ARA's Board stated that the offer was not nearly high enough and that the company was worth a lot more.*[33]

Nevertheless, ARA was far from out of the woods. Management worried that Siegel would raise more money and increase his offer, confronting the Board with a financial *fait accompli*, or that another player would come along and launch a different takeover attempt now that the company was in play.

Attention therefore remained focused on Siegel and his associates as they visited potential investors across the country to line up additional financial backing. Relying on their extensive nationwide financial and banking contacts, ARA management was able to carefully track Siegel's attempts. Fred Sutherland, who was the company's treasurer at the time, recalled that ARA's management deter-

On July 11, 1984, former ARA executive William M. Siegel (right) invited Neubauer to a lunch in his suite at New York's Sherry–Netherland Hotel. During the lunch, he informed Neubauer that he and an investor group planned to buy ARA Services. This set in motion a chain of events that would change ARA forever. *(Photo courtesy of WOLF von dem BUSSCHE.)*

mined it was unlikely Siegel would successfully raise additional capital to bolster his takeover bid:

> They went around and talked to some banks. We knew they were out looking for the money. As we looked at it, we concluded pretty quickly that Siegel was not in a very strong position. Since we knew a lot of banks, we actually got intelligence to see that.[34]

Unable to secure the additional financial backing he needed, Siegel withdrew his offer on July 31, less than three weeks after he had initially approached Neubauer. "It became clear to us that there was a crack between Siegel and his group," said Neubauer. "His group wasn't going to fight us straight up unless Siegel brought us along. ... So that effort fell apart."[35]

While this cleared a major hurdle, a giant one still remained. Former ARA General Counsel Martin Spector recalled this defining moment for the company:

> After we defeated Siegel, we went down to Goldman Sachs for a meeting. We asked them what our chances were of remaining independent. They told us now that we were on the radar screen, sooner or later, someone else with much more financial depth and know-how would come along and take us over.[36]

The writing was on the wall and easy to read. ARA's management understood that other takeover attempts would soon come. "We had various approaches by people both in this country and outside this country who wanted to take us over," said Neubauer.[37] Hostile takeovers were not uncommon at this time, and ARA Services, with its strong cash flow and numerous divestible segments and divisions, remained a prime target.

As more corporate raiders began focusing on ARA, company leaders started weighing various defensive strategies. With public attention fixed on the company's stock, the suppliers, customers, and employees became increasingly nervous. So, after many meetings and consultations, along with much debate and consideration, an ambitious plan to eliminate the hostile takeover threat began to take shape.

### Charting the Company's Future

Neubauer recognized that if the company was acquired through a takeover, it would likely be divided and pieces of it divested. This prospect bothered him on several levels because he also knew it would break up the company's management team—a cohesive and dynamic group that created real value in a strong and growing company.

In addition, Neubauer was strongly committed to the welfare of ARA Services' employees, many of whom had spent their entire working lives with the company. He understood that many of these individuals could lose their employment if the company was acquired and divisions were sold off. Neubauer also recognized the negative and disruptive impact of this event on the company's suppliers and clients.

ARA Services had made great strides in recent years. Systems had been strengthened and improved, and the focus of the company had become better defined. There was new energy among employees, along with a strong optimism for the future. A takeover was liable to negate many of these positive effects and was almost certain to slow the company's progress. Lee Driscoll, retired Board member and general counsel, explained how the threat of a takeover attempt, described by him as a "catalyst," galvanized Neubauer into action:

> He thought we were a sitting duck because at that point, the stock was selling for a fairly low amount, and ... it might have sold for considerably more. ... There were a lot of financial opportunities.[38]

After weighing his options, Neubauer concluded that to control its own destiny and create the greatest value and opportunity, ARA would need to stage a management buyout and return to being a privately held business. This way, he reasoned, the company could remain whole, it could continue to grow, employees would be supported and stabilized, its vital suppliers would remain intact, and its customers would be well served.

"This was more than just a typical financial defensive move, but rather a decision of the major executives to stick together as friends and preserve their own culture," wrote *Nation's Restaurant News*. "Thus they avoided being ripped apart by the highest bidder."[39]

# AMERICA'S HOSTILE TAKEOVER ENVIRONMENT IN THE 1980s

ARA SERVICES WAS NOT ALONE IN FEND-ing off an unwelcome takeover offer in 1984 when former company executive William Siegel launched an attempt to take over the company. Similar efforts occurred regularly throughout corporate America, causing an environment of nervous watchfulness. New words and phrases such as "greenmailer," "poison pill," "shark repellent," and "churn and burn" were coined and used in conjunction with numerous hostile takeover attempts. Corporate raider names like T. Boone Pickens, Ronald Perelman, and Carl Icahn became known to businesses both large and small.

In an article in *The New York Times*, economics writer Charles V. Bagli described the tone of the 1980s takeovers:

*In the 1980s, takeover battles were like Wild West shootouts, and descriptions of the strife relied on the imagery of violence: greenmailers and raiders with their bear hugs and Saturday night specials were pitted against white knights and corporate managers who fended off their attackers with poison pills and shark repellent. There was even a famous "Predators Ball" to celebrate the mayhem.[1]*

Known as the decade of mergers and acquisitions, the 1980s embraced the conventional wisdom that the parts of a target company were worth more than the entire entity. And ARA Services, with its wide variety of service segments, was a highly tempting takeover target with its healthy earnings, excellent revenue growth, and strong cash flow.

Recognizing the implications of a hostile takeover attempt, Joe Neubauer and ARA's management were understandably shaken when William Siegel raised the possibility of such an attempt. "We thought it meant they would take the company apart, sell off the pieces, and make a profit by dismantling the corporation," said Martin Spector, retired general counsel of ARA Services.[2]

With the ultimate defense in mind, ARA Services eventually decided to transform itself into a privately owned company and remove its stock from the market in an effort to ensure its long-term health. "We needed to take control of our own destiny, or somebody was going to take control of it for us," said Fred Sutherland, then ARA Services treasurer.[3]

As former Board member Jim Hodgson recalled, it was not long before Neubauer proposed a plan that would enable the company to do what was in the best interest of shareholders, employees, and clients:

*We were worried, but ... Joe Neubauer had the idea that we should save ourselves. His idea was to go private, and even though it would be expensive, it would preserve the company and allow him to put to work his enormous talents at building an organization.[4]*

Neubauer's next job was to determine if such a dramatic restructuring of the company was feasible; and if so, set a management buyout plan into motion.

**Navigating Uncharted Territory**

To contemplate the best method of developing a successful management buyout, Neubauer and a core group of key executives once again retreated to an off-site location. At the same time, Neubauer ensured that his senior management team remained tightly focused on keeping ARA's day-to-day operations running smoothly.

It quickly became clear that few blueprints were available for the type of management buyout Neubauer wanted to propose. According to *Nation's*

*Restaurant News*, his plan was characterized by a high degree of personal—and financial—responsibility on the part of the management group that would bid for the company:

*An especially unique aspect of the deal was that a much larger proportion of equity than is customary went to executives, giving the managers a direct stake in the action.*[40]

Sutherland described the unusual equity structure of the deal:

*One interesting thing about the buyout was the equity. We put together $100 million worth of equity, and we borrowed $1.2 billion on top of that. So we had a lot of leverage. We had 12:1 debt to equity.*[41]

Working with a sophisticated team of lawyers, financial analysts, buyout experts, and other specialists, Neubauer and his team carefully examined the prospectuses of similar buyouts that had previously occurred and determined how they could adapt parts of these plans to meet their specific needs. Once they clearly determined that a buyout was best for all the parties connected to the company, they considered how the buyout would be structured, how much funding would be necessary, and where they would acquire it.

Determined that most of the equity should come from within the company, Neubauer solicited members of ARA's Executive Corps, 62 of the company's top managers, and asked each individual to personally commit to the plan. Within ARA, the Executive Corps was widely recognized as one of the company's most valuable assets. The group had responsibility for the day-to-day management of the firm's activities, while simultaneously planning for the company's long-term progress and expansion.

The investment requirements for the Executive Corps managers, as developed by Neubauer and his core management buyout planning team, were substantial, according to Sutherland:

*[We told the Executive Corps leadership], "You are now eligible to be owners. Here is the rule: You must invest a minimum amount in the company,*

*which is 50 percent of your salary and 100 percent of any after-tax option proceeds that you get from the company being sold."*

*Managers had stock options in ARA, which was typical. At the buyout, the company was being sold, so all the outstanding options were to be cashed out. So the rule was if you're a manager, you have to invest an amount of one half your salary plus the after-tax proceeds from any options you held that were being cashed out. That meant that the managers were not walking out with anything. ... The management shareholders had the full risk of the stock.*[42]

Neubauer and other key executives then took the plan to key employees from every division of the company and asked for their support. Lynn McKee, executive vice president of human resources, recalled the situation:

*You literally had these people coming out, company leaders like Joe Neubauer, John Farquharson, and Fred Sutherland, and they delivered the message directly to all of us. So there was enormous credibility associated with that, and it was a powerful message when they told us that they were willing to invest their futures and their lives and the lives of their families in this organization, and they invited us to invest our careers and funds, as well.*

*I remember being in a meeting with John Farquharson [former ARASERVE president] where he took off his suit coat and turned his chair around so that he was leaning on the back of the chair as he talked to this group of employees. He clearly explained to them what was going on and what the company planned to do. He told us we were going to take the company private. He talked very sincerely about his personal commitment and explained the risks associated with it, but he said he thought it was a risk worth taking. Like all our executives at the time, he was straightforward and thoughtful in explaining the opportunity. It made a huge difference.*[43]

With their top managers and key employees well informed and now firmly behind the plan, Neubauer and his core management team then widened the base of financial commitment for the management buyout. First, they approached numerous individuals who had acquired ARA shares through stock swaps when their own companies had been acquired by ARA in previous years. They also invited key suppliers and solicited institutional investors to participate in the buyout. Davre Davidson and Bill Fishman, the company's two founders, also agreed to invest. Neubauer recalled the unconventional nature of the funding plan:

*Nothing about the structure was conventional. It was a colorful patchwork quilt of valued partners and longtime friends, stitched together by a single,* common thread—*their belief in our company and our people.*[44]

After spending weeks diligently coordinating capital and carefully putting together a well-articulated management buyout agreement, Neubauer and his core group of top managers were ready to announce the plan at an upcoming meeting of the company's Board of Directors. Neubauer had recommended, and the Board had approved, a five-member special committee to handle the proposed management buyout. The committee included only

# MANAGEMENT BUYOUTS

MANAGEMENT BUYOUTS (MBOs) WERE relatively new in the 1980s, although they became increasingly common by the latter part of the decade. When members of management, assisted by lawyers and investment bankers, purchase the company that employs them, they participate in a management buyout. Such transactions are commonly called leveraged buyouts, or LBOs, because the purchase of the company is financed with money borrowed against its assets and the projected cash flow.

ARAMARK Chairman and CEO Joe Neubauer explained that the 1984 management buyout of ARA Services was not a typical transaction. Unlike the typical LBO, Neubauer's management buyout plan was structured to keep as much equity as possible within the company. "This wasn't a conventional LBO," Neubauer explained. "We didn't want to trade public ownership for financial ownership. This was a management buyout."[1]

While 75 percent of the money needed for management to buy ARA Services came from outside sources, not one of those sources was permitted to hold more than 6 percent of the total stock value. Additionally, 25 percent of the equity remained within the company, divided among the 62-member Executive Corps and the 10,000-member retirement benefit plan participants.

Four years later, ARA would buy back 50 percent of the stock held by outsiders and then increase the number of ARA managers who were eligible for ownership from 62 to more than 300. By 1990, that number had increased to more than 900 company managers.[2]

Neubauer's management buyout plan proved to be a huge success, with ARA shares skyrocketing after the buyout. It protected the company from takeover and possible divesture and preserved the company's core culture—one dedicated to service excellence.

Creating this type of ownership opportunity for managers should be the goal of every management buyout, according to an economics writer for American Capital, an equity partner in management and employee buyouts. Doing so always fosters a high degree of company loyalty among the buyout participants:

*MBOs create an opportunity of a lifetime for those lucky enough to have the chance of participating in the ownership of their company. It is often the case that managers have done more than any group to have created the value a company has in the market place. It is only appropriate and natural that managers should gain a foothold through MBOs in the wealth-creation capability of America's businesses.*[3]

The New York Times
Wednesday, August 1, 1984
From The New York Times on the Web
© The New York Times Company.
Reprinted with Permission.

# ARA Offer Ended; Future Bid Studied

### By Lee A. DANIELS

William M. Siegel said yesterday that a group of investors he heads had withdrawn its offer to acquire ARA Services Inc. in a leveraged buyout for $60 a share, or $732 million. He cited the "negative response" of ARA's management and directors.

However, Mr. Siegel, a former ARA executive who lives in Los Angeles, said through a spokesman that he remains interested in the company and was reviewing the alternatives available to him for "a possible future transaction."

ARA, based in Philadelphia, is the world's larg[...]
Its stock ro[...]
Big Board[...]
Some anal[...]
belief that[...]
one else n[...]
Monday, [...]
rumors th[...]
draw his [...]

John K[...]
Merrill L[...]
drawal w[...]
ever done[...]
before," [...]
said 'no [...]
pate in th[...]

Last n[...]
ARA's n[...]
leverage[...]
the com[...]
"inadequ[...]
of the ce[...]

Alan[...]
ARA, s[...]
idea" of[...]
also sai[...]
reaction[...]
ARA's [...]

"It's [...]
been f[...]
Mr. C[...]
was n[...]
bids fo[...]

---

# ARA Ex-Official Plans to Press Bid On a Hostile Basis

### By FRANCINE SCHWADEL
*Staff Reporter of* THE WALL STREET JOURNAL

PHILADELPHIA—A spokesman for William M. Siegel said Mr. Siegel intends to "proceed on [...]quire ARA [...] continuing [...]illion bid.

[...]posite trad-[...]5, down $2. [...] Mr. Siegel's [...]ecide today [...]ld be. ARA [...]animously" [...]r. Mr. Siegel [...] for the bid [...]d buyout.

Mr. Siegel, a former division president of ARA, was part of another investor group that won a proxy battle last year to gain control of Bradford National Corp. in New York. He wasn't available for comment.

In a leveraged buyout, a small group of investors acquires a company in a transaction financed largely by borrowing. The debt ultimately is paid w[...] generated by the acquired compan[...] its assets.

Mr. Siegel in[...] management in[...] tions and inclu[...] owners of the [...] services inclu[...] care, cleaning[...] ing homes. In[...] earned $53.7[...] enue of $3.0[...]

Mr. Woo[...] prises in[...] investors[...] meeting w[...] But ARA[...]

return[...]
said. The g[...]
he said.

In a brie[...]
company's [...]
the actions i[...]
the board" [...]
licited offer[...]
Mr. Sieg[...]
and ARA r[...]

d re[...]
ow[...]
baske[...]
y own[...]
all tea[...]

Wall Street Journal
Wednesday
July 18, 1984

Reprinted with permission of the
Wall Street Journal, Copyright © 1984
Dow Jones & Company, Inc.
All Rights Reserved Worldwide.

---

# ARA's directors turn down takeover offer

### By James Asher
*Inquirer Staff Writer*

The directors of ARA Services Inc., the giant diversified services company that is an object of an unsolicited takeover bid, have backed management and rejected the $60-a-share offer, the company said yesterday.

In a brief statement, Joseph Neubauer, chairman and chief executive officer of the Philadelphia company, said the board "formally and unanimously" reaffirmed [management's earlier] rejection of the proposal" made last week by a group of investors that includes William M. Siegel, a former ARA executive.

In the statement, Neubauer confirmed that the directors met on Monday, a meeting that the company denied late Monday afternoon.

Other ARA officials would not elaborate on the statement.

Siegel was closeted with his financial advisers during most of yesterday and was not available to comment on the statement.

Robert Hodes, Siegel's attorney, said his group still considered the buy-out proposal "a serious [...] to say what Siegel': [...] be except to say, "It [...] is over."

Earlier in the day [...] cussions were unde[...] this situation."

ARA's rejection [...] the buy-out offer, how[...]

Prior to the com[...] Siegel was reluctant "[...] at this time" about a p[...] takeover, tender offer [...]

But, he reaffirm[...] assume control of the [...] our intention to take th[...] vate," Siegel said empha[...]

Officials at ARA, wh[...] employees worldwide and 14,800 stockholders, were silent on several questions, including whether negotiations could

continue if the price per share were increased

In addition, ARA refused to say what defensive actions it would take if Siegel decides to press his takeover attempt by making a tender offer directly to shareholders. In a tender offer scenario, Siegel would bypass management and the board of directors and ask the 14,800 shareholders to part with their stock.

In the event of a tender offer, Siegel has an extra advantage because 7.6 million of the 12.04 million shares of common stock are owned by just over 100 large institutional investors. With a majority interest—63 percent—in the hands of a few shareholders, Siegel's quest to wrest control is made easier.

Siegel is no stranger to controversial takeovers. In 1983, he headed a group that took control of the Bradford National Corp., a New York financial services company.

To assume the chairmanship of Bradford National, Siegel fought a tough proxy fight with hostile management and even a lawsuit before winning control of the board and outing manage[...] [...]taining prox-[...] outstanding [...] vote himself

[...] would amount [...]t, was made [...]rly president [...]sion, and two [...]" McCombs [...]o owns the [...]l team, and [...]n, the owner [...]etball team. [...]l $3 billion. [...]t up $100 [...]n Lambert, [...]iticorp to [...]e cost. In such a leveraged buy-out, the outstanding debt is paid from the assets of the acquired company.

Philadelphia
Inquirer
Wednesday
July 18, 1984

Used with permission of
THE PHILADELPHIA INQUIRER
and DAILY NEWS Copyright © 2007.
All rights reserved

---

WSJ Wed. 10/17/84

# Boesky Group Acquires 6.5% Holding in ARA

[...]NAL *Staff Reporter*
[...]investor Ivan [...]ntrols [...] [...]nge [...]0,300 [...]ased on the New York Stock[...] Sept. 12 and Oct. 11 at $63,875 to $67.75 a share.

According to the filing, the group acquired its ARA shares "in connection with risk arbitrage and other investment activities."

On Sept. 12, ARA's senior managers proposed a leveraged buyout of the company for $62 a share in cash plus debentures. ARA stock that day jumped $10.50 to close at $64.

Senior managers later sweetened their offer, increasing the cash portion to $62.50 a share and raising the face value of the debentures. ARA's board approved that offer in early October, and the transaction is expected to be completed before the end of the year.

In New York Stock Exchange composite trading yesterday, ARA closed at $62.50, down 25 cents. The Philadelphia-based company provides a broad range of services, including food service, transportation, cleaning, health and child care.

Reprinted with permission of
Wall Street Journal, Copyright © 1984
Dow Jones & Company, Inc.
All Rights Reserved Worldwide.

# ARA Rejects Suitors

## Leveraged buyout pl...
## 'inadequate,' chief say...

By **ROBIN L. PALLEY**
...News Staff Writer

...hone calls, Mr. Woods
...tacted ARA directors,

...e chief executive of ARA
...ces, the $3.1 billion divers...
...rvices company, says that...
...ent and the executive co...
...the ARA board are "strongly
Mr. Neubauer said the
...t Monday "to review
ARA management and
to Mr. Siegel's unso-
..." to a surprise $720 million
...d buyout proposal that has
...ompany as it...
...his bid last Thursday
...quickly rejected it...
...e best interest of th...
...lders."

...Calif., is chairman...
...lesaler of compute...
...He also has oil inte...
...jor shareholder in...
...Calif.
...group are Texas busi...
...and Charles Thomas...
...anching, car dealer...
...McCombs also is...
...ver Nuggets profes...
...d Mr. Thomas is a...
...ston Rockets, another...

Philadelphia
Daily News
Friday 7/13/84

Used with permission of
THE PHILADELPHIA INQUIRER
and DAILY NEWS Copyright © 2007.
All rights reserved.

---

# ARA's Suitor Met Coolly by Managers, Asks Board Support

By FRANCINE SCHWADEL
Staff Reporter of THE WALL STREET JOURNAL

PHILADELPHIA—William M. Siegel, whose
$720 million bid for AR...
rebuffed by the company's...
still is trying to win suppo...
diversified services concer...

Mr. Siegel, a former div...
said he planned to teleph...
ARA's chairman and chie...
a pitch soon to other offic...

But ARA's manageme...
opposed to the proposed $...
out, which it described as...
best interest of the comp...

In a leveraged buyou...
acquires a company in a...
by borrowing. Ultimate...
generated by the acqui...
by the sale of its asset...

In New York Stock Exchange comp...
ing Friday, ARA closed at $55, up 50 cents. The
52-week high for the stock was $55.25; the low
was $40.25.

ARA provides services involving food, transportation, child care, cleaning and care of elderly
in nursing homes.

Mr. Siegel said he is optimistic, partly because he
believes ARA's board will be willing to review his
group's offer. "I know a number of directors, and I
know of their responsibility to shareholders and
their integrity," he said.

## Board was Polled

Harry Belinger, vice president of public affairs
at ARA, said the board was polled by telephone
and "wholeheartedly and unanimously concurred"
with management's rejection of Mr. Siegel's offer.

But Jack W. Evans, an outside director who is
president of Cullum Cos., Dallas, said he could
change his position after details of the offer are
presented to the board, possibly this week.

Although Mr. Evans initially supported management in rejecting Siegel's group's offer, he said,
"I'm not going to say (the offer) is good, bad or
indifferent until I see it. ... I'm going to listen to
both sides."

## Opposition Called Firm

Mr. Belinger, however, said ARA's opposition
is firm. "We're not interested in selling," he said.
"Whatever attempts are made, we'll try to resist."

Mr. Siegel said his group hasn't decided how
to proceed if management persists in opposing
the group's plan to take ARA private. The plan
would leave ARA management in charge of day-
to-day operations and would include top managers
among the owners of the new company.

In addition to Mr. Siegel, 53, of Bel Air, Calif.,
the group includes B. J. McCombs, majority owner
of the Denver Nuggets professional basketball
team, and Charles Thomas, majority owner of the
Houston Rockets basketball team.

A lawyer for the investors said Mr. Siegel wants
to buy ARA because he believes "it can make
more money than it does and also that it has been
undervalued in the market." In the fiscal year
ended Sept. 30, 1983, ARA earned $53.7 million,
or $4.51 a share, on revenue of $3.06 billion.

From 1969 to 1980, Mr. Siegel was president
of ARA's largest division, then called ARA Food
Services Inc.

Wall Street Journal
Monday
July 16, 1984

Reprinted with permission of the
Wall Street Journal, Copyright © 1984
Dow Jones & Company, Inc.
All Rights Reserved Worldwide.

---

Wall Street Journal Wed. Aug. 1, 1984

# ARA's Suitor Cancels $720 Million Bid But Investor Says He Remains Interested

By FRANCINE SCHWADEL
Staff Reporter of THE WALL STREET JOURNAL

PHILADELPHIA—William M. Siegel said
his investor group withdrew its $60-a-share, or
$720 million, leveraged-buyout offer for ARA
Services Inc., which rejected the bid last month.

Mr. Siegel said, however, that he "remains
interested" in ARA and is reviewing his alternatives "in connection with a possible future
transaction." The offer was withdrawn, Mr. Siegel
said, "in view of the negative response" from
ARA's management and board.

In New York Stock Exchange composite trading yesterday, ARA closed at $49.50, up $2.50,
on volume of 574,200 shares.

Mr. Siegel, a former president of ARA's food
service division, declined through an assistant
to elaborate on his announcement. A lawyer for
Mr. Siegel also declined to comment.

Other services provided by ARA are transportation, child care, cleaning and care of the
elderly in nursing homes. In the fiscal year ended
Sept. 30, 1983, it earned $53.7 million, or $4.51
a share, on revenue of $3.06 billion.

## Mr. Siegel's Options

Mr. Siegel is known to have spent several
hours Monday reviewing with lawyers the word-
ing of his two-sentence announcement, an indication that his interest in ARA remains strong.
His options now include sweetening his bid by
raising the price or by offering management a
larger ownership role.

He also could plan a tender offer on proxy
fight. Mr. Siegel still hasn't commented on a
statement two weeks ago by his spokeswoman
that he intended to "proceed on an unfriendly
basis" with his takeover bid. He initially sought
management approval for his buyout proposal,
saying he would give ARA management a 10%
stake in the new company.

In a leveraged buyout, a small group of
investors acquires a company in a transaction
financed largely by borrowing. The debt ultimately
is paid with funds generated by the acquired
company's operations or by the sale of its assets.

There was some indication that Mr. Siegel
may have lost financial backing when ARA
rejected its offer. Mr. Siegel had said that a bank
syndicate led by Citicorp of New York would
provide about $650 million, while he and other
investors would contribute about $100 million.
A Citicorp spokesman said the bank holding
company never has lent money for a hostile
leveraged buyout but declined to comment on
Mr. Siegel's financing.

## ARA's reaction

Alan K. Campbell, ARA's vice chairman,
called the Siegel group's withdrawal of its
unsolicited offer "appropriate." Looking ahead,
Mr. Campbell said, "We have no idea what he
(Mr. Siegel) has in mind, if anything."

Mr. Siegel announced his bid July 12 and
ARA management quickly rejected it as "inad-
equate and not in the best interest of the company and its shareholders." Mr. Siegel continued
to seek approval for his plan, but he was rebuffed
by the board the following week.

Mr. Siegel, 53 years old, of Bel Air, Calif., was
involved in a hostile takeover last year as part of an
investor group that won a proxy battle to gain control of Bradford National Corp. Mr. Siegel now is
chairman of Bradford National, a New York-based
wholesaler of computerized financial products.

Other investors in Mr. Siegel's group were
Texas businessmen B.J. McCombs and Charles
Thomas, majority owners of the Denver Nuggets
and the Houston Rockets professional basketball
teams, respectively. Gary Woods, an associate of
Mr. McCombs, declined to elaborate on Mr.
Siegel's announcement.

The inv...
templated...
ment would...
the success...
the investor...
problems in...
adding that...
sions with a...

ARA spo...
the offer reach...
at the same tim...
told the press i...
ing the multin...
has interests in...
tion, day care...

Within hou...
a statement tru...
approval of th...
tives oppose th...
not only becau...
Belinger said.

"It's a bad t...
have to deal wi...
when we're h...
Olympic effor...
Olympic spon...
more than $4 m...
portation for th...

Reprinted with permission of the Wall Street Journal,
Copyright © 1984 Dow Jones & Company, Inc. All Rights Reserved Worldwide.

The special committee of ARA Services' Board of Directors met at the Four Seasons Hotel in Philadelphia to negotiate details of the management buyout plan with Neubauer's group.

outside Board members, none of whom were ARA employees or former employees. "The committee reported back to the Board as to the progress of the negotiations and the discussions as to what made the most sense," said Ron Davenport, former ARAMARK Board member.[45]

### Starting the Process

At the time, Neubauer understood that the Board of Directors could be conflicted about his position with the management buyout plan. The Board, which represented company shareholders, was obligated to make decisions only in the interest of ARA's individual shareholders, not for Neubauer and his group of investors. Neubauer was the CEO of a publicly held company, while also the leader of a group of investors trying to take over that same corporation. It was vitally important for Neubauer to remain friendly with the Board, but also to remove himself from it.

On the Monday after Labor Day in 1984, Neubauer and his management buyout group placed their proposal on the table, offering the Board $1 billion for the company. Neubauer announced they would complete the transaction in 100 days, although many outside experts believed that goal was too optimistic.

At the end of the Board meeting, a press statement announced the terms of the management proposal, outlining the price that other interested companies would have to beat. The pressure was on, and Neubauer's management buyout group was in a race with time. Neubauer explained the urgency of his group's position:

*Lederman said to me, "You understand now that you just put the apple on top of your head, and you're inviting everybody to shoot arrows at it." Because once you announce that you're up for sale, anybody else can up your bid.*[46]

After deciding not to make a second offer for ARA, Siegel contacted Neubauer to offer his support. "He called me and said, 'I just want you to know we are here to help you,'" Neubauer stated. "It was a remarkable call and one I will never forget for the rest of my life. It just tells you that people care for you as a human being, and care for you as an organization, as opposed to just caring for [your success in a monetary way]. He was in our corner."[47]

### Normal Day-to-Day Operations

While company executives were dedicated to the task of executing a successful management buyout plan, day-to-day operations at ARA Services continued in normal fashion. Indeed, the original hostile takeover was still a threat when the company served at the Los Angeles Olympic Games. All activities at the company remained on a standard "business as usual" basis during the full period of the buyout, despite the daunting enormity and financial complexity of the undertaking.

Field managers continued serving customers with the same high degree of excellence that had become an ARA Services hallmark. Additionally, they were responsible for continuing to expand ARA's large customer base, while keeping employees assured of the company's stability. Their efforts served as a valuable contribution to the company at this critical time.

Harry Belinger, vice president of public affairs at ARA at the time, credited Neubauer with keeping the distraction of the buyout separate from the day-to-day business of supporting the company's people and serving customers worldwide:

*When we refused the takeover and made our own bid, Joe [Neubauer] kept all that separate from the company. He said, "I want everybody to continue to do their job," and he actually got those who were involved in the proposal— to buy the company—out of the headquarters and set up elsewhere. So, there was all this activity going on, but the people at headquarters were not exposed to it. Joe very skillfully kept that separate so people were not distracted from doing their jobs.*[48]

### Taking the Show on the Road

Raising $1 billion in 100 days represented a huge order, as Neubauer and his team worked overtime to secure the necessary financial commitments. Their credibility throughout the financial marketplace aided them greatly in this endeavor, according to Lynn McKee:

*We've always had a leadership team in this organization that can go to the financial markets and talk in great detail about this business. It is very clear to any outsider who talks to Joe Neubauer or Fred Sutherland that they truly understand the business—how to motivate employees and how best to serve customers. They really know how it works, how to make money, and how to succeed in this business. They have been very hands-on and involved in [this way] for years. That grasp of span and scope really speaks well to key players in the debt and equity markets.*[49]

Neubauer and his team traveled extensively across the country, visiting major shareholders, company employees, and banks. They made arrangements to sell bonds to bond funds and insurance companies. This proved challenging, according to Neubauer's comments in *Forbes* magazine: "I remember walking up and down Wilshire Boulevard, peddling bonds, and it was tough to sell [them] because at the time Drexel had a very big market share, like 93 percent. ... The day after we borrowed the money, we didn't know whether the customers were going to be there."[50] During this process, ARA had been concerned about the heavy amount of debt the company would be taking on, but this was tempered by the trust that the ARA community placed in Neubauer and his team, according to Hodgson:

*When it comes to making a judgment on that kind of thing in business, you have to determine the risk and the return. As far as we were concerned, however, with this matter in the hands of an astute financial man and as effective a leader as Joe Neubauer, we had a lot of faith.*[51]

Additionally, Neubauer and his team put up money of their own, mortgaging their homes, reinvesting their bonuses, and tapping their individual retirement accounts. "Some of [ARA's managers] even used their credit cards to advance the money," said Neubauer.[52]

At the same time, company executives met routinely with the Special Committee of the Board to provide updates and hear the recommendations of lawyers and financial analysts. All the while, they remained aware that a higher offer could come at any time, and the Board of Directors would be obligated to consider it.

### Neubauer's Core Group

Neubauer's management buyout team was completely devoted to Neubauer. "People would walk through fire to support Joe Neubauer," said Martin Spector.[53] They would spend hours discussing their progress, debriefing after meetings with the Special Committee, and providing updates on their financial status.

By then it was nearing the end of September 1984, and the Special Committee would soon meet in the hope of approving the plan for the buyout. Unfortunately, two banks that Neubauer's group had been counting on for large amounts of money both unexpectedly turned them down. Yet this setback was quickly displaced by even more disturbing news.

Waiting at the station for a train to take them from New York to Philadelphia, Neubauer and Sutherland learned during a call to headquarters that a large and powerful British company had suddenly surfaced, and it was interested in buying ARA Services.

### A Threat from Abroad

The potential new bidder, Trust House Forte, was a huge, British-based hotel, food service, and catering company. Key Trust House Forte executives were eager to quickly meet with ARA's management, leaving Neubauer and his core group little time to prepare for this crucial meeting.

Representing ARA, Neubauer, Spector, and Francis Palamara, another member of the management buyout team, first met with the Trust House Forte executives, who explained that they wanted Neubauer and his team to continue managing the company. In addition, they pledged to make the company much larger by combining their own extensive U.S. operations with those of ARA.

ARA executives riveted on the Trust House Forte overture, since the company was a giant player with large international holdings, and its financial powers presented it as a serious threat. Indeed, Neubauer's management buyout team knew that if the British company offered a serious bid for ARA, there was little they could do to stop it. They simply could not match Trust House Forte's huge financial reach and resources.

At a second meeting, Trust House Forte made an alternate proposal and offered to buy ARA's food service company, suggesting that the company's other business lines join to form a separate company. Neubauer, however, was not impressed with this plan, since he had determined there was greater value in keeping the company, its employees, and its service offerings intact.

*The world recognized ARA Services' 1984 management buyout as one of the most successful corporate restructurings. A positive report called "A buyout that worked" was published in the July 23, 1990 issue of Forbes magazine. (Reprinted by Permission of Forbes Magazine © 2007 Forbes LLC. Photos by Sarah Leen.)*

---

*As many of the leveraged buyout deals put together by financiers are hitting the walls, a deal put together by managers is hitting new levels of prosperity.*

## A buyout that worked

**By James Cook**

JOSEPH NEUBAUER, who in late 1984 led the insider buyout of what is now Philadelphia's ARA Group, Inc., works alongside some demanding employees. "One manager who just bought into the company came up to me a while back," relates Neubauer, "and he pointed a finger right at me and said, 'Mr. Neubauer, you better not screw it up.'"

The admonition is both an indicator of why ARA is so successful and a reminder of how far the company has come in five years. When Neubauer and 61 other managers closed the buyout in December 1984, ARA had bought in its 12 million outstanding shares for $917 million in cash. The recapitalized company's debt came to a breathtaking $1.2 billion, teetering on a $100 million pinpoint of equity. But there was hidden stability, too.

Primary in this regard was the desire to succeed brought to their jobs by ARA's new manager-owners. Says Neubauer, now 48, who had been head of a division of PepsiCo's Wilson Sporting Goods before he joined ARA in 1979 as chief financial officer: "This wasn't a conventional LBO. We didn't want to trade public ownership for financial ownership. This was a management buyout."

And so it was. Altogether, 75% of the equity came from outside the company, from institutional investors and from interested suppliers but no individual outsider got more than 6% of the stock. The largest block went to various company insiders—to members of ARA's 62-man Executive Corps (which got 18% of the equity) and to the 10,000 participants in its employee retirement benefit plan (7%). So, from the start, 25% of the equity was held inside the company, in contrast to six Nabisco and other 1980s-era Wall Street deals in which outside financiers took the lion's share of the action, spread a few equity crumbs among the company's managers, and walked off with enormous fees and profits.

It also helped matters that ARA's businesses are more stable than most. From its mixture of food services (60% of sales), uniform and linen rental (14%), nursing homes and child care (17%), and magazine and book distribution (9%), ARA could predict its prospective cash flow fairly accurately. Thus, despite an increase of roughly $100 million in its interest charges as a result of the buyout, ARA stayed in the black from the very beginning. So accurate were the cash flow projections, in fact, that within two years Neubauer was able to reduce ARA's debt by $200 million—without sacrificing its capital program or selling off any of its core operations.

"We did not want to dismember the company," Neubauer says, "and we didn't have to." Neubauer did, however, remove some gangrene. He sold a trucking business, for example, which was losing $20 million a year. But that would have gone anyway.

He also cut the number of nursing homes by 20% in five years. "We've been trimming around the edges," Neubauer says. "We can reduce volume and improve profitability by getting rid of marginal assets."

As ARA's operating margins began to rise (they have widened from 8.6% to 10.6% today), Neubauer concluded that ARA had better things to do with its financial resources than reducing its debt. He began borrowing again in order to expand the company. In two years he laid out nearly $400 million on a half-dozen major acquisitions to strengthen its basic food service, linen rental and day care businesses.

At the same time, Neubauer accelerated ARA's growth by taking over businesses its new customers had previously operated themselves—a $16 million food service contract with the University of Virginia, for example, and a $24 million contract to feed 105,000 schoolchildren in the Duval County, Fla. school system.

As the acquisitions began to pay off, the debt underlying the company became more and more manageable. Total debt still runs around $1.2 billion, as it did when the buyout took place, but sales will hit $4.5 billion this fiscal year, while earnings before interest and taxes will go from $150 million to $250 million.

"We're doing $1 billion more business and earning $100 million more than we did the day we took the company private, and we've done that on the same asset base, that's what our strategy is all about," says Neubauer, adding: "High debt levels are not what cause corporate problems. It's how you manage the debt and the business, and the ability to control and live with debt is something we worked on very, very hard."

Determined to share ARA's values with the people who were actually creating those values, Neubauer in 1988 bought back 50% of the stock held by outsiders; they were paid $265 for shares that cost them $55 two years earlier. With the repurchased equity, he began widening the base of managers eligible for ownership from an original 62 to over 300 in 1987 and nearly 900 this year.

As inside stockholders retire or leave the company, ARA buys them out at a price set by outside appraisers. Last year that came to $18.50 a share on average, this year to $22.50. Not bad for stock that cost the original investors $3.50 a share. Neubauer owns over 11% of ARA's stock, at last appraisal, that was worth nearly $35 million.

Is Neubauer planning to take the company public again? He vigorously denies it, insisting that the company has nothing to gain from tapping new public owners. ARA has no trouble borrowing money, as it demonstrated in April with a $125 million debenture offering. Moreover, Neubauer figures ARA can cultivate its opportunities better in private.

Which, after all, is why Neubauer engineered the buyout in the first place. "A former ARA chief executive made a run at us," he says, "and though he eventually went away, our stock was no longer in very safe hands, so we decided to take the company private."

The situation today could not be more different. "Inside the company," says Neubauer, "we now own two-thirds of the stock and over 92% of the voting control, so we are indeed masters of our destiny." ∎

*ARA distribution* **Cash flow stability.**

ARA's Joseph Neubauer with a baker at an ARA cafeteria in Philadelphia
**"Mr. Neubauer, you better not screw it up."**

# ARA's STREETWISE LEADERS

**B**USINESS WRITERS ACROSS the country all agreed that ARA's management buyout was a huge success because of the highly professional team of executives directed by then-Chairman and CEO of ARA Services, Joe Neubauer, who planned and structured the buyout's terms.

In a 2005 interview, Robert J. Callander, ARAMARK Board member and retired vice chairman of Chemical Bank, discussed what makes ARAMARK's leadership so special:

Well-respected corporate executive and longtime Board member Robert J. Callander has been associated with the company for more than 25 years.

*In looking at the company over the years, the great success is that we always refer to the people that run the business not as managers or executives but as "operators." That's what Davre Davidson and Bill Fishman were, you know, they actually made the sandwiches fairly early on. So the company's success has been [due to the fact] that we have a group of very good operators.*

*Some might or might not have gone to the Harvard Business School. Many of them worked their way up with a lot of savvy, a lot of street smarts, and a lot of good business sense and aggressiveness regarding getting things done.*

*Of course, as the company matures, you end up with more educated people, but one thing you want to make sure of is that the men or women running the company really know the business; that metaphorically, they've got some peanut butter and jelly on their hands. It isn't just MBA types doing strategy and projections and budget and so on. It's great people dedicated to great service for their customers. That's really what's made the company such a success.[1]*

After making their alternate proposal, Trust House Forte's representatives left the second day's meetings, but ARA's team remained, working long into the night to develop a strategy to counter the potential Trust House Forte bid. After much deliberation, the group decided to follow Martin Spector's plan and refuse Trust House Forte's proposal to buy the ARA food service operations but invite the British company to invest in ARA Food Services, giving it a minority interest.

The next day, the Trust House Forte team considered yet rejected Spector's plan. However, there was a silver lining: With their rejection, the Trust House Forte team explained that they would not pursue a hostile takeover attempt of ARA Services. Further, they would leave the door open to the possibility of a future alliance with the company.

Having dealt with yet another challenge, Neubauer's team returned to preparing for another key meeting with the Board's Special Committee.

### $1 Billion Not Enough

Neubauer's management team remained optimistic that the Special Committee would approve its buyout plan and recommend that the full Board of Directors do the same. The Special Committee, however, wanted to ensure that enough had been done to acquire the best possible price for the company's shareholders. As a result, committee members asked Neubauer and his group to raise their bid amount by $15 million.

Management's offer was based on an appraisal process, and the management buyout offer of $1 billion reflected that. Responding to this new request

from the Special Committee, Neubauer and his team believed their offer was more than fair. The two groups negotiated through the night and finally agreed to a new bid acceptable to both sides. More trouble, however, loomed ahead.

Members of the Board and the Special Committee now raised the concern that management had somehow dissuaded Trust House Forte from making a formal offer for ARA Services. They believed such an offer may have been higher than the $1 billion offer proposed by Neubauer and his group.

Members of the Special Committee explained that they could not approve management's buyout plan until this matter had been resolved. And so, on the afternoon of October 4, 1984, just hours before a gala party scheduled to celebrate the 25th anniversary of the merger of Davre Davidson and Bill Fishman's businesses—and hopefully to announce the successful launch of the buyout—management and the Special Committee met to review the discussions with Trust House Forte.

As Special Committee members met to deliberate the matter, Neubauer and his group waited at the Four Seasons Hotel. Members of the Executive Corps and other party guests waited at the nearby Franklin Institute for Neubauer to arrive with the news. For several hours, people stood around in the rotunda in their formal wear, hoping for word. Finally, it came. The Special Committee announced it would give provisional approval of management's buyout plan, contingent on a conversation with Trust House Forte executives.

Neubauer and others on the management team were thrilled and confident that the plan would now move forward. After days of hurdles, roadblocks, and sitting around in black tie, it was time to celebrate, as management and Board members jointly delivered the good news. Once the buyout was finalized, ARA Services would be best positioned to serve its clients and customers, and best able to take care of its suppliers, its shareholders, and its people. The party, which had been delayed for several hours due to the meetings, began in earnest. The champagne bottles could be opened at last.

### A Race with Time

While Neubauer and his team had earned the Board's blessing to proceed, it was now necessary to execute the details of the buyout. A multitude of financial and legal issues still needed to be successfully addressed—and time was of the essence. Until the plan was approved by the shareholders, ARA Services remained vulnerable to other takeover attempts. Members of the management buyout team worked around the clock until the deal was consummated. Sutherland recalled the intensity of the negotiations, which involved 27 different parties, including bankers, lawyers, and investors:

*It was the most intense and exhilarating business experience I have ever had. It meant 14- to 18-hour business days, six or seven days a week. I would close negotiations in New York, drive home, and fall in bed at 1 or 2 A.M. At 5 A.M., while I was sleeping, documents would be delivered to my house by courier. I would get up at 6 A.M., get the papers from inside the screen door, and read them on the train back to New York, where there would be more negotiations. With 27 parties negotiating, it was pretty complex.*[54]

This hard work paid off as the aggressive deadline grew closer, and the buyout deal began to fully come together. By this time, strong financial partners were in place, according to Neubauer:

*We received commitments from all the banks. The four major investors along with the management team were JPMorgan, Chemical Bank, Goldman Sachs, and Metropolitan Life Insurance Company. Those were the four big ones.*[55]

As November neared an end, everyone remained confident that the deal would close by December 20—the 100-day deadline set by Neubauer. ARA Services would borrow a total of $1.2 billion to finance the buyout, "teetering," as *Forbes* magazine put it, "on a $100 million pinpoint of equity."

Representatives of all participating banks met in the boardroom of the Morgan Guaranty Trust Company on Wall Street in New York on December 17, 1984, to sign the final financial agreements. The day before, however, one bank, which had committed $50 million, announced that it was not ready to sign.

At Philadelphia's Franklin Institute in 1984, ARA Services celebrated the 25th anniversary of Davidson and Fishman joining forces. By coincidence, negotiations for the management buyout concluded the same night as this gathering, and Neubauer and his management buyout team were pleased to announce the good news at the celebration. Shown, left to right, are Harry Glick, a longtime ARA Services executive responsible for negotiating many of the company's key acquisitions; Davre Davidson; Charlotte Davidson; and Bill Fishman.

Though this rattled some nerves, the matter was resolved by the end of the day. With this final piece of the financial puzzle in place, the signing went off as planned, and the management buyout closed on December 19, on day 99.

### A Superbly Organized Management Buyout

Financial analysts and the business press were in uniform agreement that ARA's management buyout had been well organized and handled very professionally. "Clearly, ARA is an example of an LBO that has worked," said Jack Kelly, an equity research analyst at Goldman Sachs. He pointed to three primary reasons:

*First, ARA completed the buyout early in the LBO craze of the 1980s, before the price of companies went sky-high. Second, while most chairmen are traditionally operations people, Neubauer's financial background gave him a banker's savvy. And, finally, the employees rallied to make it work.*[56]

According to *Nation's Restaurant News*, other planned buyouts had not always been as successful:

*This represents the only truly successful LBO among foodservice chains, in this editor's opinion.*

*Denny's, Foodmaker, Restaurant Associates, and Service America, among others, encountered debt or other obstacles in varying degrees. ...*

*ARA has proven the skeptics wrong and shown that an LBO can work—if the proper management principles are carefully applied and if the principals themselves remain dedicated to maximizing quality and not merely profiting from the LBO.*[57]

"Management did an outstanding job, both in terms of the financing ... and also running the business on a day-to-day basis and making it grow," said Ron Davenport, former ARAMARK Board member.[58]

In a *Nation's Restaurant News* article, editor Charles Bernstein credited Neubauer and his team for the successful buyout:

*What were the ingredients of this LBO that set it apart and above other such deals?*

Above left: Bill Fishman (left) shares a private moment with his protégé, Joe Neubauer, as the company finalized its historic restructuring.

Below: In celebration of the successful closure of the management buyout, a party took place at The Palace Hotel in Philadelphia. The date of the buyout agreement, December 19, occurred one day before Neubauer's self-imposed 100-day deadline to raise the needed cash for the buyout—$1.2 billion.

*First, there was the [CEO], Joe Neubauer. ... He possessed exactly the right mix of leadership and discipline, as well as financial savvy, to make this work. The chemistry of his top executives also was ideal in the situation.*

*What Neubauer did so brilliantly was to let a tiny group ... put together all the working details for the deal.*[59]

Neubauer and his management team had hit a bull's-eye with the buyout. It had successfully placed the company in the hands of its employees. According to Neubauer, this presented a major advantage:

*We have good people who are both happy in their work and good at what they do. It's their company, and they realize they are in control of their own destiny every day out in the field. ...*

*We're not Wall Street types or financiers; we're a professional services company. When we talk to our employees about their company, they know we really mean it. Our people are excited to be owners of their company.*[60]

The atrium at the top of the 32-story building is just one of the attractive features of company headquarters located at the northwest corner of 11<sup>th</sup> and Market Streets in Philadelphia. *(Photo by Lawrence S. Williams, courtesy of The Athenaeum of Philadelphia.)*

## CHAPTER SEVEN

# SURPRISING THE SKEPTICS

## 1985–1989

*First and foremost ... ours was truly a "management buyout" that was opened to a large number of ARA managers, rather than just a few top executives. Second, unlike the majority of firms that undergo a buyout, we have not sold off major chunks of our company to reduce our debt. Instead, we have depended on the growth of our company to reduce our debt.*

—ARA Chairman and CEO Joe Neubauer

**A**FTER ARA'S MANAGEMENT buyout in 1984, experts from all corners of the business and financial world kept a close eye on the company's activities. The widely publicized transaction had, after all, left the company with a staggering $1.2 billion debt. Would ARA join the ranks of other companies that had floundered financially after a leveraged buyout? Would the company have enough cash to invest in the business? Would Chairman and CEO Joe Neubauer begin selling off parts of the company to raise funds and pay down debt? Many wondered if the company would go stale, burdened with debt that would inhibit growth and eliminate the possibility of new acquisitions.

The company provided answers that would, in time, completely surprise the skeptics. The company's corporate transition from public to private ownership, with every nuance ripe for analysis, would prompt Neubauer to describe ARA as nothing less than a "maverick" company.[1]

Aware of the industry buzz and determined to keep the company intact, executives returned to work after taking the company private and, through careful planning and strategic business decisions, began implementing plans to pay down the company's debt. "Having your own money at stake does give you a sense of urgency," said Neubauer, the

company's largest, single shareholder, in January 1985.[2]

Immediately, the company's "Flash" methodology—the monthly reporting of sales and profits—enabled management to stay current with financial positions, an invaluable intelligence that provided the optimum vantage point for sound tactical decisions.

Intent on maintaining customer confidence, the company quickly initiated a "Cash is King" task force, aimed at identifying marginal assets and all possible ways to free up cash. This located any available cash that could be invested in services to customers and also encouraged all systems to save money in any manner possible. Throughout the company, executives emphasized the implementation of the most efficient and cost-effective methods of delivering quality service for a respectable profit. "We knew we had very strong cash flows, and we actually focused a little bit more on cash flow," recalled Neubauer. "We made up buttons saying,

---

Chairman and CEO Joe Neubauer, a fixture at Olympic Games all over the world, noted that the company's participation in the 1988 Olympic Games in Seoul represented ARA's 20th year of service to Olympic athletes.

'Cash is King,' and you know, we skimped on a few expenses here and there, but not vis-à-vis the customers."[3]

In fact, Neubauer later admitted, financial institutions may have loved the "Cash is King" concept, but he did not. "You know, I thought it was cute for about a week, and after that I said, 'You better get a new button that says "Customer is King." Because that's really who's king around here.' "[4]

### Business as Usual

One of Neubauer's primary goals and challenges after taking the company private was convincing both customers and employees that business would continue as usual and that the service company was still a vital organization. Neubauer remembered:

*The traditional model for an LBO is that you buy the company, turn it around very quickly, sell off assets, and make a financial killing. People said we wouldn't be able to do business like before. Even our own people expected that. I remember a contact in Chicago, where one of our competitors was telling the customer, "ARA won't be able*

*to spend any money anymore. They have huge debt." Well, I had to personally assure the customer that we would spend the money. I didn't anticipate how difficult it would be to convince our own people that we would continue to do business in the usual manner.*[5]

As soon as possible, the company started refinancing its debt through the benefit of constantly declining interest rates, which worked to improve the company's credit rating, enhanced its debt-equity ratio, and helped contribute to the continuous rise of the stock price (based on a quarterly evaluation). As a result, in 1985 alone, the company reduced its debt by more than $150 million and even reported a slim profit. Fred Sutherland, ARAMARK chief financial officer, once marveled at the speed of the company's management buyout plan. He now felt similar wonder about the amazing pace of the first year and a half after the buyout:

*We refinanced for the first seven quarters. We generated cash like crazy, we scrutinized capital expenditures, and we addressed the working capital. We really drove the cash flow. We paid off*

**1985**
As a new private company, ARA creates a "Cash is King" task force aimed at identifying marginal assets, finding any available cash to invest in services to customers, and managing costs.

**1986**
ARA moves to impressive new headquarters at 11th and Market Streets in Philadelphia.

**1986**
The company manages to pay off $200 million in debt almost two years ahead of schedule. It records its highest level of new business activity in one year in the history of the company.

**1987**
ARA purchases Szabo Food Service, Inc. of Chicago. It also acquires Servisco, Inc., a Hillside, New Jersey, company that manufactures and rents work uniforms.

*$175 million in seven quarters. So we showed the banks that this company could generate cash flow even with this debt load.*[6]

### Stunning the Skeptics

In June 1986, the *Wall Street Journal* noted that after paying off $175 million, ARA "is now more than $50 million ahead of its schedule" in paying down its original $1.2 billion in debt.[7] In a move that completely surprised industry observers and skeptics alike, the company continued to pay down its debt ahead of schedule without selling any strategic assets. The same newspaper article described Neubauer as "fiercely proud" of this accomplishment.[8] According to Neubauer, out of the $25 million worth of divestitures after the buyout, the company's only marginally significant divestiture by the end of 1986 was the sale of Sugarbush Valley Ski Resort in Vermont for less than $20 million. Neubauer said, "It simply didn't fit anymore. That business depends on the weather. Since we can't control the weather, it wasn't a good fit for us."[9] He later stated, "It's fair to say that for us, debt repayment has not replaced rational business sense as the impetus for action."[10]

The post-buyout process cemented the company's conversion from what Sutherland called "the founding management to *professional* management, for lack of a better word, which was the transition from Bill Fishman to Joe Neubauer."[11] This period also ushered in a new era for management. According to Davre Davidson, they were essentially "managing two businesses": the "successful operation of a service business" and the "management of the finances for the company." He attributed their stability and profits to "a brilliant job of layering debt, prudent use of debt instruments, and ... even lower borrowing interest rates."[12]

While the accelerated debt repayment pleasantly surprised financial skeptics, the company continued to maintain its culture of service and partnership. Enormous growth opportunities meant only one thing: It was time to expand the company again.

"We first ran the company for maximized cash flow," said Neubauer. "We did that for about a year and a half. [Then] we actually started buying more companies ... once we proved to ourselves and proved to our creditors that we could invest in the company and pay off the debt."[13]

**1987**
Focusing on core businesses, ARA divests its trucking division. ARA also begins to trim its nursing homes inventory, reducing it by 20 percent over five years.

**1988**
ARA celebrates 20 years of Olympic service to seven Olympic events since 1968.

Games of the XXIVth Olympiad Seoul 1988

**1987**
Employee ownership in the company is expanded from the original 62 executives. By the end of 1989, the company will have more than 900 direct owner–managers, and employees will own nearly 65 percent of the company.

**1989**
ARA's 120,000 employees serve more than 10 million people each day. Revenues reach an all-time high of $4.2 billion.

# STRATEGIC ACQUISITIONS

TO BROADEN ITS PORTFOLIO AND ADD muscle to its core competencies, ARA executed the following important milestone acquisitions and service enhancements from 1985 to 1989:

- **Cory Food Services**—acquired in 1985 from Hershey Foods, Inc., it enhanced the operation of ARA's Coffee System division, which was renamed ARA/Cory Refreshment Services.[1]
- **Szabo Food Service, Inc.**—acquired in 1987, the addition of Szabo, headquartered in Chicago, expanded the company's business dining services and moved ARA into providing food services to correctional institutions. By acquiring Szabo, ARA also took over important concessions operations at Anaheim Stadium and Convention Center in California and at Wrigley Field in Chicago.[2]
- **Servisco, Inc.**—announced in 1986 and acquired in 1987. This Hillside, New Jersey, manufacturer and renter of work uniforms, helped boost ARA's uniform business in the north central part of the country. It also added several accounts to the company's facilities services operation.[3]

- **Children's World Learning Centers**—announced in September 1987 and acquired in 1988. The purchase of Children's World, later renamed Children's World Learning Centers, more than doubled the size of the company's early childhood education division.[4]

### A Daring Expansion

In essence, Neubauer concluded that ARA had better plans for its financial resources than reducing its debt.[14] From an outside perspective, ARA and its entrepreneurial executives proceeded to accomplish what Neubauer once described as "everything that people said we couldn't do."[15]

ARA began borrowing again in an effort to expand the company to the tune of nearly $250 million in the first two years after the buyout.[16] The bold moves startled the business community, which had predicted that ARA would likely downsize after going private. Instead, there were two very significant and early acquisitions.

In 1987, ARA paid approximately $65 million to purchase Servisco, Inc., a Hillside, New Jersey, company that manufactures and rents work uniforms. ARA then paid around $85 million for Szabo Food Service, Inc., of Chicago, Illinois. The company also attempted to acquire Saga Corporation, a San Francisco–based food service operation, but pulled out due to the high purchase price. In the case of Saga, however, the process itself was well worth the effort. "After the buyout … they said we wouldn't be able to invest capital in existing businesses, and they were certain that we couldn't play the acquisition game," said Neubauer. "Well, we did go after Saga. We stopped only because someone else wanted to pay something higher than we wanted to

Opposite: ARA caters to the nutritional needs and tastes of more than 650,000 schoolchildren every day. The lunches that ARA prepares in some 180 school districts in 22 states are planned to meet nutritional requirements and children's tastes, in addition to strict budget constraints.

Right: Lake Powell is North America's second-largest man-made lake. Houseboating from ARA's marinas is a popular way to see the lake's 1,960 miles of shoreline and 96 major canyons.

- Lake Powell concessions in Utah and Arizona—acquired in 1989. When ARA acquired the concession rights to the 185-mile lake, it considerably increased the scope of its resort management business. ARA became responsible for a small navy of houseboats and other recreational boats that are the focal point of tourist activities at Lake Powell, one of the jewels in the National Park system.[5]
- From 1985 to 1989, ARA expanded its campus dining services to serve such notable institutions as MIT, University of Virginia, University of Chicago, Vassar, Clemson University, Vermont State College, University of Houston, College of Charleston, Barnard College, Wesleyan University, The Citadel, Duquesne University, UNC–Greensboro, UNC–Charlotte, and UNC–Wilmington.[6]
- In healthcare management services, ARA secured accounts at Albany Medical Center in New York; Summit Medical Center, Oakland, California; University of Pittsburgh Medical Center; and Loyola University Medical Center, Chicago. In the realm of school nutrition services, ARA established an account with the Lubbock Independent School District in Lubbock, Texas.[7]

pay. We certainly didn't stop because we lacked the financial wherewithal."[17]

According to *Forbes* magazine, within two years Neubauer "laid out nearly $400 million on a half-dozen major acquisitions to strengthen its basic food service, linen rental, and day care businesses."[18]

By the end of 1986, ARA's impressive financial milestones clearly revealed the reason banks were willing to loan ARA money for acquisitions. The company had managed to pay off $200 million in debt almost two years ahead of schedule. While the year's profits of $15.5 million were far below the $64.4 million in profit from 1984, it was 50 percent above company projections. The profits resulted from a record $3.75 billion in fiscal 1986 revenues and took into consideration $140 million in interest charges.[19] Moreover, in 1986, ARA's service orientation and emphasis on customer relationships resulted not only in the retention of key accounts, but also in the highest level of new business activity over one year in the company's history.[20]

**Making the Move**

After debating whether to remain in Philadelphia or relocate, in 1986, ARA Services left the Curtis Building and moved into the decidedly uptown, impressively modern ARA Tower at 11th and Market Streets. The company's offices in the art deco skyscraper offered sweeping views of New Jersey and

Philadelphia, sending a clear message about ARA's ambitious financial goals and its dedication to continued prosperity.

The change of address caught the attention of the business world and served to highlight the remarkably confident nature of both the company and its CEO. "Most firms move downtown in an LBO [leveraged buyout]," Neubauer noted. "We went uptown."[21]

After going private, ARA's continued entrepreneurship and bold business steps impressed Board member Ron Davenport, who attributed the company's renewed mission to Neubauer and "the quality of leadership" the CEO built around him. "I think being a winner is having a winning attitude, honesty, and integrity," said Davenport.[22] Robert J. Callander, now retired vice chairman of Chemical Bank who joined the ARA Board in 1986, also noticed a unique trait in the company CEO:

*Many CEOs always say, "I want candor," but do you know what they really want? They want what I call "positive candor," and that everything is going great. They don't like candor at all. Joe Neubauer wants and demands candor, and that [makes him different]. I think it enables a lot of creativity to come out of the process because he then gets to know what is really going on, good or bad, and he can take it. Joe has enough self-esteem that he can take the criticism and not take it personally, and he understands that all of his directors are extraordinarily loyal. You really do*

Above: ARA is America's premier provider of vending services. Each day, ARA stocks trucks and makes deliveries to meet the vending need of tens of thousands of customers at more than 6,000 accounts across the country. ARA launched its coffee and refreshment services operation 20 years ago to serve small offices where a full-scale vending program was not practical. As of 1986, ARA provides beverages and snacks in 200,000 locations in 39 states; annually, ARA sells more than a billion cups of coffee and more than 44 million snacks.

Opposite: When ARA completed its move to the new headquarters in 1986, the signature ARA red letters on top of the ARA Tower, shown here in an artist's rendering, clearly identified the new corporate resident at 1101 Market Street.

*feel that you're needed and wanted. And by God, you'd better perform.*[23]

**"Everybody Sells"**

Encouraging better performance was not limited to enthusiastic executives or Board members. In fact, everyone at employee-owned ARA was expected to contribute to the company's success. Toward that goal, Neubauer appointed a special sales task force in 1986 to identify ways that would help accelerate the growth of the company.

Task force members came from many lines of ARA business. Richard H. Vent, president, Air/Leisure Services Sector, presided at the first task

force meeting in Philadelphia on July 15, 1986. The motto "Everybody Sells," which was quickly adopted, emphasized the importance of effecting new sales, retaining clients, and improving merchandising.

The task force recommended a number of action steps, including the creation of the "20/20" program, which aimed at accelerating ARA's top-line sales and revenue performance. At all levels of ARA management, sales and operations leaders were charged with developing lists of 20 top clients and 20 top prospects so they could improve client retention, boost sales in existing accounts, and promote the sale of new business.[24]

In an effort to capture the best practices throughout the company, various divisions were asked to identify their most successful programs in client retention, sales, training, merchandising, or sales compensation, and then apply these programs to other areas of the business.[25]

Rallying frontline managers, ARA's corporate message of "Everybody Sells" frequently focused on the ways even small but cumulative efforts could translate into remarkable gains.[26] The following examples appeared in an ARA *Topics* newsletter: "If each manager in each of ARASERVE's 3,000 units could add just one daily customer, it would add $1 million to the bottom line. And if each director in each of our 450 Children's World Learning Centers could enroll just two more children, it would mean an additional $1.3 million."[27] The overall importance

# "EVERYBODY SELLS"

ONLY TWO YEARS AFTER THE SLOGAN "Everybody Sells" was introduced, ARA determined that the message had become a permanent part of ARA's culture. Interestingly enough, the concept had developed far beyond the original goal of improved sales figures and client retention rates. "Everybody Sells" had seeped into the very fiber of the way ARA employees delivered services.

Living Centers adopted the "Everybody Sells" concept by training employees on how to respond to the needs of residents who call ARA's centers "home." Within ARA's Magazine and Book Distribution Services division, the "Everybody Sells" concept indicated a warm, friendly smile and a willingness to help customers. For ARA/Cory personnel, ensuring that customers always had a fresh supply of coffee, refreshments, and related supplies was part of the "Everybody Sells" philosophy. Acting on that concept meant that ARA employees were willing to make the extra effort necessary to ensure the services they provided met the high standards that had become synonymous with ARA.[1] The employees themselves explained it best. According to a group manager of ARATEX Services in Columbus, Ohio:

*The "Everybody Sells" philosophy means that every employee realizes and works to project a positive image of the services ARATEX provides. Although many of our employees work behind the scenes and seldom visit our customers personally, I believe they can all contribute to the selling process by performing their jobs in a conscientious manner that enables us to maintain our reputation for quality service.[2]*

A manager from ARA Leisure Services also elaborated on the importance of quality service:

*Encouraging our people to take pride in the company and their jobs is one of the ways we put the "Everybody Sells" concept to work at Fulton County Stadium. I don't think it matters whether you're a manager or a vendor serving hotdogs in the stands—we all can do our part to provide our clients and customers with quality services. The way people dress, the way they treat customers, and the overall image they convey are all part of the "Everybody Sells" idea and have an impact on the success of our operations.[3]*

ARA's Children's World Learning Centers offered high-quality educational programs for children, who could have fun and learn valuable social skills at the same time.

of "Everybody Sells," however, was crystallized by Neubauer:

*Our growth depends on continuous improvement in everything we do. Although acquisitions, takeovers, and divestitures often dominate today's business news, I strongly believe that profitable internal growth is the most important measure of any company's success. Through improved client retention, enhanced merchandising, and new sales, we can continue to set growth records.*[28]

By the end of 1987, ARA reported that "Everybody Sells" had become much more than a "passing, catchy phrase. Today, the 'Everybody Sells' message has become a permanent part of ARA's culture."[29] Indeed, the proof that everyone did sell was found each year in the company's annual statistics. Although ARA's early childhood development capabilities more than doubled with the acquisition of Children's World, the growth in ARA's Correctional Medical Systems subsidiary resulted from a "dramatic growth in sales" in 1987.[30]

In 1988, the company noted that while the concept of "Everybody Sells" was a few years old, "its relevance has by no means diminished. This program has always emphasized the importance of client retention, improved merchandising, and new sales."[31] By the end of 1989, ARATEX, ARA's uniform rental operation, had clearly weathered the consolidation of Servisco, strengthening its position as the world's largest uniform rental company by generating substantial new business and improving customer retention rate—the very touchstones of "Everybody Sells."[32]

**Company Ownership**

Just as ARA wanted everyone to sell, management felt equally committed to broadening employee ownership—one of the company's primary goals after ARA went private in December 1984.[33] Year after year, ARA expanded the circle of ownership beyond the original 62 executives, and by 1989, there were more than 900 direct owner–managers. These steps began in 1987, when direct ownership of the company expanded from the individuals who participated in the initial buyout to more than 300 people.[34]

In 1988, management's ownership stake in the company was given another boost when the ARA Board decided to increase management's direct ownership interest in the company. The Shareholder's Enhancement Plan allowed ARA to buy most of the ARA stock that outside investors owned and sell it back to managers, a move that ultimately increased managers' ownership interest in the company from 34 to 65 percent, issuing through various grades of stock a 94 percent voting control.[35]

While financial institutions such as Chase, JPMorgan, and Goldman Sachs still owned about 20 percent of ARA, the move whittled down the number of shares held by the original equity partners from a post-buyout high of 69 percent to 35 percent.[36]

# "GOODBYE ONE READING; HELLO ARA TOWER"

WHEN ARA ANNOUNCED IT WOULD keep its headquarters in Philadelphia and move to a new 32-story building at the northwest corner of 11th and Market Streets, it was by no means a simple process.

First, the company held a press conference in late December 1984, announcing that the glass and marble structure, then known as One Reading Center, would soon be the new home of ARA Services. From then on, it would be called the "ARA Tower."[1]

Next, ARA named Ken Wells as coordinator of the company's move to the Tower. Wells, who had been one of the architects of the successful transportation system at the 1984 Olympic Games in Los Angeles, presided for over a year at the regular weekly meetings to discuss every detail of the transition. The Philadelphia firm Kenneth Parker Associates was responsible for the design and furnishing of the new office space on floors 15 through 20 and 23 through 32. A newsletter called *Tower Talk* kept ARA's headquarter employees in step with efforts to trans-

---

As this photo shows, the headquarters Tower on Market Street provided both ARA employees in 1986 and ARAMARK employees today with a wonderful view of downtown Philadelphia—a skyline vista that includes William Penn atop Philadelphia City Hall and the historic PSFS Building.

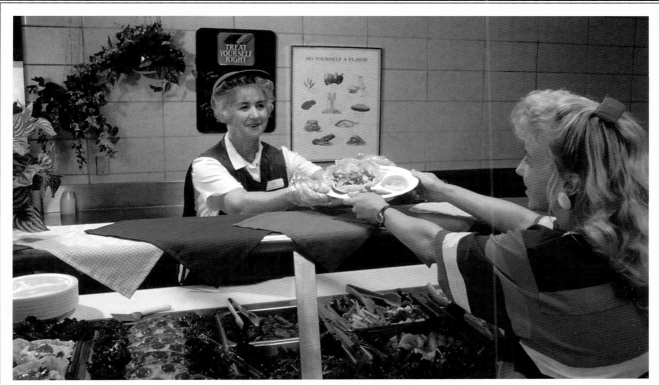

In the late 1980s, ARA launched a new food service campaign called "Treat Yourself Right" to emphasize the value of good nutrition for both adults and children.

form more than 200,000 square feet spread out over 13 floors into their new corporate home. More than a logistical problem and change of address, the move to the Tower was another step Neubauer took, with Scotty Campbell's assistance, to raise the public profile of the company. From early on, Neubauer was determined to put forward a professional image for the company. The glass and marble communicated ARA was an important professional service management company, and one that figured prominently in the Philadelphia business community.[2]

Kenneth Parker Associates used local artisans for the craftsmanship on the top two floors. The art collection was part of a program that supported emerging Philadelphia artists and would be open to art students for tours. It would later receive a Philadelphia Arts & Business Council award.

The newsletters and all communications sought to allay any misgivings about the move to employees, clients, and prospects. Could the cost be justified? Was Market Street going to be developed? The answers were emphatically in the affirmative: The cost was a necessary one, and the company worked with Philadelphia city government to accelerate development in the area.

It was a big move—one that Neubauer undertook just two years after taking the helm. Moving out of the historic Curtis Building and into the new ARA Tower served as a symbolic commitment to the city and an embrace of the future. The new building was an office space designed for the computer age, offering easy access to automated equipment through the use of compact, modular workstations—and included an electronic security system, an employee dining room, a fitness facility, and an impressive art collection throughout the building. As *Tower Talk* had previously noted, "Most ARA employees will be supplied with new furnishings. We will be bringing with us only our file cabinets."[3]

The corporate move to enhance management ownership was clearly much more than a gesture. In an effort to underscore its significance, Neubauer traveled around the country and explained the new Shareholder's Enhancement Plan to ARA managers in Los Angeles, Chicago, St. Louis, and Houston. Scotty Campbell, vice chairman and executive vice president, remembered the reaction inside those meetings: "There were a lot of whoops and hollers. Everybody was excited about what it meant."[37] When the news was celebrated in Philadelphia on March 16, 1988, a reporter for the *Wall Street Journal* captured the scene with the headline, "ARA, Betting on Pride, Approves Plan to Give Managers Voting Control":

> *At a black-tie benefit hosted by ARA Services a few weeks ago, Chairman Joseph Neubauer and members of his management team exuded confidence as they moved from one dinner table to the next, shaking hands, patting backs, and clinking glasses. "They act like they own the company," said one guest. "They soon will."*[38]

On April 21, 1988, ARA staged its second "ARA Network" teleconference, linking Neubauer to 3,600 managers in 33 cities via satellite from the studios of WHYY Channel 12, the Public Broadcasting System station in Philadelphia. The 90-minute telecast first featured taped segments on ARA's history and its new corporate headquarters. The telecast then cut to a dapper and enthusiastic Neubauer seated alone on stage in front of an "ARA Services" logo and looking directly into the camera. He addressed several important issues, from the Shareholder's Enhancement Plan to the "Everybody Sells" campaign to the importance of ARA frontline managers. Neubauer later wrote about the telecast in glowing terms: "Our videoconference was held at a most important moment in ARA history. The Shareholder's Enhancement Program had just been effected."[39]

In addition, after buying back blocks of stock from outside investors, the company extended stock ownership even more broadly to employees. Just five years after the management buyout, more than 10,000 employees owned stock in the company, directly and through retirement plans, a number that would steadily rise through the years as Neubauer continued to use corporate ownership as a way to motivate employees. The company called it "one of the largest ownership groups of its kind."[40] In essence, the program adhered to the following structure:

> *Each year, employees at or above the district manager level are given the chance to buy shares at a price set by an independent appraiser. If they lack cash, the company will lend them the money at prime, repayable over three years; it will also lend them money to pay the income taxes on the difference between the set price and the price at the time they actually buy. ... Each employee can sell up to $600,000 worth of holdings annually back to the company at the prevailing price. They can use the money to pay for an operation or to send the kids to college. Or they can use it for a trip to Hawaii. No strings.*[41]

The fact that ARA had reduced its debt and operated in the black every year since it went pri-

ARA Magazine and Book Distribution Services employees work carefully to tailor stock and determine the "product mix" of books and magazines that will sell best at a specific location.

vate had remained the key to creating an attractive investment opportunity. "Because we were doing well, and because we were able to reduce the debt, the stock kept increasing in appraised value," said Neubauer. "So people were very happy to borrow money to buy the stock and keep it."[42]

The opportunity for stock ownership and keeping ARA privately held was virtually assured through an important management buyout stipulation: As stockholders retired or left the company, they were required to sell their shares back to ARA at a price set by outside appraisers.[43] "That's what we meant when we said we wanted to keep it in the family," said Neubauer. "That's what we meant when we said we wanted to have a management buyout as opposed to a leveraged buyout.[44] We are indeed masters of our destiny."[45]

**A Focus on Core Business**

In the four years after the management buyout, it was clear that ARA Services had decided to follow the business maxim "stick to our knitting" in all of its business lines.[46] Although the concept of focusing on its core competencies had long been a hallmark of ARA Services, this was a move into a new era. The days of rapid expansion and acquisition were, under Neubauer's supervision, giving way to strategic discipline to refine the service portfolio. The focus on the delivery of quality service intensified even further after the buyout. Neubauer once called it the "management of essential services."[47] By 1988, ARA Services business segments were divided into four core groups: Food and Refreshment Services, Textile Rental and Maintenance Services, Magazine and Book Distribution Services, and Health and Education Services.

To strengthen its core businesses, ARA Services continued executing important acquisitions in the late 1980s, primarily in the food service, early childhood education, and linen/uniform rental sectors. In some cases, core businesses were further enhanced through the acquisition of new companies and new contracts, which included increased services to existing customers.

In 1989, ARA Leisure Services took over the management of the Lake Powell recreational facilities in Arizona and Utah and signed a new 15-year contract to manage the food service and gift shop

ARA took an active role in helping retail clients promote, advertise, and sell books and other printed materials. Recognizing that impulse-purchase products such as books and magazines have the greatest sales potential in high traffic areas, the division began a new business solicitation program aimed at convenience stores, video rental stores, and other locations outside the traditional customer base.

operations at Ellis Island, which helped further strengthen ARA's Leisure Services association with the National Park Service. That same year, Children's World Learning Centers landed a 20-year contract to build and operate the first on-site childcare facility for one of the world's most famous office buildings—the Pentagon in Washington, D.C.[48]

In 1988, ARA celebrated its 20th anniversary of Olympic services since 1968. The company signed on to provide food service management and consulting services for the 1988 Winter Games in Calgary, Canada, and the 1988 Summer Games in Seoul, Korea.[49] The company also accelerated its growth in core areas and took over businesses that new customers had previously operated, including a $16 million food service contract with the

Managed by ARA Services, the Canyon King paddle wheeler is available for sunset dinner cruises and special group events on Lake Powell in Arizona. Each December, it leads the Festival of Lights parade, one of many exciting Lake Powell annual events.

University of Virginia and a $24 million contract to serve schoolchildren in Duval County, Florida.[50]

While keeping an eye on growth and improving sales, the company's focus on core businesses included not only making key acquisitions and increasing existing services but also scrutinizing disappointing or underperforming assets. According to *Forbes* magazine, the company set out "to remove some gangrene."[51]

ARA's beleaguered trucking business was the first to go. In late 1987, ARA/Smith's was sold to American Carriers, Inc., creating one of the nation's five largest motor carrier operations at the time.[52] Nursing homes were also carefully analyzed, and 20 percent were cut over five years. Neubauer described the cuts as "trimming around the edges. We can reduce volume and improve profitability."[53]

In many ways, the focus on core business was not simply a matter of zeroing in on certain sectors and expanding the related businesses. At ARA, renewed attention to core business meant better understanding of each service sector and of the individual needs of each client.

Consider the story of Jack Donovan. When he joined the company in 1988 as regional sales director for campus services in Chicago, one of his first challenges was to land the residential dining contract at the University of Chicago, the very place where Joe Neubauer had completed his MBA. On directions to "camp out" on campus and learn everything possible about the university, Donovan found himself talking to students and faculty, visiting the library, and reading a collection of speeches that the university's first eight presidents had written. Ultimately, Donovan incorporated quotes from those presents into the company's successful 1989 proposal and showed how ARA's proposal remained consistent with the university's vision and mission. Donovan never forgot the university's reaction:

*We had maybe 10 people on the dais, and we went through a three-hour presentation and question-and-answer session. Toward the end, one of the Resident Masters, who was very influential, raised her hand and said, "I want to know who wrote the proposal." We gave them the team answer, and she said, "No, I want to know who did the research and actually put pen to paper." We gave the team answer again. She said, "No, I want to know who actually was responsible specifically for the research on the university." And I said, "Well, that was sort of my part." She then said, "I just want to congratulate you and the team because I've lived on this campus for 22 years, and when I read your proposal, I learned things about this university that I did not know. I think you've done a remarkable job of demonstrating an understanding of us."*

*Of course, we smiled because we figured that was a very significant differential that others*

*probably had not captured. We won the contract, and we're still there, by the way. We discovered after that contract award that we were higher than the principal competition for the bid in terms of price ... but the group of people who made the decision had a comfort level since we had understood what they were truly trying to achieve.*[54]

**Continued Emphasis on Service Innovation**

By 1989, ARA's 120,000 employees served more than 10 million people each day. Their work included everything from providing food services to businesses, hospitals, conference centers, correctional facilities, school districts, colleges, and universities to providing physician staffing and management support services for emergency rooms. The company was involved in refreshment services, uniform rental, book and magazine

---

ARA's outstanding Olympic experience in Seoul, Korea, helped spark an expansion into food service businesses in Korea in the early 1990s.

sales, healthcare for prison inmates, long-term care for the elderly, childcare, environmental services, and industrial cleaning. At the close of 1989, ARA management decided to reorganize its food service operations, aligning them with the other service lines and moving from a system based on geographic divisions to one with separate and distinct lines of business that were organized by and dedicated to the type of venue where key services were provided. In a way, many agreed, the change was long overdue.

"I think for a long period of time, particularly during the management buyout, privately held portion of its history, [ARA] was almost like a holding company model, in the sense that these operators were charged with aggressive growth goals and financial results targets, and that if they were able to deliver those numbers, there weren't many questions as

to how they did it," said Chris Malone, former senior vice president of marketing. "There was a real belief that corporate overhead should be kept at a minimum, and that was certainly a part of their success over time. They were able to hire the best people that would make the right decisions at the business or unit level and who were able to compete very nimbly on that basis."[55]

The reorganization of ARA Services resulted in new names and some reassignments for the four key business units: 1) ARASERVE provided food and refreshment services for ARA's business and institutional clients through five service divisions known as Business Dining, Campus Dining, ARA/Cory Refreshment Services, Healthcare Nutrition, and School Nutrition; 2) Distributive Services, whose services ranged from uniform rentals and creating safe manufacturing environments to distributing magazines at airports, offered through ARATEX, ARACLEAN, and ARA Magazine and Book Distribution Services; 3) Health and Education Services, which included ARA Living Centers, the medical services group Spectrum Emergency Care, Correctional Medical Systems, and Children's World Learning Centers; and 4) Leisure/International Services, the most diversified of the service groups responsible for services to parks and convention centers as well as food services through its international operations in Canada, the United Kingdom, Belgium, Germany, and Japan.[56]

Before and after the reorganization, ARA management always gave their frontline managers remarkable autonomy, challenging them to be "true renaissance people." Neubauer once noted that "because our business is so location- and client-specific, there is no way we can sit in Philadelphia and make the day-to-day decisions for managers in Texas, California, Alaska, or even Ohio and New York."[57] Ira R. Cohn, president of Business and Industry Group, viewed it this way:

*As large as the company is, it's still just an amalgamation of thousands of individual units. The people at the top reflect the people in the individual units, they have a lot of autonomy, and many of them have grown up through the organization. So whether you run a small business cafeteria or a retail operation in a hospital or patient feeding in a hospital, state prison, campus, or*

ARA's clients include correctional facilities, where ARA manages the food service for inmates.

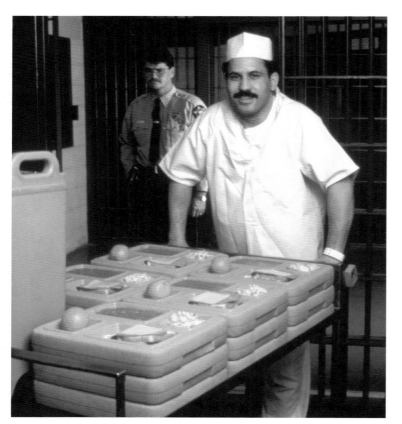

school, you're running your business. You're dealing with problems day in and day out. The management culture reflects what we ask our managers to do, which is to think on their feet, solve problems, address concerns, and manage the P&L [profit and loss].[58]

In 1989, a year when revenues reached an all-time company high of $4.2 billion, Neubauer looked to the past to help predict the future:

Since December 1984, ARA has been somewhat of a maverick compared to other companies that have completed a buyout. First and foremost is the fact that ours was truly a "management buyout" that was opened to a large number of ARA managers, rather than just a few top executives. Second, unlike the majority of firms that

ARA's dieticians oversee the preparation of meals and provide individual nutrition counseling for patients at more than 300 client healthcare facilities, including Toyosu Hospital, ARA's first healthcare client in Japan serviced through ARA's affiliate, AIM Services. AIM Services expanded its various businesses throughout the year and concluded 1989 with a client list that included nearly 200 accounts.

undergo a buyout, we have not sold off major chunks of our company to reduce our debt. Instead, we have depended on the growth of our company to reduce our debt. And we have expanded ARA through acquisitions to strengthen our core business and thereby position ourselves for continued growth well into the next decade and beyond.[59]

Chairman and CEO Joe Neubauer (center) celebrates Opening Day at Baltimore's new Oriole Park at Camden Yards, standing between Baltimore baseball great Boog Powell (left) and NBC weatherman Willard Scott (right) during an NBC *Today Show* interview on April 6, 1992. Camden Yards was the site of a great new service idea that brought team history together with great ballpark food. "Boog's Barbeque" remains a very successful fan dining experience at the ballpark, and the idea has worked in other new parks, as well.

CHAPTER EIGHT

# GROWING WORLDWIDE

## 1990 – 1994

*It's wonderful to look back on 10 years of employee ownership and see continuous growth in revenues and earnings. ARAMARK today is in a very solid financial position. Our record of financial achievement gives us the flexibility to take advantage of the right opportunities. Our employees are true heroes. Our financial success is a reflection of ARAMARK's exceptional efforts in serving customers better each and every day.*

—"The Power of a Dream,"
ARAMARK's 1994 report to employees

THE BUSINESS CHALLENGES of the early 1990s were daunting. High unemployment rates, looming government deficits, and stymied economic growth created an economic malaise characterized as a recession in the United States. The rest of the world appeared somewhat immune to this economic downturn, so American businesses turned to more favorable markets overseas. ARA was no exception.

Granted, ARA already had a foothold on foreign soil. Cofounder Bill Fishman, after all, had long ago been called the company's "expansionist" who was responsible for promoting the company's push into Canada and the European markets in the late 1960s and early 1970s. That move had resulted in food and vending services in Canada, the United Kingdom, Germany, France, and Belgium.[1] ARA's food services had been a fixture in Japan since 1976, when ARA Services and Mitsui & Co. Ltd. in Tokyo started a highly successful joint venture called AIM Services. Now, despite a recession at home, with barriers to communism and world trade crumbling, ARA leaders decided to expand their efforts and transform into a global company.

"While a recession may cause other companies to pull back, we view it as an opportunity for us," explained CEO Joe Neubauer. "I say that because we're in control of all our business lines. If you spun off 90 percent of our divisions and operated them individually, you'd find that we hold either the first or second position in the market for each. That's what I mean by being in control."[2]

ARA's globalization push was not low-key. The day after the Berlin Wall crumbled, ARA began moving into the former East Germany, subsequently signing a contract with the Leipzig Fair, the world's largest industrial exhibits facility. Following Germany's reunification, ARA created a food service operation that was crucial to the 800-year-old fair's future success and expanded ARA's growing presence in Germany. By mid-1991, when ARA announced the acquisition of a contract food service operation called SCP Cater Partner located near Düsseldorf, Germany, ARA had established catering and vending services for more than 500,000 people daily at some 500 locations in Germany—including Mercedes Benz, Siemens, IBM, and the Leipzig Fair facility.[3]

As the European common market continued to expand, ARA also established contracts in Hungary and the former Czechoslovakia. At the same time, it

---

WearGuard, which specialized in providing uniforms for small to midsize businesses, was a perfect complement to ARA's existing uniform businesses and added significantly to one of ARA's core businesses, ARATEX Services, Inc.

expanded existing businesses in Germany, Belgium, and the United Kingdom that included food services as well as housekeeping and maintenance services. Though ARA's entrance into the Japanese market had started in 1976 with a joint food service business with the Mitsui Group, the company significantly expanded its Japanese influence in 1990 by providing uniform rental services through a new company, ARATEX/Japan. According to Steve Duffy, an ARA uniform services executive who helped expand the uniform business in Japan in 1990, the very concept of renting uniforms was novel to Japanese culture.[4] The situation had presented some unique challenges, as Duffy explained:

*It was difficult for people to understand rental versus purchasing, and ... to try and come up with a product that meets the market's needs, while not having a very diverse product line. Everybody wears a uniform [in Japan], but they all wear a different one, and everybody wants a high degree of personalization. You can't do that for everybody because you wouldn't have enough room in the stockroom for every uniform in the world, and that's a challenge we face ... Another unique challenge is that in Japan, the concept of direct selling is foreign. In fact, it's not really looked upon favorably. ... So figuring out a way to get to the consumer was a real challenge because most business is done through introduction.[5]*

Despite the challenges, the company prospered, reporting $500 million in overseas business by the end of 1990 and predicting that overseas revenue would double within five years.[6] With its overseas business growing significantly, the company managed to thrive in the challenging business climate of the United States. Unlike scores of domestic companies that struggled at home, ARA's financial performance records appeared to grow only stronger, as the company reported continuous growth in revenues and earnings year after year. By taking advantage of business decisions and strategies set in motion long before any hint of a market downturn, ARA continued to grow in the first decade of employee ownership.

While a record number of companies were defaulting on corporate bonds in the economic recession, ARA was exceptionally cash-rich in fiscal year 1990, with revenues of $4.6 billion, a cash flow of $185.7 million, and profits of $51.8 million. Although its post-buyout debt remained at $1.1 billion, these new figures reflected continuous corpo-

---

**1990**
ARA expands into the former East Germany, establishes contracts in Hungary and the former Czechoslovakia, and expands existing business in the United Kingdom, Germany, Belgium, and Japan.

**1992**
ARA launches "Project Growth" to increase sales, cross-sell services, retain existing customers, and grow existing accounts.

**1992**
ARA services Baltimore's new Oriole Park at Camden Yards when it opens. ARA Leisure Services also lands prestigious accounts at the Pennsylvania Convention Center and the San Jose Arena.

**June 15, 1991**
Cofounder Bill Fishman, 75, dies in his home in suburban Philadelphia.

**1992**
ARA revenues reach a record $4.9 billion.

ARA solidifies its leadership in the uniform services business when it acquires WearGuard, one of the nation's largest direct marketers of work clothes and casual wear.

rate growth and expansion, with ARA spending more than $680 million on capital expenditures and $48 million on new businesses from 1984 to 1990. By April 1991, 900 ARA executives owned stock in the company, which represented 66 percent of the company's stock and 94 percent of the voting power, a factor that Neubauer noted as a contributor to ARA's success. "Our people are more intense," he said. "This is their company."[7]

The company continued to benefit from the ubiquitous "Everybody Sells" campaign, and a "New Accounts Score Board" began appearing in company newsletters to list recently acquired or expanded businesses. By the close of 1990, newspapers and wire services were filled with headlines such as the following, proclaiming ARA's growth at some high-profile locations: "Business dining: ARA aims for small-business accounts;"[8] "[ARA's] School Nutrition Services wins accounts with educational efforts;"[9] and "Ellis Island opens door to tourists: ARA launches food service center at renovated New York landmark."[10]

"In short, the 'Everybody Sells' strategy we introduced several years ago has become more significant than ever before," Neubauer noted in January 1991.[11] The company remained either first or second in the market in nearly all of its lines of business, from food service to uniform rentals to healthcare services for nursing homes, child care centers, and prisons. The company's Food and Leisure Services division, responsible for about 60 percent of ARA's total revenue, continued to capitalize on its branded food products, ranging from Itza Pizza and Gretel's Bake Shop goods to Allegro pasta and Leghorn's chicken. The brands not only helped distinguish ARA from its competition but also resulted in higher profit margins than ARA's standard food items.

In a business era where competition was keener than ever, ARA reported that more than 95 percent of its service accounts renewed annually—a clear reflection of the CEO's message that retaining clients was as important as acquiring new ones.[12] In the stubborn business climate that characterized the first few years of the new decade, ARA continued to post impressive gains while emphasizing one of Neubauer's critical business touchstones:

*What's very important is to develop a positive reputation, doing what you say you're going to do and then deal fairly. You can be tough. That's okay. You can drive tough bargains. That's okay, too, but*

**1993**
ARA develops ARAKOR, an historic joint venture in South Korea with an affiliate of Daewoo Corporation that became the first major contract food service enterprise in the country. By the end of 1993, ARA's international operations approached $1.1 billion in annual revenues.

**1994**
ARA purchases the Harry M. Stevens Company, the oldest concessions business in the United States, with rights to service Shea Stadium, the Houston Astrodome, and Fenway Park.

**1994**
Neubauer unveils "Mission 10–5," a campaign that identified key growth opportunities with the goal of increasing the company's revenue by 10 percent annually over the next five years.

**1994**
ARA becomes known as ARAMARK on October 11, 1994. In addition to the new name, the company has a new corporate theme of "Managed Services, Managed Better" and a new corporate icon—the Starperson.

# AN INTELLECTUAL VISIONARY: WILLIAM S. FISHMAN

IT WAS JUST ONE INTRO-duction, just one moment in the Philadelphia front-line managers' meeting on a cold December night in 1989, the last of the six-city Great Performances series of meet-ings. Many managers had been introduced, recognized, and applauded. This one turned out to be different, though.

It was Bill Fishman, the man who cofounded ARAMARK with Davre Davidson and had retired from the company five years earlier. Because of his declin-ing health, Fishman now attended few corporate functions. Joe Neubauer, whom Fishman had selected to succeed him, saw his former boss sitting in the audience and decided to intro-duce him.

"As soon as I said 'Bill Fishman,' the applause started," Neubauer recalled. "And it got louder and louder and louder. Six hundred people were on their feet, clapping as hard as they could. It was a thunderous ovation. And it lasted for at least five minutes. Standing on the stage you could feel the pure emotion— an outpouring of love for a man who gave so much and who meant so much to each and every person in that room. When it finally ended, I stepped to the microphone and said, 'No one could add anything to that.' And no one could."[1]

Fishman, an intellectual visionary who loved fishing, piloting airplanes, and polishing his Phi Beta Kappa key, was deeply loved as a mentor, colleague, and friend by all who knew him at ARAMARK, then known as ARA Services. When he died on June 15, 1991, at his suburban Phila-delphia home, he would always be remembered for his business acumen, generosity, humor, and legendary kindness.

---

*when you say you're going to do something, you've got to do it. You've got to develop a reputation for integrity, particularly in service businesses.*[13]

This message was never lost for John Orobono, who first worked for ARA as a purchasing analyst in 1972, left the company from 1976 to 1981, and then returned to run ARA's Distribution Center in 1981. Orobono, now senior vice president of sup-ply chain management, recalled, "I work for a great company that has a great reputation. We do it the right way. ... All that adds up to integrity and can-dor. You do business. You go to market with people you have confidence and trust in, just as we go to market with building this unlimited partnership that we all talk about."[14]

### The "Strength of Excellence"

While stressing integrity and professional busi-ness partnerships, the company's top management stressed the value of good relationships with em-ployees, too. Over time, as more and more ARA employees owned stock in the company, executives religiously gave credit for the company's success to frontline managers and frontline workers. When

Born in Indiana in 1916, Fishman graduated in the top 1 percent of his class at the University of Illinois at Urbana, immediately entered the business world, and quickly made his mark. By the late 1930s, Fishman was considered a pioneer in the field of automatic vending, eventually becoming president of Chicago's Automatic Merchandising Company, which in 1959 was bought out by Davidson Brothers, founded by Davre and his brother, Henry. The two relatively small vending machine companies formed Automatic Retailers of America (ARA), which would become the world's leading service management company.

Fishman served as president of ARA from 1964 to 1976, CEO from 1975 to 1983, and chairman from 1977 until he retired in 1984. Of the two founders, many considered Fishman a visionary entrepreneur whose adventuresome spirit would never die. He insisted that ARA look at the entire world as its potential marketplace and is credited with taking the first steps toward making ARA a global company. His peers repeatedly lauded his business achievements, and in his cofounder's honor, the company established the Fishman–Davidson Center for the Study of the Service Sector at the University of Pennsylvania's Wharton School in 1982.

Throughout Philadelphia, Fishman was well known for his civic, cultural, and educational interests. He gave generously to a wide range of charities and greatly supported educational institutions, as well as medical research. His financial and personal contributions served as a catalyst for the creation of the National Museum of American Jewish History on Independence Mall, and he was the first chairman of the Business Leadership Organized for Catholic Schools (BLOCS) in the city. He also served on the Board of the Philadelphia Museum of Art, the Franklin Institute, and the Philadelphia Orchestra Association.

Yet for all of his accomplishments, Fishman was perhaps best known for his warmth and lack of pretense, equally comfortable in an ARA kitchen as in the boardroom. Joan Voli, a receptionist who has worked with ARAMARK since 1957, still remembers sitting right outside Fishman's office at the Curtis Building. It was her job to lock the office every night at 6 P.M. One night, however, due to a broken watch, she inadvertently locked Fishman and the company pilot in the office. "He said, 'Why are the doors locked? It's not six o'clock yet,'" she remembered. "I showed him my watch, and my watch had a little after six. So in a couple of days, he had his executive assistant buy me a new watch. Mr. Fishman was unbelievable. There will never be another William Fishman."[2]

Fishman's first wife, the former Clara Sylvan, died in 1980. He was survived by his second wife, Selma Demchick Ellis Fishman; three sons, Alan, Fred, and David; four grandchildren; two stepchildren, Joshua Ellis and Jill Feninger; and two sisters, Ruth Zimbler and Georgia Fishman.

John R. Farquharson, then president of ARASERVE, won the Operator of the Year award from *Nation's Restaurant News* in 1990, he was quick to give credit to his staff. "I'll see that the soldiers in the ARA army get the recognition they deserve for this award, as they are the ones who earned it," he said. "I'm just a part of the army."[15]

When addressing this ARA "army," Neubauer's message was as consistent as his thoughts on ARA's business in 1990:

*The business hasn't changed significantly since its inception 30 years ago. Our senior-level executive team is clearly in place, while our 4,000 or so frontline managers are really the key to what we do. We have an army of people who own shares in this company and put their livelihood on the line every day. We have a lot of quality-control programs in place and spend a good amount of time talking to clients and customers. There isn't a person in this company I can't learn something from, whether it's a customer or an entry-level employee. This is a business you have to love, and at ARA we do. People ask me how I sleep at night, and I tell them I sleep very well. We have excellent people, and quite honestly, we're the best at what we do.*[16]

ARA lost one of these excellent people on June 15, 1991, when the 75-year-old Bill Fishman died in his home in suburban Philadelphia following a long illness. More than 1,000 mourners attended his funeral—family and friends, leading civic and business leaders, and a swell of current and former ARA employees. In an announcement to employees, ARA Chairman and CEO Neubauer echoed their sentiments when he referred to Fishman as a "mentor, a valued colleague, and a dear friend."[17]

Anyone who knew Fishman realized that he always had a vision for the future of the company both at home and abroad. As he once told a *Forbes* magazine writer, "We are in the business of anticipating and managing services that meet basic needs and expectations."[18] In the year when he died, ARA chose "Strength of Excellence" as the theme of its 1991 annual report. The concept served as a fitting tribute to the man who would always be remembered as the company's visionary:

*For ARA, the "Strength of Excellence" captures the motivating spirit that has fostered the company's dynamic growth for over three decades. And it represents the essential, underlying foundation that will support ARA's reach for new and higher levels of accomplishment in the years to come.*[19]

### Core Business Expansion, Consolidation

In 1992, ARA continued its "Strength of Excellence" theme, not just in the copy of its annual report. Despite what Neubauer called "an extremely sluggish worldwide economy," ARA posted an even better financial performance than it did the previous year, as revenues rose slowly to a record $4.9 billion. The company conducted a coast-to-coast series of "Strength of Excellence" meetings to recognize the vital contributions of frontline managers and present them with specially designed Olympic-style medals in recognition of the crucial role they played every day in the company's success.[20]

Despite the economic conditions, ARA continually refined its core businesses, which for a while included tweaking the names of these services on a yearly basis: Food, Leisure, and Support Services was also known as Food and Leisure Services; Uniform Services was also called Textile Rental and Maintenance; and Health and Education Services,

Tom Vozzo, a rising WearGuard sales executive who stayed with ARA after the acquisition in 1992, inspects a WearGuard product. Today, he leads the company's entire uniform business. *(Photo courtesy of ©RickFriedman.com.)*

which included Magazine and Book Distribution Services, became grouped under Distributive Services.[21] As surely as ARA refined the names of its core services, it also continued to complete important strategic investments that remained critical to future growth and market dominance.

In a move that solidified ARA's strength in the uniform services business, in 1992, ARA acquired WearGuard, headquartered in Norwell, Massachusetts, one of the nation's largest and most effective direct marketers of work clothes and casual wear. Tom Vozzo, a WearGuard executive who stayed with ARA after the acquisition and eventually became president of the company's Uniform and Career Apparel division, remembered the acquisition, which paved the way for the purchase of additional uniform companies later in the decade:

*Bill Leonard, then-president of ARATEX, made the decision to buy WearGuard. At the time, ARATEX was the largest rental company in the United States and in the rental industry. They have the phrase, "Always rent a uniform; never sell it." You make more money on renting than you do on selling, but Bill also said that they weren't covering the whole marketplace because they never sold uniforms. Bill's vision was to take the largest rental company in the United States and the largest direct sale company of working clothing and combine them as one company. That was the business rationale behind the WearGuard acquisition. And it has worked.*[22]

ARA soon announced other strategic corporate moves. ARA Living Centers, the company's long-term care subsidiary, became a separate company "to respond more effectively to the country's ever-changing healthcare needs." Children's World

Learning Centers, operating nearly 500 centers in 22 states, continued as the country's acknowledged leader in high-quality child care with more accredited centers than any other company. ARA also acquired two companies to broaden the scope of its Emergency Department contract staffing services and continued expanding services abroad.[23]

## Project Growth

ARA's persistent expansion and corporate refocusing efforts reflected the introduction of a significant new program called "Project Growth."

Launched in 1992, the program was essentially a refinement and upgrade to the "Everybody Sells" campaign that called upon ARA executives to "leave no stone unturned" as they examined market forces, potential growth opportunities, and the company's ability to act on those opportunities. After a series of focus group sessions, Project Growth initiatives materialized like veritable marching orders

Recognizing that even small businesses have professionally developed logos, WearGuard developed proprietary machinery to produce uniforms with attractive company emblems featuring custom personalization.

for ARA's army. They included the adding of sales-people, improving facilities, aggressively pursuing new markets, cross-selling services, and growing existing accounts. Tangible results of Project Growth included a shared sales incentive program in the Business Dining Group, improved marketing brochures for Children's World, and increased sales efforts by Campus Dining Services.[24]

Neubauer said, "Project Growth is all about improving our 'top line'—ARA revenue and sales—with the goal of growing our business profitably and achieving higher client satisfaction."[25]

### The Unforgettable Summer of 1992

With the momentum of Project Growth setting the pace, the summer of 1992 was nothing short of a combination home run and gold medal for ARA. The company codesigned the food service area, and in a move that pleased legions of baseball fans, provided outstanding food and service to help open the

tremendously successful, retro-style ballpark known as Oriole Park at Camden Yards in Baltimore on April 6, 1992. According to the ARA newsletter, *Update*, by the end of opening day: "President Bush had thrown out the first ball; ARA Chairman and CEO Joe Neubauer had appeared on the *Today Show* with Willard Scott and former Oriole great Boog Powell, and the league-leading array of over 200 dining clubs, concession stands, retail stores, and lounges that ARA operates at the stadium has passed the test of almost 50,000 demanding fans, media professionals, and visiting dignitaries. In the process, ARA Leisure Services had cemented its national reputation for stadium

Throughout the 1992 baseball season at the new Oriole Park at Camden Yards in Baltimore, Maryland, ARA's services received rave reviews from sellout crowds that flocked to this "field of dreams."

Above: At the opening in 1992, ARA enhanced the fan experience at Camden Yards in Baltimore with gift shops that offered everything from novelty items to team merchandise such as Oriole T-shirts and pennants.

Right: In Barcelona, Ed Nelson (wearing tie) supervised the food service in the athletes' main dining room. "Seeing this facility, which was nearly two years in the making, move from paper into actual operation was incredible," said Nelson, a district manager from the Campus Dining division who coordinated the service in the Olympic Village dining room.

food service excellence." (Incidentally, Baltimore beat Cleveland, 2–0.) [26]

ARA officials were obviously ecstatic after the success of the high-profile, widely televised event. "After this, there should be no doubt that we are the leading expert in the country for food and retail merchandising services at sports facilities," said Charles Gillespie, president of ARA Leisure Services.[27] By late summer, ARA declared a "Triple Play for Leisure" by announcing that the Pennsylvania Convention Center in Philadelphia; the brand new Colorado Rockies; and the San Jose Arena, home of the San Jose Sharks had all chosen ARA Leisure Services

to provide food, beverage, and merchandise services to their facilities.[28]

For former Stadiums and Arenas President Sean Rooney, the opening of Oriole Park at Camden Yards triggered it all. "It really started a building boom," said Rooney. "It gave us an opportunity to help design and build out to enhance the fan and the customer experience, just to make the overall experience that much better. That really changed our business."[29]

As the summer of 1992 continued, ARA celebrated its 40th year of continuing service to Memorial Hospital in Danville, Virginia, the company's first Healthcare Nutrition Services account that was, remarkably, still on a 30-day contract. After the ceremony, Neubauer wrote that he was "just as proud of ARA" for its four decades of service in Danville as he was of Opening Day in Baltimore. "More than anything, these two events speak to our past strength and future opportunity, not only in new sales but in client retention as well," he said.[30]

Neubauer stands with Olympic athletes during official ceremonies. He later remarked, "Among the most exciting highlights of 1992 was ARA's gold medal performance at the Summer Olympics in Barcelona." *(Photo by IMPACT STUDIOS LTD.)*

Yet, even Neubauer had to admit that "among the most exciting highlights of 1992 was our gold medal performance at the Summer Olympics in Barcelona."[31] For the eighth time since 1968, Olympic officials called on ARA to manage the food service for the world's finest athletes, thousands of officials, volunteers, and international media who gathered for the spectacular event in Spain.

### Capitalizing on Performance

The company's high-profile efforts and outstanding records at the Olympic Games often resulted in new opportunities for ARA in countries that hosted the games. In 1993, for instance, just one year after the highly successful Barcelona Summer Olympic Games, ARA expanded its international reach by acquiring a majority interest in the HUSA Group, a contract food service company serving hospital, school, and government customers in Spain.[32]

After introducing the American bagel to Seoul at the 1988 Summer Olympic Games in South Korea, ARA returned in 1993 to develop ARAKOR,

a historic joint venture with an affiliate of Korea's Daewoo Corporation that became the first major contract food service enterprise in Korea.[33] Located at the new Daewoo Center in Seoul, the cafeteria was designed to serve 7,500 customers from 31 client companies at the center. The cafeteria quickly earned a reputation for being the largest of its kind in Korea, offering multiple menu selection. When it opened in the fall of 1994, Korean representatives performed a traditional *kosa* ritual to bring good blessings to the new facility. The cafeteria promptly served an average of more than 6,000 luncheon meals, complete with traditional Korean dishes and popular Western entrees. There was an extended takeout selection, as well. "The enormous success of this new contract service operation is exceptional in a land where most businesses, hospitals, and schools rely on home-prepared meals and minimal institutional food service," said Richard Vent, president of ARA's Leisure/International Services.[34]

When *Update* featured a special report on international operations in its January/February 1993 issue, Vent reported that ARA's Leisure/International Sector had increased its revenues by more than 400 percent during the last six years. What ARA called "an unprecedented period of growth and expansion" had resulted in: 30 major accounts in what was formerly East Germany; new sales offices in Budapest, Hungary, and Prague in the former Czechoslovakia, where the company signed a service contract with an 8,000-employee chemical plant; fully owned companies in Germany, the United Kingdom, and Belgium; 70 percent ownership in Versa Services Ltd., Canada's largest service management company; majority ownership in the HUSA Group in Spain; and in Japan, AIM Services, a joint food service venture with the Mitsui Group, as well the start of ARATEX/Japan, a uniform rental business.[35] Noting that additional joint venture operations were in the planning stages for Korea (ARAKOR) and Mexico, Vent predicted continued growth opportunities for ARA:

> *In the United States, about 85 to 90 percent of the business food service market now is contracted, compared to 35 to 40 percent in the United Kingdom.[36] In Germany, the number is only 20 percent, and in Korea, it's almost zero. So we haven't even scratched the potential market. All this means great opportunities for us since we are the only food service contractor with a major international presence.[37]*

By the end of 1993, ARA's international operations approached $1.1 billion in annual revenues, and ARA was recognized as the leading provider of global service management. According to news reports in July 1993, "a careful balance of acquisitions and joint ventures coupled with aggressive

internal growth has fueled ARA's continuing success abroad. ... In the field of contract food service, ARA's sales outside its home base lead the industry."[38] Ira Cohn, then vice president of ARA International, predicted that the company's global reach would keep growing. "It's the ground floor for a whole new industry in many countries, and we're ideally positioned to take advantage of the opportunities," he said.[39]

No one recognized this more than Steve Duffy who, after helping to expand the uniform business in Japan in 1990, coordinated ARA's efforts to build a uniform factory just northwest of Tokyo in 1994. "The potential in Japan is exponentially larger than what we face in the United States. ... It's the most highly uniformed country in the world when you look at the percentage of people wearing uniforms. It's not uncommon for the president of a company like Toyota to wear a uniform. ... It's a very, very large market."[40]

In 1992, ARA's food service team at the Summer Olympic Games in Barcelona served nearly 2.5 million meals to athletes, media, volunteers, security staff, and special visitors such as these schoolchildren.

**The Advent of Outsourcing**

One business practice that gave ARA an edge when it came to successful global growth was "service outsourcing," a development that ARA executives called one of the most important "economic tools" of the 1990s.

An acknowledged leader in the outsourcing field, ARA reasoned that the rest of the world was finally catching up to an idea it had long embraced. "Private companies worldwide from Texas to Tokyo are embracing the same principle: Let's do what we do best, and let someone else handle the rest," wrote Neubauer. "It is a realization that companies should focus on what is central to their business—and outsource the rest to specialized providers like ARA." As an example, he cited the University of Virginia in Charlottesville, which relied on ARA to manage food services for the faculty and student body, coordinate food services for the stadium and the hospital, and provide child care on campus through the Children's World Learning Center. "Over the years, we have achieved much in a business environment not fully appreciative of the value of outside service management," he continued. "Now, the tide of global business is moving in concert with our mission, offering

# OLYMPIC AND BALLPARK FOOD OVER THE YEARS

WHEN IT COMES TO TRANSFORMA-tional food trends at ballparks and Olympic stadiums, nothing says it better than the press headlines and event write-ups:

*Sushi, Rotini, Bratwurst, plus 9 Innings of Baseball: Baseball may be as American as apple pie, but ballpark food is quickly becoming an international affair.*[1]

*Ballpark Food is Haute Stuff: While the standard hamburger or hot dog has by no means left the building, sports fans of broadening diversity and with increasingly sophisticated palates are pushing ballpark chefs to new heights of eclecticism.*[2]

*Olympic Heritage Continues at Lillehammer: Visitors to Norway and the Olympic Games wishing to sample the local cuisine selected from specialties like reindeer steak, brown cheese, and pickled herring.*[3]

By the early 1990s, sports fans with tastes refined for more than just hot dogs, beer, and the customary bag of peanuts were making themselves heard—and getting results. According to a survey conducted at six major league stadiums by ARA Services in 1990, everything from lasagna and sushi to bratwurst and imported beer was now offered at stadiums around the country.

"The fans want variety and fun in what they eat and drink," said Tim Lawler, ARA general manager at Three Rivers Stadium in 1990, home of the Pittsburgh Pirates. "That's why we're adding an imported beer cart this season and introducing an authentic Polish sausage on our menu."[4]

You could try sushi at Anaheim Stadium, along with *yakitori* (barbecued chicken on a stick) and *yakisoba* (Japanese noodles). You could savor Mexican tacos, nachos, and burritos at Chicago's Wrigley Field.[5] Or, munch on a Cleveland Dog—an all-beef hot dog topped with fried purple cabbage, cheddar cheeses, diced onions, tomato, dill pickle, and Cleveland's own authentic stadium mustard—when the Cleveland Cavaliers kick off the season at Gund Arena.[6]

While stadium food was no doubt well on its way to being revolutionized when Baltimore's

even greater opportunity to capitalize on the velocity of today's outsourcing trend."[41]

The outsourcing movement played on the strengths of ARA's frontline managers, who were historically encouraged by corporate executives to run their divisions like independent entrepreneurs. Sean Rooney, who was appointed general manager of the Spectrum in 1989, said:

*Back when I started, we were a privately held company, and I think it all comes [down] to the people, the management team, and the entrepreneurial spirit of the individuals. Joe Neubauer*

*instilled a mindset in us that we should see it like our own business.*[42]

This approach was even reflected in the company's approach to marketing. Each business unit had its own marketing group dedicated to developing and implementing marketing programs, and merchandising sales efforts targeting clients in specific trade channels. It was not always easy, according to Dan Jameson, who joined the company with the Szabo acquisition. As explained by Jameson, who was later named senior vice president, sales and marketing, Correctional Services, there were some "grow-

---

Oriole Park first opened in 1992, the grand debut of this retro "field of dreams" forever changed the image of what is expected in a ballpark. In short, fans no longer wanted just the game; they expected the entire "fan experience."

In Baltimore, that ultimate "fan experience" meant a selection of more than 200 concession stands, dining rooms, retail stores, and lounges in the stadium and the adjoining warehouse building. It implied fresh food, prepared in the most appetizing way possible, giving fans a chance to smell the aroma of sizzling burgers and see their selections cooked to order. It brought the atmosphere of a street festival into the stadium through the use of food courts. In Baltimore, this concept was realized in Eutaw Street, an area comprising stores, cafes, and picnic areas, where people meet before, during, and after the game. Here, fans can even greet former baseball great Boog Powell as he promotes his Boog Powell's Pit Beef sandwich and signs autographs—a baseball player–recipe concept that ARAMARK has since taken and rolled out in other stadiums.[7]

"Fans no longer go just to see the games," said Hugh Gallagher, president of concessions for ARA Leisure Services, in 1992. "They want a total entertainment experience. Food, beverage, team souvenirs, and sportswear are a big part of that."[8]

The food service demands and the changing landscape of food requirements are slightly different when it comes to the Olympic Games. While it is important to keep the guests, print and

broadcast journalists, and volunteers well fed and entertained, the main focus is on the athletes and on advance preparations to fulfill the staggering food demands of the multi-week event.

"ARA takes great pride in its tradition of Olympic food service," said John Scanlan, ARA's former vice president of special events, just after the Winter Olympic Games in 1994. "It was a real thrill to be in Lillehammer. Preparations started two years [before the event]. And each day offered a unique challenge as we sought to satisfy the nutritional needs of figure skaters, hockey players, skiers, and others."[9]

At each Olympics, local cuisine is offered, with a nod to local traditions, too. "Many Norwegians consider breakfast the most important meal of the day," said Scanlan. "If you enjoy a hearty breakfast, you would have enjoyed yourself in Lillehammer."[10]

When a person steps in a ballpark or an Olympic athlete walks through an Olympic Village cafeteria that is managed by ARAMARK, the company wants to provide them with a pleasant experience.

"It's about the food, it's about the service, it's about the facilities management," said Jack Donovan, national vice president of sales and marketing at the time. "But what it's really about is creating a transformational experience for the fans. If somebody walks out of that park as a better fan than when they walked in, we've done our job."[11]

Above: With its world headquarters based in Philadelphia, ARA took great pride in providing a unique fan experience and exceptional food services at every event staged in the 1990s at the Spectrum, Philadelphia's multipurpose coliseum.

Below: In ARA's state-of-the-art Olympic kitchens, a team of up to 100 chefs prepared the huge quantities of food served during the event.

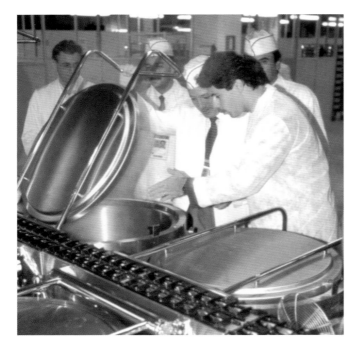

ing pains, but most of the time, they let us manage our own business. They've always let us manage our business portfolio, giving us the resources, the tools, and the capital necessary to grow this business."[43]

The company's 1994 report to employees reinforced this message: "Each 'Frontline Manager' today can provide and manage a portfolio of services. And this approach to outsourcing is considered, by many business thinkers, as the wave of the future."[44]

Throughout its history, ARA leaders had been serious, though informal, students of market trends. In June 1993, ARA asked its executives to officially study the changing needs of their highly competitive, global marketplace. Through an impressive ARA initiative called the Executive Leadership Institute (ELI), a group of executives representing ARA's diverse lines of businesses participated in four one-week sessions. Taught by professors from the nation's finest business schools at Harvard, Columbia, Cornell, and the Wharton School at the University of Pennsylvania, ARA executives covered such topics as Managing the Cycles of Change, Leadership through Teamwork, Market Analysis, and Businesses Development.[45]

The ELI was designed to help executives "explore new concepts in customer service, challenge status quo thinking, and apply new methods and fact-based analysis to business problems and opportunities." It would, ARA predicted, "turn managers into leaders."[46]

### The Pursuit of "Mission 10–5"

As 1994 approached, ARA entered its 10th year of employee ownership. ARA continued its outstanding legacy of Olympic service by filling the important role of Food Service Management Advisor for the 1994 Winter Games in Lillehammer, Norway. ARA's continuing success and steady growth potential sparked strong investment activity among company employees who were eligible to participate in the 1994 Installment Stock Purchase Opportunity. During the annual exercise period, which ended on January 15, approximately 90 percent of

the 1,400 outstanding grants were exercised. In all, ARA employees purchased approximately 2 million shares of stock, valued at close to $24 million.[47] By the end of the year, company employees would own nearly 75 percent of the company, nearly double the 1984 figure. The number of original employee–owners would triple by the close of business

In 1994, Neubauer (below right) received the prestigious Horatio Alger Award, which is presented to American business and civic leaders who have achieved success despite humble beginnings. Accepting the award, Neubauer followed in the footsteps of ARA cofounder Davre Davidson, who received similar recognition in 1967.

# "MANAGED SERVICES, MANAGED BETTER"

On October 11, 1994, ARA Services officially became ARAMARK. National and international advertising announced the milestone, which included a new corporate name, logo, and theme of "Managed Services, Managed Better." Central to the ARAMARK logo and fundamental to the new ARAMARK culture was the Starperson, the new icon that immediately appeared in advertising, on uniforms and letterheads, and on coffee cups and uniform trucks.

"Our Starperson stands for you—the secret of our success," said Chairman and CEO Joe Neubauer to ARAMARK employees. "At ARAMARK, the product first and last is our employees. The food served, the uniforms delivered, the books and magazines distributed, the healthcare and child care provided are important, but not as important as the service attitude and impact that each employee makes every day. That's who the Starperson is."

No true baseball fan can resist a new baseball cap, available in any number of gift shops at Angel Stadium in Anaheim, California.

in 1994, as 3,100 additional managers became eligible to purchase stock.[48]

In January of that same year, unexpected tragedy rocked southern California in the form of a catastrophic earthquake. ARA's 1,700 employees in the greater Los Angeles area rallied to meet the challenges of the disaster. Every employee was fortunate enough to escape serious injury—and immediately focused on continuing to provide food, housekeeping, and uniform services to clients' facilities just two days after the earthquake, while getting all 12 Children's World Learning Centers facilities back up and running.[49] Everyone was relieved that no great harm came to any of the company's employees, and nobody was surprised that those same employees returned to providing services as soon as possible.

Still early in the year, the Horatio Alger Association of Distinguished Americans tapped Joe Neubauer to receive the prestigious Horatio Alger Award in 1994, following in the footsteps of ARA cofounder Davre Davidson, a 1967 award winner. Every year, award winners were chosen from among hundreds of the nation's foremost business and civic leaders who have achieved high levels of success despite humble beginnings and difficult childhood circumstances. At a nationally televised black-tie awards dinner in Washington, D.C., in April 1994, Neubauer accepted the distinguished award in front of family, friends, and his ARA colleagues. Davidson noted, "Joe is a wonderfully decent, intelligent, and successful human being who epitomizes the American dream. ARA, American business, and indeed America itself have been enriched by his leadership."

The continued growth of ARA—through acquisitions, new service contracts, and client retention—certainly seemed to support Davidson's statement. New clients ensured that ARA remained at the forefront of emerging school food service trends in the 1990s, providing lunch every day to more than 1 million students in more than 280 school districts nationwide.[50] There was growth in tourism in 1994, which translated into a 5 to 6 percent growth in ARA's national parks services business.[51] In June, the Dodger Stadium organization in Los Angeles announced that ARA Services would be managing food and beverage services for one of the greatest franchises in baseball, joining the nearly 14.5 million Major League baseball fans nationwide served by ARA every season.[52]

To enhance its growth prospects, ARA also continually worked to refine its core businesses, which included divesting companies that no longer fit. In July 1994, ARA sold Woodhaven Foods, its northeast Philadelphia food-distribution center, to SYSCO, along with other distribution centers in Cincinnati, Chicago, Greensboro, and Birmingham.[53] Fred Sutherland recalled: "We systematically decided, 'We can't be everything to everybody. Here's what we're good at. Here's what we're not so good at.' So we sold [some areas of the business], but we did it over time."[54]

In the fall of 1994, Neubauer unveiled a strategy designed to focus on the company's opportunities for growth and increase the company's revenue by 10 percent annually over the next five years. Called "Mission 10–5," the strategy was designed to

At the 1994 All-Star Game at Three Rivers Stadium in Pittsburgh, Pennsylvania, the company provided spectacular food service for fans and players alike, including this pasta station for custom-made entrées.

move revenues to the $8 billion level by the end of the decade. The program was remarkably ambitious, designed to equal or exceed the average growth of all of the company's key competitors.[55] Acknowledging he had raised the bar, Neubauer was nonetheless aggressively determined to see this mission accomplished. "We're going to insist on growth performance in everything we do," he said. "We're going to maintain all the good things that we've been doing over the last 10 years, but we're now looking for growth."[56]

To that end, the company concluded a decades-long courtship of Harry M. Stevens Company, finally purchasing the oldest concessions business in the United States, with the rights to service Shea Stadium, the Houston Astrodome, Miami Arena, the Meadowlands, and Churchill Downs.[57] Ignoring ongoing baseball and hockey strikes, Neubauer noted that strikes are merely short-term disruptions in a business with "excellent long-range growth prospects."[58] The media described the transaction between Stevens and ARA as a "marriage of giants."

## ARA Becomes ARAMARK

On June 21, 1994, ARA Services, a $5 billion global company known as the world's leading provider of managed services, prepared to launch a completely new look, a new logo, and a new name: ARAMARK.

After nearly two years of research and evaluation by an internal task force headed by Mike Cronk, president of the Business Services Group, Neubauer announced the name change to ARAMARK during a nationwide videoconference that originated in Philadelphia and was simulcast to 25 locations across the United States. The announcement, by all accounts, was dramatic news. As nearly 1,000 top-level managers listened intently, Neubauer explained the company name change:

*Very simply put, we have outgrown our current trade name. Look carefully at the first three letters of our new name. They represent our roots and our link to the past. The last four letters are our future. They signal to the world that we intend to become the recognized standard against which all managed services are*

*measured. We chose the name ARAMARK because it signals to the world that we will set the mark—the standard—for managed services throughout the world.*[59]

From September 19 to 29, Neubauer and top management met with nearly 4,000 frontline managers in seven cities from Los Angeles to London and presented the new name and corporate identity. In highly choreographed and spirited meetings, the company admitted it "pulled out all the stops." In addition to introducing the new Mission 10–5 campaign and the new corporate Vision Statement and Guiding Principles, everyone received a glimpse of the new Starperson corporate icon (above), as well as a sneak preview of new corporate-wide advertising campaigns that included a new look for all vehicles, uniforms, and stationery. A cast of Broadway actors put on a performance called *Dreamers and Doers* that recreated the early years of the company, including the 1984 unsuccessful takeover attempt that led to the employee ownership of ARA. "Simply the best—that's how I feel about you," Neubauer said in meeting after meeting, echoing the theme song's title. "All your hard work and focus have produced quite a company."[60]

On October 11, 1994, ARA officially announced the new ARAMARK name, along with the new corporate theme of "Managed Services, Managed Better" and the new corporate icon—the Starperson. According to *Update*, "Complete with outstretched arms and a 'ready to serve you' attitude, the ARAMARK star personifies the star quality that ARAMARK people deliver day in and day out."[61] Every line of business immediately assumed the

ARAMARK name, with three exceptions: Spectrum Healthcare Services, WearGuard, and Children's World Learning Centers, which continued to operate under their existing, well-established brand names, newly endorsed as ARAMARK companies.

The press did not always adopt ARAMARK's serious tone in its quest for new corporate identity. "Hold that hot dog," wrote one Denver newspaper reporter. "ARA Services, the food service company that supplies Denver sports fans with classic ballpark fare, has officially changed its name to ARAMARK."[62]

By the time ARAMARK celebrated its 10th anniversary as a privately held firm on December 17, 1994, there was no question that ARAMARK's 130,000 employees—serving 15 million people at 500,000 locations in 11 countries every day—had embraced the name change and Neubauer's enthusiasm for the role each employee played in the service industry:

*From coffee cups to catalogs to corporate headquarters, we're showing a fresh new face to the world. Our corporate identity program is more than just a cosmetic face-lift. It's a strategic tool to help us build brand awareness in the global marketplace. Each element—logo, Starperson symbol, and positioning statement—is a message in itself. Who we are. What we do. How well we do it. Even the positioning of those elements communicates an important fact about our company. The Starperson always comes first, because it symbolizes each of you. Your service is ARAMARK's only product. YOU are ARAMARK.*[63]

The new ARAMARK logo lights up the Philadelphia skyline from corporate headquarters at 11th and Market Streets.

## CHAPTER NINE

# COMPANY ON A MISSION

## 1995–1999

*Who am I? I used to be called ARA. Now my name is ARAMARK. ... I'm wherever America works or plays. I'm there for your workers. For your customers. For you. And I'm proud to be of service.*

—Advertising copy,
The Starperson, ARAMARK's new icon

THE BRAND NEW, TWO-TON ARAMARK sign stood firmly in place atop corporate headquarters in downtown Philadelphia, when the company previously known as ARA kicked off 1995 with a new corporate identity. By all accounts, the newly positioned company with an 18-foot-tall, signature red Starperson icon perched on its building rooftop was off to an impressive start.[1]

Working around the clock, ARAMARK managers at the Superdome in New Orleans prepared vast quantities of jambalaya, gumbo, and alligator sausage; 1,500 Po' Boy sandwiches; and 20,000 hot dogs for the 72,000 fans attending the Sugar Bowl on January 2.[2] Two months later, the Atlanta Committee for the Olympic Games named ARAMARK as the food service manager for the 1996 Summer Olympic Games, an announcement that made it the only company in history to manage food service at 10 Olympic Games over four decades.[3]

Company officials were excited over the late 1994 acquisition of Harry M. Stevens Company, the oldest concessions business in America, which brought Churchill Downs, Shea Stadium, Fenway Park, and 17 additional sports venues into the ARAMARK Leisure Services fold.

Moreover, Campus Services announced six new accounts worth a total of $25 million in annual sales, and ARAKOR, the company's joint venture

with the Daewoo Corporation in South Korea, had seven food service units up and running. With an international presence in 11 countries, ARAMARK moved in March 1995 to increase its foreign market share by combining its domestic and international operations under a new name: Global Food and Support Services.[4]

Kristen Goodhardt and Donna Lowenstein of Uniform Services and Healthcare Support Services, respectively, won a contest to rename the employee newsletter, *Update*, as *The Mark*, reflecting the new ARAMARK identity and the company's commitment to hitting "the mark" and providing excellence in managed services.[5] In addition, Disney World, arguably one of the world's most renowned entertainment venues, chose ARAMARK to provide food service to its 38,000 cast members at 22 locations across the park's sprawling 43-square-mile site in Orlando, Florida.[6]

In the first few months of 1995, ARAMARK employees prepared to embrace the company's aggressive plan for unparalleled growth. According to the two main objectives of Mission 10–5, frontline

---

Given once a year since 1996, the Davidson Cup quickly became the most coveted annual employee award and honor at ARAMARK.

managers were charged with leveraging and expanding different services to existing customers while bringing in new customers through the company's new "Managed Services, Managed Better" initiative. Mission 10–5 had definitely launched.

### Mission 10–5

Announced by CEO Joe Neubauer in the fall of 1994, Mission 10–5 made previous growth programs like "Everybody Sells" and "Project Growth" look like Little League sluggers in a batting cage with a pro baseball player. Five out of the six Mission 10–5 goals focused on increased sales and marketing along with the development of a sales culture aimed at growing revenue throughout the company. Neubauer was very clear: The goal of Mission 10–5, the company's most ambitious growth initiative ever, was to increase revenues by 10 percent a year for the next five years.

Although ARAMARK had posted record earnings for many years, revenues for the last five years had remained relatively flat—$4.6 billion in 1990, $4.8 billion in 1992, $4.9 billion in 1993, and $5.1 billion in 1994. The company was mired in single-digit revenue growth. Neubauer suspected that risk-averse practices had set in and the owners were more interested in protecting their equity than growing the company.[7] Neubauer commented:

*The problem with slow revenue growth is that it limits our options and forces us to focus on reducing costs to increase earnings. While we've done a good job of controlling costs, that can only take us so far. In addition, much of our bottom-line growth over the last 10 years is attributed to interest rate reductions, a force that's largely beyond our control and one that appears to be on the rise. That's why now is the time for us to control our own destiny via top-line growth as well.*[8]

There was another problem, too, one that had a tremendous impact on a privately held company, particularly one owned by employees. According to an article in *Forbes* magazine, "Since the internal share price is based on profit growth, employee wealth suffers if profits drag. By the early 1990s, Neubauer realized he might face just such a problem."[9]

From the very beginning, Neubauer was determined that the company's restaging—complete with a new name, new logo, new icon, and new vision statement—would help lay the foundation for what he called "the next level of ARAMARK growth."[10] With

**1995**
ARAMARK is appointed food service manager for the 1996 Summer Olympic Games.

Disney World selects ARAMARK to serve its employees in Orlando, Florida.

**May 19, 1995**
Cofounder Davre Davidson dies, nearly 60 years after he started the business that would grow into ARAMARK.

**1995**
Mission 10–5 begins in earnest, designed to help accelerate the company's revenue growth.

Two key acquisitions enhance ARAMARK's uniform and career apparel services: Gall's, Inc., and Todd Uniform, Inc. One year later, ARAMARK purchases Crest Uniform.

**1996**
CEO Joe Neubauer launches "Unlimited Partnership," a blueprint for how to expand and deliver an increasing array of company services to clients.

With the 1994 purchase of Harry M. Stevens Company, the oldest concessions business in America, ARAMARK took over food services at the legendary Churchill Downs, home of the Kentucky Derby and the first jewel in the Triple Crown of thoroughbred horse racing.

Mission 10–5 in place, the company highlighted the crucial role of the frontline managers in building customer satisfaction and equity and guaranteed managerial and executive training through such established venues as the Executive Leadership Institute to assure high-quality staffing as growth continued. In the process, "policies and practices would become standardized across business lines, and resources and best practices would be shared wherever and whenever possible. ARAMARK would focus on growth rather than bottom-line profit; on teams instead of silos; and make a top priority of identifying, recruiting, and retaining more management talent than there were positions available to ensure the company's 'bench strength' was second to none."[11]

In his address to the company's global human resources conference in Philadelphia, not long after Mission 10–5 was in place, Neubauer immediately

pointed out who was ultimately responsible for the success of the company's latest growth campaign:

*The question no longer is, "Can we hit 10–5 growth?" The question is, "Can we sustain it?" And the answer to that question is right in this room. The old story of "we don't have enough talent" isn't my*

**1996**
ARAMARK decides to sell 80 percent of its interest in Spectrum Healthcare Services, a subsidiary that provides emergency-room physicians and nurses, as well as medical care in prisons.

**1998**
ARAMARK sells its Magazine and Book Distribution Services division.

ARAMARK expands into the private education business when it launches Meritor Academy, a network of private education K–6 schools. *(Photo courtesy of James Schnepf.)*

**1997**
After revenue growth of 8.6 percent in 1995 and 9.4 percent in 1996, Joe Neubauer announces that ARAMARK met the Mission 10–5 goal of achieving double-digit growth in a single year by growing the business 10 percent in fiscal 1997.

**1998**
The company buys back approximately 1 million outstanding ARAMARK shares through a onetime tender offer.

**1999**
The company adds nine new conference centers to its list of 80 and notes that it is the "world leader in conference center management." *(Photo courtesy of James Schnepf.)*

*problem. It's YOUR problem. We have plenty of capital, plenty of ideas, and the market is receptive to what we want to do. But people are our critical competitive advantage. So this company will march on the strength of our HR capabilities.*[12]

Brian Mulvaney, ARAMARK's senior vice president of human resources, knew the pressure was on, and so did everyone else. "You don't get the kind of return on net assets we've had by burning the furniture," Mulvaney said. "But we have to align our people and our resources with the new strategy for it to continue. We can't come up with some dramatic new product. We're a service organization. If we do it better than everyone else, we succeed. If we don't, we fail. It's really as simple as that."[13]

### Gathering Momentum

ARAMARK's push to grow received some good news in the spring when the eight-month-old baseball strike was suspended. Finally, ARAMARK could get back to business in nine of baseball's best-loved stadiums.

Other critical developments continued to work in ARAMARK's favor. After striving for five years to win the account, Campus Services landed Case Western Reserve University in Cleveland, Ohio, as a client. Healthcare Support Services won back Roxborough Memorial Hospital in Philadelphia and

doubled the account's volume by providing the hospital with additional services. Expansion in food services was international, too, as ARAMARK Mexico prepared to double in size and the company's European partnerships continued to expand. ARAMARK Uniform Services landed more than 25 new accounts, including Duke Power in North Carolina, one of the top 20 volume accounts in the country. Two key acquisitions in 1995 enhanced the development of ARAMARK's uniform and career apparel operations, which had expanded significantly in 1992 with the purchase of WearGuard. The purchase of Gall's, Inc. gave ARAMARK ownership of the largest mail-order supplier of public-safety equipment in the United States, opening up markets in law enforcement, fire safety, and protection; emergency medical response; and security guard industries. Later in the year, ARAMARK purchased the rental operations of Todd Uniform, Inc. and launched a major, five-year, $500 million capital investment program in its uniform business, which included building new plants and upgrading existing ones. The division continued to grow in 1996, when ARAMARK purchased Crest Uniform, a leading provider of uniform apparel to the restaurant, hotel, and healthcare industries.[14]

In an effort to bolster the disappointing performance of its Magazine and Book Distribution Services division, ARAMARK made what many thought would be key revenue-boosting acquisitions when it purchased Meader Distributing Company and Rainier News in 1995. The division also consolidated its sales and marketing programs at 24 distribution centers nationwide under one national marketing group and formed a number of new partnerships with Wal-Mart and three regional food market chains. "Our goal is to be the nationwide distributor of choice," said Jeff Spencer,

Above and right: Through Galls, safety professionals can purchase everything from uniforms and badges to security and public safety equipment required by an expanding public-safety workforce.

vice president of sales and marketing, Magazine and Book Distribution Services.[15]

One year after purchasing the Harry M. Stevens company, ARAMARK made a move that bolstered the new acquisition's facilities component by forming GMARA, a 50 percent venture between General Motors (GM) and ARAMARK; ARAMARK eventually bought out GM's interests and changed the name to ARAMARK Industrial Services. ARAMARK then acquired two additional companies: Diversified Facilities Services, a small company in Atlanta that had developed a niche for providing facility maintenance and operations in the correctional environment; and Facilities Resource Management, a boutique facilities business in Connecticut with about 30 clients and revenues of $25 million that specialized in higher education services, purchased by ARAMARK in 1998. These acquisitions proved the cornerstone for ARAMARK's official move into facilities services.

**Hitting the Mark**

The August 1995 edition of *The Mark* contained a special tribute to a handful of ARAMARK men and women who had made outstanding contributions to advancing the ambitious corporate objectives of

Gall's, Inc., based in Lexington, Kentucky, retained its well-respected brand name but dropped the apostrophe after ARAMARK Uniform Services acquired the company.

---

Mission 10–5. "Catch Our Rising Star!" proclaimed the headline, pointing to these exceptional managers who hit the mark.

Tony Urso was recognized for leading a team of 37 ARAMARK employees who stocked fortune cookies, chocolates, and Rolodex cards for his customers, growing the business at Amoco's world headquarters in downtown Chicago by nearly 240 percent in one year. Kelly Tyler, a district manager of Children's World in the Puget Sound region of Washington, had added 40 new programs and $800,000 in new revenue. Lloyd Gatherum, correctional medical services regional manager, had overseen the implementation of a statewide healthcare services program for Alabama's 17,000 state prison inmates—$20 million in new business. Ed Jenkins, Campus Dining Services frontline manager, had done "the impossible in four months" at Abilene Christian University in Abilene, Texas, when he and ARAMARK's interactive design team and District Manager Steve DiPrima recreated the residential

# REINVENTING THE UNIFORM BUSINESS

THROUGH A SERIES OF ACQUISITIONS, ARAMARK's Uniform and Career Apparel division began to reinvent its uniform business. By the end of the 1990s, ARAMARK offered a total solution to image enhancement programs for a wide range of companies and businesses, which meant that ARAMARK Uniform and Career Apparel Services could design, manufacture, sell, rent, and even clean uniforms for every client.

ARAMARK's purchase of WearGuard in 1992 did more than give the company access to America's preeminent direct-mail retailer of work clothes. WearGuard gave ARAMARK the wherewithal to expand its offerings as well as its uniform services philosophy. "We want to go to every customer in each of our targeted markets and offer them a whole solution," explained Fred Sutherland, then-president of ARAMARK uniform services group, in 1996. "We want to say to them: 'Here's a full line of work clothing—for employees behind the scenes and for those in front of your customers. You can rent or buy anything you like. If you want to personalize the clothing, or if you want something unique and distinctive designed just for you, we can handle it.'"

ARAMARK Uniform Services, the anchor of ARAMARK's Uniform and Career Apparel Services division, was well known in the late 1990s as America's leading supplier of uniforms and career apparel, providing rental, purchase, and lease services to more than 1.5 million people at more than 450,000 locations.[1] By adding to this base, ARAMARK morphed from a uniform service business into a total career apparel solution.

### WearGuard

In 1992, ARAMARK purchased WearGuard, a premier direct-mail retailer of work clothes serving the personalized work clothing needs of

In 1992, WearGuard was the country's leading direct-mail retailer of work clothes, which allowed ARAMARK to significantly expand its uniform services business.

more than one million businesses. For a company that had previously only rented uniforms, ARAMARK's newly acquired ability to sell work clothes opened up an entire new stream of customers and revenue.

Fitting into the ARAMARK culture wasn't always easy. "WearGuard had a unique identity," remembered Tom Vozzo, who first joined ARAMARK with the WearGuard acquisition and eventually became vice president and director of marketing. "Back in the early 1980s, they had an on-site fitness center and an on-site daycare. So they did a lot of employee-oriented benefits to get some of the best and brightest employees to work there. ... So for several years, we were trying to keep our own culture within, and we really didn't let ARAMARK in. But over the years, we saw the value of a bigger corporation. We knew we needed to adopt more of the ARAMARK philosophy. ... There's a bigger mission in place."[2]

### Acquiring Gall's and Todd

In 1995, ARAMARK acquired two more uniform companies: Gall's, Inc., and Todd Uniform, Inc.

Gall's, Inc., which became Galls under ARAMARK Uniform Services, is the largest mail-order supplier of public-safety equipment and accessories in the United States. Based in Lexington, Kentucky, Galls markets brand-name and private-label public-safety equipment and accessories to such industries as law enforcement, fire safety and protection, emergency medical response, and the security guard industry, as well as other safety professionals in the public and private sector. The company, founded by businessman Phillip Gall in 1902, started out selling camping gear and sportswear. The store became popular with police officers and began to offer law enforcement products. Gall's Police Equipment became a separate business in 1967 and changed to Gall's, Inc. in 1972. The company grew substantially when it entered the mail-order business, a step that eventually grew the regional company into a national company that handled almost 800,000 orders a year.[3] ARAMARK's purchase of Gall's coincided with a nationwide expansion of public safety in response to an ever-expanding population base.

Samuel Coxs, supply management specialist at the Smithsonian Institution and a Gall's client when ARAMARK purchased Gall's, always marveled at how seamlessly the company provided uniforms for nearly 760 security guards in nine Washington, D.C., museums: "They got us to the point (where) it's incredible how they are able to do what they do with uniforms, correct sizes—everything—and in a quick turnaround period."[4]

Todd Uniform, based in St. Louis, Missouri, and acquired by ARAMARK in 1995, was known as one of the country's largest uniform services companies. While Gall's provided direct access to the corrections market, company officials felt that Todd provided additional geographic markets for the uniform services business, particularly in the Midwest. ARAMARK folded Todd into its Uniform Services.

### Crest Uniform

In September 1996, ARAMARK bought Crest Uniform, a high-end catalog marketer focused primarily on the hotel, restaurant, and healthcare markets. Just as Gall's and Todd provided an introduction to specialty markets, Crest opened up ARAMARK's ability to tap into the hospitality and healthcare markets, which typically required tailored blazers and slacks, along with fashion-designed ensembles and a broad range of business and casual shirts, blouses, and sweaters. By 1996, ARAMARK knew that nearly 20 percent of workers in the United States were employed in the hospitality and healthcare fields, a statistic that promised significant growth opportunities.[5]

According to Vozzo, the Crest acquisition was "the third leg of the stool. You have rental, direct sales, and design and manufacturing capabilities for custom-made uniforms. That fills out the group."[6]

By its third year under the ARAMARK umbrella, the design team at Crest Uniform counted among its customers such familiar names as Chevron, Wal-Mart, McDonald's, Goodyear, Kentucky Fried Chicken, Denny's, and Pizza Hut. When it added the U.S. Postal Service in 1999, it was the first time that postal workers had ever "gone to an outside vendor for uniform design," said Karen Macek, Crest vice president of design. When the Crest design team was named the winner of numerous awards by the National Association of Uniform Manufacturers and Distributors, "[the Postal Service] asked us to create new uniforms for their retail clerks nationwide. Our designers have creativity and a unique ability to translate customers' needs into product design."[7]

dining facility, featuring eight ARAMARK brand concepts. And rising star Tom Vozzo, WearGuard vice president of marketing, was recognized for launching WearGuard into the international marketplace by leading a direct-mail retailing charge into Canada and the United Kingdom that produced more than $3 million in new sales and was poised to generate as much as 30 to 40 percent overall additional sales for the company in five years.[16]

"Nobody in the United Kingdom had what we're offering in both products and services," said Vozzo at the time.[17] He credited ARAMARK not only with having the "classic deep pockets" that allow such expansion to take place but also the foresight to train and develop managers to help make it happen. ARAMARK "develops executives," he said. "It's great to be part of an organization that cares about the senior management."[18]

Neubauer noted that these managers represent "thousands of ARAMARK managers who have bonded deeply with their customers. They have enriched the relationship. They have brought added value through new ideas and better ways of doing things, which have increased the value of our 'managed service' in the eyes of our customers. In every case, they have accomplished these things by remaining faithful to the legacy and spirit of our cofounder, Davre Davidson."

For everyone at ARAMARK, the legacy and spirit of Davidson was felt more keenly than ever that spring. He died on May 19, 1995, nearly 60 years after he bought his first peanut vending machine and started a business that would grow into ARAMARK.

In an emotional tribute, a special remembrance written about the company cofounder's life recalled how Davidson, "motivated by an entrepreneurial spirit and a keen business sense ... built a small peanut vending business into today's premier global managed services company. You could say that he was ARAMARK's original frontline manager—a hands-on manager responsible for providing the best possible service to customers with a high level of integrity. Today, ARAMARK's approximately 4,000 frontline managers need to look no further than the legacy of Davidson to learn what it takes to please customers, continuously improve, grow the business, and give something back to the community."[19]

**Unlimited Partnership**

When James E. Preston, chairman of Avon Products, Inc., joined the ARAMARK Board of Directors in 1995, he immediately recognized that Neubauer did not want ARAMARK customers to be viewed as transactions:

*[Neubauer] wanted to build partnerships. And he wanted to instill in the people of the company a philosophy that when you're dealing with people, we're not just interested in a transaction that might lead to some profit in the short term. What we're interested in is building a partnership. In order to build a partnership, we need to understand in great depth what their concerns are, what their wishes are, what their desires are, and to be as creative as possible in what we do in order to better fulfill their wants, needs, and desires. To build long-term relationships with customers is probably the most profitable way*

In the summer of 1999, ARAMARK turned 50 Boeing *Delta Rocket* workers into fashion models. At the new 1.5-million-square-foot Boeing Delta IV Launch Vehicle Factory in Decatur, Alabama, workers participated in a fashion show that introduced WearGuard's new casual work wear for the plant's employees.

ARAMARK CEO Joe Neubauer celebrates a special evening with company cofounder Davre Davidson. Neubauer always referred to Davidson as a great businessman and an "exceptional person."

*to build a business. … You want to prove to them that what you're trying to do is not simply sell a product, but provide a service of long-lasting benefit.*[20]

For years, ARAMARK's managers had created value for clients by taking on supposed "non-core" functions such as food service or uniforms and enabling clients to focus on what they do best. ARAMARK's managers recognized that, with many clients, the company had moved far beyond the traditional "supplier" role into full business partnerships that continued to expand over time. ARAMARK began calling these special relationships "Unlimited Partnerships," recognizing that ARAMARK would do anything necessary to satisfy clients and help them succeed at their core businesses. It wasn't long before ARAMARK was driven by a unique "no limits" culture, anchored by an unrivaled need to succeed, and dedicated to customizing services to meet the needs of individual customers.[21]

Unlimited Partnership—Phase II of ARAMARK's corporate identity program—was launched in January 1996, just one year after the debut of the company's new brand and its Mission 10–5 initiatives. Both a philosophy of service and an "exportable" blueprint of ways to deliver those services, Unlimited Partnership was key to a growth mindset—a way of approaching the business and clients. While the company was still driven to accomplish 10 percent revenue growth each year, the Unlimited Partnership program connected faces, clients, desires, and possibilities to those black-and-white financial numbers and made the quest for growth almost a byproduct of developing partnerships with the customer. To Neubauer, it helped explain exactly *why* ARAMARK managed services better than anyone else:[22]

*We're asking all ARAMARK employees to look closer at the potential for expanding our partnerships with our customers. What more can we be doing to create economic value? Where is the untapped potential in the relationships we've created? What other needs can we help address by creating new solutions? … Through partnerships that have "no limits," we will unleash and focus the entrepreneurial passion that is at the core of our uniqueness as a company. In this way, we will take another important step toward achieving our ultimate goal … world leadership in managed services.*[23]

In many ways, the Unlimited Partnership program worked as a business model to articulate the ARAMARK method of doing business through customized solutions and providing additional services—as opposed to the standardized "off the shelf" programs of its competitors. As Terry Crump, vice president of sales and marketing for ARAMARK Campus Services, once put it: "We're like golfers. Every course, every customer, is different. We have more clubs in the bag than the other guys, and we know when to use them and how to use them better than our competitors."[24]

**From Partnership to Growth with "No Limits"**

Over the next four years, the Unlimited Partnership initiative dominated ARAMARK's push for even higher levels of growth, as evidenced by the themes of its consecutive annual reports: "The Power of

# DAVRE DAVIDSON

TO HAVE A FULL LIFE, DAVRE J. DAVIDSON believed that you had to have four things: family, community, business, and education. When he and his wife Charlotte started a peanut vending business in 1936, his office was the front seat of a 1932 Dodge Sedan and his warehouse was the back seat and trunk. Their first week's receipts amounted to $7.56. "My aspirations were modest," he admitted. "After all, one had to be a committed optimist to consider opening a business in the depths of the Great Depression."[1]

Davidson, the founder of a Depression-era business that turned into the multibillion-dollar service management company known as ARAMARK, was 83 years old when he died of heart failure on May 19, 1995, at Cedars–Sinai Medical Center in Los Angeles.

"Davre was not only a great businessman and leader, he was an exceptional person," recalled CEO Joe Neubauer. "To him, success was always 'we,' and failure was always 'I.' He truly believed that he was here to serve others, and he lived his life true to that belief. He was a success story in many ways—as a husband, father, educator, and community leader. With his passing, we've lost far more than a mentor and a friend, but the lessons he taught us about life and businesses will endure."[2]

In 1959, Davidson and his brother Henry acquired Bill Fishman's business to form ARA, later known as ARAMARK. The company's first-year revenues were $37 million. For 16 years, Davidson served as ARA's CEO and as the company's first Chairman of the Board before retiring in 1977, a time when revenues surpassed $1.5 billion and the company employed 90,000 worldwide. Davidson continued to serve on the Board of the company he founded and often used the phrase "People, Planning, Progress" to describe what he believed were the key elements to ARAMARK's continuing success. A pioneer in every sense of the word, his colleagues knew that Davidson never stopped searching for the innovations that could give the company a competitive advantage.[3] But if you asked him the secret of his success, his son Harold once explained, "Without hesitation,

---

Unlimited Partnership" (1995); "The Value of Unlimited Partnership" (1996); "The Growth of Unlimited Partnership" (1997); and "We Create Value One Customer at a Time Through Unlimited Partnership" (1998). Tucked inside these annual reports and various company newsletters were countless examples that illustrated ARAMARK's long history of providing and maintaining customized solutions for its customers as well as creating the "no limits" culture that anchored Unlimited Partnership:

• When ARAMARK executives first walked into Fenway Park in 1995, Rich Roper, vice president of operations, Leisure Services, took one look at one of baseball's most venerable ballparks and decided that "limitations are a state of mind. The job was listening ... to their fans. The fans were pretty clear about what they didn't like and what they wanted." It worked.

"We told ARAMARK we were searching for a 'best practice' food operation," said John Buckley, Boston Red Sox executive vice president for administration. "We had seen what they did at Camden Yards in Baltimore. We wanted that for Fenway Park. Rich has a can-do attitude. How else can you explain him finding a way to sell seafood chowder at Fenway? That set the tone. There was no 'us' or 'them.' We were one team."[25]

• San Diego Zoo Manager Jean Saxon wanted to create a "total experience" to attract more visitors, though that included safari-themed outfits, which seemed too expensive. Jeff Black, ARAMARK Uniform Services general manager, came up with a solution. "We told Jean, 'We'll buy the uniforms and lease them to you. We'll also stock, maintain, and clean them. And we'll do it all for a lot less than what you expect to

he would have said, 'Marrying Charlotte.' They were married for 56 beautiful years. Charlotte was the balance, the strength, and the support my dad needed to attain great achievements. They were truly a team."[4]

In 1982, Davidson and Fishman were honored by the company they founded when it established The Fishman–Davidson Center for the Study of the Service Sector at the University of Pennsylvania's Wharton School. It was Davidson's hope that the center would continue "analyzing and solving the very unique problems of managing businesses where the only product is service."[5]

Recipient of the Horatio Alger Award, Davidson was a leader of many professional and philanthropic associations in the Los Angeles area. His charitable giving extended to Cedars–Sinai Medical Center, the University of Southern California, Junior Blind of America, the Orthopaedic Hospital Foundation, and Claremont Colleges, among others. Forced to leave college for economic reasons as a young man, he later received an Honorary Doctorate of Humane Letters from Lincoln (Ill.) College. When he died, he was survived by Charlotte; his two children, Dr. Harold A. Davidson and Celia Davidson Farkas; and three grandchildren. When Charlotte passed away nearly four years later, her family noted in 1999 that "we are consoled that Charlotte is now re-united with Davre, the love of her life."[6]

In 1994, when ARAMARK unveiled its new name and logo, Broadway actors recreated the start of the company in a production called *Dreamers and Doers*, a direct tribute and reference to Davre and Charlotte Davidson. As Joe Neubauer and other frontline managers watched as the *Dreamers and Doers* play captured the love and interdependency of this great partnership, he called it "one of the greatest thrills in my business career. It had an impact on all of us who experienced it. It transcended business. [The Davidsons] dreamt and they did, and they taught all of us that there can be no enduring achievement without a dream. And there is no dream realized without hard work."[7]

In a lasting tribute to the Davidsons, ARAMARK initiated the Davre J. Davidson Entrepreneurial Award in October 1996 to honor the passion, entrepreneurship, and risk-taking that defined the company founder. The award, presented during a ceremony each year that is highlighted with a tape recording of Davre's enduring messages to the company, has quickly become the most coveted prize at ARAMARK.[8]

---

pay.'" Since 1996, ARAMARK has helped San Diego Zoo achieve the distinct look it wants for employees and boost attendance by an average of 5 percent annually.[26]

- In the midst of the "numbing commercialism, sweltering heat, unreliable transportation, suffocating security, and mindless terrorism" that threatened to define the Summer Olympic Games in Atlanta in 1996, ARAMARK rallied to customize solutions and perform under pressure to keep services to athletes and others free of interruptions. The ARAMARK team excelled undaunted. "They designed a dining room and a kitchen, and they helped build it on a parking lot. ... Because if there's anything that seems to get a team of ARAMARK managers' juices flowing, it's a challenge. An opportunity to redefine, yet again, the power of partnerships without limits."[27]

- In 1996, "ARAMARK placed Farley's Fruit Snacks in vending machines all across the Midwest, creating significant additional annual revenue for us," said John Baran, Farley's office services manager. "Then before I could even say "thank you," they showed us how to save 25 percent on our office coffee service! Our revenues are up, our costs are down. What's not to like?" As Brian Drew, ARAMARK sales director, explained, "We made a team effort to build a partnership with Farley Foods, and it's working."

- When Sprint Corporation hired ARAMARK in 1998 to serve as the food service provider for its new world headquarters in Overland Park, Kansas, ARAMARK's interactive design team worked with the telecommunications company to design the six cafeterias and satellite food facilities that would feed more than 10,000

Jerome Bill, ARAMARK's food service director at the Olympic Village in Atlanta, and his staff of expert chefs provided around-the-clock food services during the Olympics and celebrated the occasion by creating this incredible ice sculpture.

*Forbes* magazine also noted:

*ARAMARK makes its money on stuff its customers need but don't want to bother with. ARAMARK prepares and serves food to the 1,000 inmates at the Lubbock County jail in Texas and fancier fare to the cuff-links crowd at Goldman Sachs' corporate offices in lower Manhattan. ARAMARK launders and delivers weekly the yellow-and-red shirts worn by McDonald's workers worldwide. It distributes magazines like this one, in 20,000 locations, from airports to supermarkets, in 22 states. ... Above all, ARAMARK is a people business. It does over $6 billion with just $2.7 billion in assets. Its real asset is its relationship with its customers and its employees.*[30]

employees at the complex. A driving design factor was Sprint's unique desire to "keep its people on site," said John Zillmer, president of ARAMARK's Business Services Group. "The main reason is that the road infrastructure in the area around the headquarters will not be able to handle a mass of people leaving at once to go out to lunch."[28]

In many ways, the Unlimited Partnership "no limits" initiative reflected ARAMARK's historical effort to establish and maintain the best partnerships possible with customers. There was no magic formula, no secret to success. As Neubauer once said:

*If we have one underlying theme it's that we're very customer-oriented. We don't have any pre-conceived notions about what our customers need or want. We listen to them, work with them, shape their needs, and deliver a quality product, whether it's a banquet for 1,000 people or linen services for a hospital.*[29]

Unlimited Partnership worked. In 1995, ARAMARK revenue grew 8.6 percent, still shy of the 10 percent goal but more than double the unacceptable 3 percent the company recorded the previous year. In 1996, revenue went up 9.4 percent. And in 1997, Neubauer announced, "We delivered on our Mission 10–5 goal. We grew the ARAMARK Corporation's continuing business operations 10 percent in fiscal 1997. Achieving double-digit growth for a $6 billion company is an extraordinary achievement. ... It means we're beginning to deliver on the growth potential of our unlimited partnerships."[31]

### Responding to the Market, Refining Core Businesses

In an environment so focused on growth and unlimited partnership potential, any company segment that turned in a disappointing performance was ripe for review. When Neubauer noted in the 1996 report to employees that "losses in the magazine and book business and a disappointing performance at Spectrum Healthcare Services kept earnings short of our plan," everyone knew the writing was on the wall for these two divisions.[32]

By the late 1990s, fast-moving changes in the healthcare industry had made it a very different and more volatile business sector, with a less predictable growth potential. The introduction of managed care and health maintenance organizations, shifts from inpatient to outpatient services, and changes in healthcare insurance reimbursement systems all had an effect on the company's healthcare services. Consequently, by the end of 1996, ARAMARK decided to sell approximately 80 percent of its interest in Spectrum Healthcare Services, a subsidiary that provided doctors and nurses to emergency rooms and prisons. Though the company introduced a new management team to contain costs and built a stronger marketing and sales infrastructure, the "focus on recovery" that Neubauer once predicted for the company's Magazine and Book

Distribution Services division never really materialized; after $5 million in losses in 1996 and nearly $15 million in 1997, ARAMARK moved in 1998 to divest itself of this segment, which Neubauer ultimately decided "was not core to our business design or creating sufficient economic value."[33]

### Pressured to Go Public

By the final years of the 1990s, questions about the company's status had begun circulating: When would ARAMARK, a $6 billion-plus company that went private in 1984, go public?

The pressures were obviously building, and Wall Street analysts were more than eager to discuss the reasons. If the company remained private, how could the shareholders realize full value for their stock? By staying private, was the company keeping the stock value lower than it would be on the open market? As a public company, analysts predicted

Right: After adding nine new conference centers, ARAMARK declared in 1999 that it was the world leader in conference center management. *(Photo courtesy of James Schnepf.)*

Below: Galls is recognized as America's largest mail-order supplier to safety professionals, catering to the special needs of law enforcement, fire-fighting, emergency medical response, and security guard industry personnel.

# MANAGING THE 1996 SUMMER OLYMPIC GAMES

IN EARLY 1995, ARAMARK ANNOUNCED THAT it had been tapped as food service manager for the 1996 Summer Olympic Games. It would be the company's 10th Olympic Games event. ARAMARK noted that overseeing 5 million meals served by more than 3,000 food service employees in 17 days would be a huge challenge for even the most experienced company. However, the Games were a perfect fit for a company that defines itself by the level of its service.[1]

The three-week-long Olympic Games in Atlanta "tested the company's 'no limits' culture like never before." Amid terrorist attacks, security restrictions, heat, and traffic congestion, ARAMARK proved it was up to the challenge of the "world's single most demanding food assignment." But before it was over, ARAMARK showed once again that its ability to customize solutions and perform under pressure produced another outstanding result for a client that the company first served in 1968.[2]

ARAMARK brought its best practices and the strength of nine past Olympic Games performances to Atlanta for the Games and delivered a tremendous managed services show before a world audience on a world stage. To make this happen, Charlie Gillespie, sports and entertainment president, and John Scanlan, vice president for special projects, assembled a team of 7,000 workers and 200 managers.

They designed and helped build the athletes' dining facility and a state-of-the-art modular kitchen in a parking lot and kept it open 24 hours a day. They placed the entire Olympic Games kitchen online, computerizing the ARAMARK World Menu from which 3,500 athletes chose their meal selections. The menu, developed through the company's Culinary Resource Center in Philadelphia and based on athletes' dining preferences at previous Olympic Games, offered 550 international recipes that embraced every cultural, religious, and ethnic need. For the first time at any Olympic Games, ARAMARK provided onsite nutritional analysis of athlete meals and answered general nutrition questions.

Jerome Bill, ARAMARK's food service director of the Olympic Village, agreed to keep a diary for *Nation's Restaurant News*, regularly reporting on just how far ARAMARK pushed to provide everything the athletes needed. For instance, on July 12, Bill wrote:

*One of the international dishes ARAMARK is serving the athletes is Korean kimchi. It is actually imported from Korea and shipped to Atlanta in large tubs. However, the cabbage for the kimchi is cut by the chefs here and added right before the dish is served. After sampling the kimchi, some Korean athletes informed one of the ARAMARK servers— who also happened to be from Korea—that the cabbage was being cut too small. The server talked with the athletes and then relayed to the chef directions on how to cut the cabbage properly for authentic Korean kimchi.*[3]

On July 16, Bill filed the following summary:

*So far, the food service operation has been the talk of the village. Apparently, it is one of the only operations that has not experienced major problems during the past week. It would seem that our experience with several previous Olympics is paying dividends.*[4]

Outside the Olympic Village, ARAMARK served millions of other meals to spectators and Olympic employees in eight different venues. This included food and beverage services at the 83,000-seat Olympic Stadium, and food, beverage, and retail merchandise sales across the street at Atlanta–Fulton County Stadium, site of Olympic Games baseball and a stadium client of ARAMARK's since 1966. There were "1,900 points of service within a 1.5-mile radius in downtown Atlanta known as The Olympic Ring, where the ARAMARK team put their 'no limits' culture on the line every day."[5]

Struggling against traffic backups and security restrictions, ARAMARK delivered services to

Above right: ARAMARK also offered concession services throughout the city at the Olympic venues. *(Photo by Matthew Stockman.)*

Below: The Olympic dining facilities run by ARAMARK in Atlanta, Georgia, in the summer of 1996 offered more than 550 international recipes and dishes in an attempt to meet the cultural, religious, ethnic, and nutritional needs of the world's most outstanding athletes. *(Photo courtesy of www.garymeek.com.)*

basketball fans at Morehouse College; field hockey fans at Morris Brown College; badminton fans at Georgia State University; and swimming, diving, and water polo fans at Georgia Tech.

ARAMARK also provided 10,000 green logo hats, 10,000 polo shirts, 4,000 chef coats, and countless other uniform and cleaning services during the Games. It was also responsible for refreshment services at exclusive hospitality venues throughout Atlanta for top clients from 96 countries and major corporations. Around-the-clock meals were served to hundreds of journalists, 1,200 Olympic officials, and 500 volunteers. ARAMARK set up special day care centers for Olympic Game visitors and employees through Children's World Learning Centers, and the seven Spectrum Healthcare Services Emergency Care facilities were placed on heightened alert during the Games. It was a precaution that turned out to be critical when a tragic incident triggered by a terrorist bomb killed two spectators and injured more than 100 at Centennial Olympic Park.

Russ Chandler, mayor of the Olympic Village, said, "The 1996 Centennial Olympic Games don't happen without ARAMARK." By the end of the Olympics, there was obvious relief mixed with pride. The headline of ARAMARK's September employee newsletter proclaimed that "ARAMARK Gets the Gold!" Inside the newsletter, the article noted: "That makes 10 now. About what you would expect from the world's best managed services company."[6]

that ARAMARK's shares would command at least double the multiple applied by its appraiser.[34] By staying private, how could the company expand its equity base for the inevitable acquisitions that ARAMARK seemed poised to make to expand its core businesses? For acquisitions, companies need currency. That currency is often publicly traded stock, which becomes a factor in any acquisition where dealmakers are looking to minimize taxes and create rollover value to benefit shareholders.

Analysts noted that without publicly traded shares, ARAMARK "continued to face obstacles in growing against the likes of top international competitors."[35]

By all accounts, Neubauer listened but didn't waver. "Joe Neubauer vows he'll keep ARAMARK private," stated a late 1997 headline in *Forbes* magazine:

*Neubauer says that he will keep ARAMARK private for the foreseeable future. Despite pressures from some managers who would like to cash out, Neubauer has steadfastly refused to play the usual buyout game of flipping the operation to the public and walking away a wealthier man. Instead of selling stock to the public, he uses it to motivate employees. ... Neubauer has seen to it that he and some 14,500 employees now own 80 percent of the company. He himself owns 13 percent, worth some $160 million. The remaining 20 percent belongs mostly to institutions like Chase and Goldman Sachs. "Populist capitalism," Neubauer calls it. "Sitting here today, I don't see any reason why this company needs to be public."*[36]

In response to mounting pressure to take the company public, Neubauer did just the opposite. In 1998, he created more employee capitalism and attempted to complete a process the company started in 1984 when it initiated the management buyout. Paying $531 million, the company bought back approximately one million outstanding ARAMARK shares through a onetime tender offer and sold them back to employees. The offer initially created controversy for outside shareholders such as Chase, JPMorgan, Metropolitan Life Insurance, and Goldman Sachs, but it ultimately went through after ARAMARK adjusted its price and lowered its quest to own 100 percent of the outstanding stock. After the buyback, employees owned 93 percent

of ARAMARK, with about 6,000 owners through individual stock ownership and about 14,000 owners through employee benefit and retirement plans. Clearly, employee ownership in ARAMARK had expanded dramatically, from 40 percent in 1984 to 93 percent in 1998. Neubauer argued that employees now owned "nearly all of the value they create for the corporation."[37]

When ARAMARK pushed to buy them out, institutional investors like Chase and Goldman Sachs sold their entire holdings in ARAMARK in 1998, reportedly realizing a compounded 30 percent annual return on their investment since 1984.[38] MetLife, however, refused to sell, releasing only about 25 percent of its shares. The employee benefit plans indicated that they, too, preferred to keep more than 500,000 ARAMARK shares in their portfolio, while selling around 400,000 shares back to the company.

For years, Neubauer marveled at the few major players who had refused to sell. MetLife, he remembered, "basically said, 'We don't want to sell. We think we're going to make more money on you than we made on Microsoft and Coca-Cola.' I said to the chief investment officer, 'We're just a hot dog and dirty laundry company. What are you talking about? This is not a global brand name or some technology stuff. This is just hot dogs and dirty laundry.'"[39]

Nobody believed him.

As the company finished 1998 almost entirely employee-owned, a leaner ARAMARK focused on three core business segments: ARAMARK Food and Support Services, ARAMARK Uniform and Career Apparel, and ARAMARK Educational Resources. While keeping its child care business, the Educational Resources division expanded into the private education business with the launch of Meritor Academy, a network of private, early education K–6 schools that enroll students as they

Opposite: In Westlake Village, California, parents did not want their children to leave the nurturing, familiar environment of ARAMARK's Children's World Learning Centers when it was time to leave preschool and kindergarten and enter another elementary school. This led to the creation of Meritor Academy, ARAMARK Educational Resources' foray into providing K–6 education in a private setting.

"graduate" from the programs offered by the Children's World Learning Centers. In Food and Support Services, news reports focused on ARAMARK's ability to change with the times.

Special reports highlighted ARAMARK's revised food service options at the University of Tennessee and the University of Delaware, and the installation of a retail, marketplace-style food court at Goldman Sachs' Manhattan headquarters.[40] For the 11th time since 1968, ARAMARK managed food services at the Olympic Winter Games in Nagano, Japan, in collaboration with AIM, the corporation's affiliate in Japan. This unique partnership continued a company tradition that was three decades in the making.[41]

No one seemed to miss the large stake ARAMARK had in the $250 billion industry, which was growing at 15 percent or more a year through outsourc-

ing. According to *Forbes*, "Neubauer and ARAMARK are sitting squarely in the middle of one of the hottest growth areas in U.S. businesses: outsourcing—the contracting out by schools, hospitals, prisons, and corporations of tasks unrelated to their main missions."[42]

### Skin in the Game

When Lynn McKee, vice president of executive development and compensation, looked around ARAMARK after the 1998 employee ownership expansion, she recognized one overwhelming feature—employees throughout the organization were invested in the success of the company. Just as Neubauer had always preached, the best way to keep employees engaged and motivated was to make sure they had the chance to own the company and share in its success. McKee recognized immediately what that brought to the table:

*It was an ownership culture. People had skin in the game, if you will. You were invested in the success of this company. You worked hard to ensure*

---

Students at Meritor ranked in the 80th percentile nationally in standardized reading and math testing. *(Photo courtesy of James Schnepf.)*

*the success of this company because you know, at some point in time, your own economic success would follow.*[43]

After all those years of hearing about a "no limits" Unlimited Partnership culture, by 1999, ARAMARK employees had clearly made the shift "from just being a uniform or a food company to being a multiservice company that can provide multiple services for any one of those clients ... more aware of what was happening with the competition and what changes were taking place in the marketplace overall," said McKee. "We also had a stronger need, as a business group, for increasing the amount of talent that we were bringing into this organization. So we really ramped up our executive development efforts over those years as a way to be able to get a common vision and a common mindset throughout the organization about how to approach the business."[44]

Dining services and meeting planning are part of ARAMARK's comprehensive business services provided to all conference center clients, where ARAMARK creates value by turning local menu specialties into events that have lasting memories for out-of-town visitors. *(Photo courtesy of James Schnepf.)*

The 1999 report to employees recognized the tremendous contributions employees had made to the company. Noting the title, "We Celebrate!" Neubauer explained:

*We celebrate 40 years of incorporation. We celebrate 15 years since the management buyout that took our company private and set the stage for employee ownership and the tremendous growth we have enjoyed. We celebrate five years as ARAMARK and the success of Mission 10–5. And most importantly, we celebrate our people—thousands of gifted people who deliver value to our customers every day, give of themselves in their communities, and who have given our company a notable past and a promising future.*[45]

In March 1999, FORTUNE® magazine named ARAMARK the No. 2 Most Admired Company for Outsourcing Services, just behind ServiceMaster. With revenue approaching $7 billion, ARAMARK now employed more than 150,000 employees serving 15 million people at 500,000 locations in 15 countries every day. As the company's revenues and worldwide reputation grew, so did its list of accomplishments. To wit:

• ARAMARK's "Passion for Service" continued to inspire community partnerships through community service. Through service partnerships with Big Brothers Big Sisters of America, Junior Achievement, and Reading Is Fundamental, ARAMARK employees "celebrate a heritage built around serving others."[46]

• Declaring itself the "world leader in conference center management," ARAMARK added nine new conferences centers to its list of 80 in 1999 and reported a 100 percent retention rate since 1994. While averaging a minimum of eight support services at each conference center partnership, the record number of services was 16 for the U.S. Postal Service at the William F. Bolger Center for Leadership Development in Potomac, Maryland, where ARAMARK managed dining and catering; an upscale cocktail lounge; sales and marketing, meeting planning and setup, audiovisual, and cleaning services for 44 conference rooms; mail service; the stockroom; the front desk, including reservations; accounting; transportation; janitorial services; grounds maintenance; facilities maintenance; general support, including secretarial, office, and computer; housekeeping; recreation rooms; and security.[47]

- ARAMARK expanded its U.K. business into the hospital sector and landed an important offshore hotels contract with British Petroleum (BP) Amoco. In 1999, ARAMARK also acquired Phoenix-based Restaura, Inc. to enhance its food management and services sector. The acquisition added about $180 million a year to ARAMARK's dining and refreshment services.[48]

### The War for Talent

As ARAMARK approached a new fiscal year, a new decade, and a new millennium, Neubauer stood before a conference of human resource executives on September 27, 1999, concluding that "by any measure, Mission 10–5 has been a huge success. We have done what we set out to do: to get this company growing again. We now have something essential that we did not have five years ago when we launched the growth mission. We have *market momentum.*"[49]

With Mission 10–5 successfully executed, ARAMARK began to focus on the next challenge for the undisputed global leader in managed services. By December, the challenge was identified, and goals were defined: "Now we must wage—and win— the war for talent," Neubauer announced.[50]

With the shortage of management talent projected to continue well into the next century, ARAMARK unveiled a broad-based campaign to ensure that the corporation had access to the highly skilled managers it needed to continue growing at a rapid pace. Neubauer even suggested that this war for talent "may be the most critical campaign in our company's history."[51] Four task forces identified four key strategies of the campaign:

ARAMARK manages a wide array of services ranging from dining and catering to landscaping and facility maintenance. *(Photo courtesy of James Schnepf.)*

- *Retaining ARAMARK's Existing Talent.* "Our retention and promotion data show that ARAMARK managers have tremendous opportunities for advancement," said Ed Evans, team leader and senior vice president for human resources, ARAMARK Uniform Services. "We must communicate to managers the wide range of opportunities that exist."[52]

- *Developing ARAMARK's Talent.* "We need to make sure our people have the skills that match our future needs," said Jack Donovan, serving at the time as president, ARAMARK Campus Services. "People development and succession planning must be a core part of our strategic planning and business planning processes."[53]

- *Improving ARAMARK's Workforce Diversity.* Stung by some recent discrimination lawsuits, ARAMARK was determined to not only improve its employment track record but also prepare for a future where 85 percent of new workforce applicants will include women, people of color, or immigrants. "Our growth goals can be realized only by maximizing our ability to recruit, retain, and advance a diverse workforce," said Joan Mazzotti, team leader and senior vice president and associate general counsel, ARAMARK Food and Support Services. "We need to create an environment that allows all employees to contribute to their fullest potential."[54]

Toward that goal, ARAMARK launched the Kaleidoscope Initiative, which included expanded efforts to target women and people of color for recruitment and advancement, a greater focus on diversity in ARAMARK's career development systems, diversity education for all levels of management, and a sustained communications effort.[55]

- *Branding the ARAMARK Opportunity to Attract Talent.* "Our success depends on our ability to attract top management talent," said Jim McManus, team leader and president, ARAMARK Business Services. "But the pool of qualified people is shrinking. The people we need are more mobile and have higher expectations than ever before. We need to develop a campaign of activities that communicates the right message about ARAMARK to them."[56]

In an end-of-the-year interview, editors at *The Mark* asked Neubauer to comment on priorities for fiscal year 2000 and beyond. "Five years ago, we launched Mission 10–5. Today, we can all declare victory," he began. "We did it. And we did it together." Noting that "people drive economic value creation at ARAMARK," Neubauer then emphasized that the future of the company and its ability to build on the success of Mission 10–5 depended on the skills of the ARAMARK team, "people who know how to keep customers and build unlimited partnerships." An ARAMARK leader, he noted, has the ability to build strong relationships with customers, peers, bosses, and subordinates from diverse backgrounds; has an entrepreneurial spirit and finds opportunities where others may not see it; has a passion to serve; and brings to the table a diversity of experience that simply creates better leaders.[57]

Neubauer described a fifth leadership trait that he admitted was "a seemingly odd combination, but it is distinctly ARAMARK. We are confident, not arrogant, because we are successful at what we do. We are winners, but we are also humble because we serve others, and we do it in their 'homes.' We are the best, but our goal is to make others look good, to make the lives of others productive."[58]

Lynn McKee recognized this particular leadership trait right away. "Humble confidence," she said. "It's a Neubauer term, and it's true. It's very characteristic of the people at ARAMARK."[59]

Chairman and CEO Joe Neubauer commends the efforts of ARAMARK employees, who helped make the company's return to Wall Street a success. *(Photo courtesy of ©Candace diCarlo.)*

## CHAPTER TEN

# PRESERVING THE CULTURE
## 2000–2002

*Ideas and Entrepreneurs. The heart and soul of ARAMARK. Our heritage and our blueprint for the future. Our company began more than 60 years ago with a single idea from one man, Davre Davidson. He saw a need others didn't. And he stepped up to meet it. Ever since, we've been a company of entrepreneurs, of "dreamers and doers."*

—Introduction, 2001 annual report

ARAMARK FACED MANY CHALlenges in the first years of the new millennium, including international and national expansion, acquisitions, intense competition in the midst of tight labor markets and a slowing economy, national tragedy, and a corporate restructuring. At every turn, the core business units embraced a three-pronged formula for success that emphasized the need to retain customers, build relationships, and win new business. "The key to winning, now as always, is your entrepreneurial drive," wrote Chairman and CEO Joe Neubauer to ARAMARK employees. "This is our true point of difference and the envy of our competitors."[1]

For ARAMARK to take advantage of growth opportunities, Neubauer proposed redirecting the company's entrepreneurial drive and once again taking the company public, 17 years after he led the management buyout. In changing the company's structure, Neubauer nonetheless vowed to preserve the culture and the entrepreneurial spirit of ARAMARK's 200,000 employees and support their quest to be the world leader in managed services.

The ambitious plan faced daunting market forces, but no one doubted they could achieve success. "Nowhere But Up For ARAMARK," read one newspaper headline. From 2000 to 2002, the dreamers and doers were at it again.[2]

### Core Strength

In 2000, ARAMARK strengthened its food service leadership position in key markets through new acquisitions and strategic partnerships, both nationally and internationally.

ARAMARK acquired the food and beverage concessions and venue-management business of Ogden Corporation and also acquired the prison food service division of Wackenhut Corporation. The Ogden acquisition, priced at $236 million, included 140 contracts to provide concessions at ballparks and arenas, including Veterans Stadium in Philadelphia and The Waterfront Entertainment Center in Camden.[3] By acquiring Wackenhut's Correctional Foodservice Management, ARAMARK added an estimated $70 million in annual volume and a client base of 103 facilities to its existing 275 correctional facilities services.[4] In addition, ARAMARK formed strategic joint ventures in Ireland and the United Kingdom with Campbell Bewley Group, the largest food service company in Ireland, and in Chile

ARAMARK Chef Doug Bradley helped coordinate 1.2 million meals for 10,000 athletes from nearly 200 countries during the 2000 Summer Olympic Games in Sydney, Australia. *(Photo by Donald Miralle.)*

with Central Restaurantes. ARAMARK's International Services now managed first-class food and facility services in more than 15 countries, with particularly strong growth in Canada, Belgium, and Germany, and double-digit revenue growth in the United Kingdom and Spain.[5]

A surge in coffee consumption, the hot beverage of choice to keep employees happy and businesses moving, meant a 40 percent increase in coffee business for ARAMARK's Refreshment Services, which in 2000 provided one billion cups of coffee, 400 million servings of soda, and 200 million snacks at 100,000 locations in the United States.[6] "When we partner with our clients to make refreshments part of a more comfortable workplace, the result is happier, more productive employees. We're not just selling coffee, we're providing employee satisfaction," said Richard Wyckoff, former president of ARAMARK Refreshment Services.[7]

Coffee services were an important contract element in June 2000, when the Boeing Company selected ARAMARK to provide food, vending, and coffee services to the company's 103 locations and 200,000 employees around the country.[8] The deal began with a simple e-mail message from Boeing to Jay Leyden, former vice president of sales for

ARAMARK business services. "The folks at Boeing asked if we would come to Seattle for a negotiating session," Leyden said. "In this high-tech world, sometimes there is a gift worth hundreds of millions of dollars on the other side of an e-mail, waiting to be opened."[9]

Landing the contract was particularly important to ARAMARK, given its historic connection to Boeing. Founder Davre Davidson always considered Douglas Aircraft his first workplace customer. Douglas later became McDonnell Douglas, which then became part of Boeing when the two companies merged in 1997. Neubauer was thrilled when ARAMARK landed the Boeing account. "This win is gratifying," he said. "It is built from a long-term partnership that has a great deal of value and historic significance to us."[10]

With sales of $7.3 billion in fiscal year 2000, ARAMARK recorded an all-time high of more than $800 million in new business, while still focusing on organic growth and customer retention. In its 12th Olympic appearance since 1968, ARAMARK recreated its "World Menu" and served 1.2 million meals to Olympic athletics and staff in Sydney, Australia. The company also won accolades from both Democrats and Republicans for its services during the national conventions in Los Angeles and Philadelphia.[11]

**2000**

The Boeing Company signs a 10-year agreement with ARAMARK—worth more than $40 million per year—for food, vending, and coffee services to more than 200,000 employees.

**2001**

ARAMARK executives decide to take the company public after 17 years as a private company.

**2000**

ARAMARK provides food service to Olympic athletes in Sydney, Australia; Democrats at the national convention in Los Angeles; and Republicans at the national convention in Philadelphia. *(Photo by Donald Miralle.)*

**September 11, 2001**

Seven ARAMARK employees die during the terrorist attacks in New York City and Washington, D.C. Along with the rest of the country, ARAMARK mourns the loss of life. Employees in both cities respond to the tragedy with remarkable skill and dedication.

ARAMARK "went global" with long-term client Citigroup in 2000, expanding existing food services from nearly 40 Citigroup locations in the United States to the new corporate headquarters in London. The company revamped London operations to meet the dining needs of 4,000 employees, up from the original 400, as Citigroup's employee population increased.[12] ARAMARK also took over management of Citigroup's private boat launch in London, ferrying customers down the Thames River for business meetings. This global partnership, which began in the United States with individual contracts for vending and food service, proved yet another example of ARAMARK's drive to establish "Unlimited Partnerships" with its clients. In a year when revenue growth reached double-digits in the United Kingdom, ARAMARK's 2000 report to employees featured the company's expanding international businesses. The report included photographs of key members of the ARAMARK Citigroup team visiting London landmark Big Ben.[13]

While ARAMARK's Food and Support Services accounted for about 75 percent of sales in eight different sectors, Uniform and Career Apparel and Educational Resources accounted for the remaining 25 percent. Although Educational Resources felt the impact of higher labor and healthcare costs in an overall challenging year, Uniform and Career Apparel reported better results than the year before, delivering a 13 percent jump, thanks to organic and new growth.[14] During the year, Uniform Services acquired Sunshine Uniform Rental of Orlando, Florida, which processes uniforms for more than 6,000 people in the Orlando area.[15] It later added Crescent Laundry, Inc., of Tyler in east Texas, bolstering its presence in the region.[16]

**Changing the Structure**

In January 2001, while ARAMARK prepared to provide the "total fan experience" at both conference championship games for the National Football League at Giants Stadium in northern New Jersey and Network Associates Coliseum in Baltimore, Maryland, corporate executives were gearing up to make a big corporate play of their own.

Company officials had determined that after 17 years as a private company, it was time to return to the public markets. The idea had always been a part of the corporate mindset. "People thought that [I] had a three-year plan, a five-year plan, a seven-year plan, a 10-year plan," Neubauer said. "Frankly,

**November 31, 2001**
ARAMARK purchases the managed services division of ServiceMaster for $800 million.

**2002**
ARAMARK opens a $20 million flagship laundry processing and distribution facility in Burbank, California. It is so modern and technologically advanced that the media labels it "A Plant for the 21st Century."

*FORTUNE*® magazine names ARAMARK America's No. 1 Company for Diversified Outsourcing Services.

**December 11, 2001**
ARAMARK returns to Wall Street under the symbol "RMK."

**2002**
Neubauer announces "Mission One," a strategic initiative designed to accelerate ARAMARK's growth, retain and develop a talented workforce, and ensure unlimited and enduring partnerships with each and every client.

from the beginning we thought we would remain private for an intermediate period of time, and then we would take it public again."[17]

Launching the company IPO "wasn't that hard a decision to make," explained Executive Vice President and Chief Financial Officer Fred Sutherland. He continued:

*We had become a victim of our own success. If you retired or you left the company, typically, the company would then buy back your stock at the appraised value like in any private company. The equity value compounded at 30 percent a year, so it was turning into a big number. If you have 10 or 15 percent of the equity value turning over every year from people who are retiring or leaving, then the amount of money the company had to use to buy back stock from retirees and departures compounded at 30 percent a year. We said, "We're going to reach a point where the balance sheet is just not going to support it all. We have to create an independent market in the stock. We can't have the company as the only buyer." In a nutshell, that's why we went public.*[18]

Employees who invested in the company had realized a phenomenal return on their investment as the stock compounded at a 30 percent annual

Above: ARAMARK provided quick, professional service and tasty refreshments to delegates at the 2000 Democratic National Convention in Los Angeles.

Below right: When the Republicans traveled to Philadelphia for their national convention in August 2000, ARAMARK provided everything from quick lunches to elaborate gala dinners.

Opposite: ARAMARK's Olympic Team at the 2000 Olympic Games in Sydney, Australia, included executive chefs from Japan and Korea. Pictured here are Yukio Onodera (left), Makoto Takano (second from right), and Hirokazu Tokuhara (right) from AIM Services, ARAMARK's affiliate in Japan. Peter Wright (second from left), works for SSL Spotless Services, a leading managed services provider in Australia and joint venture partner with ARAMARK during the Olympics. *(Photo by Donald Miralle.)*

rate over 17 years. "We could see that people retiring from the company would cost us several hundred million dollars a year in the next several years," Neubauer said. "We had to provide a market for it. That's when we started thinking about taking the company public."[19]

Determined that returning to the New York Stock Exchange (NYSE) was the best course of action, company officials began pursuing that goal. Architects of the plan worked hard to achieve a new capital structure that would preserve the company's entrepreneurial approach to business.

Ultimately, they concluded, the total number of shares offered to the public would be less than 20 percent of its outstanding shares. From this initial public offering, or IPO, ARAMARK expected to raise about $600 million.

With the company going public, one concern was how financial analysts would classify ARAMARK. Was it a business service company or a food service company? "It wasn't totally clear who should cover the company from an analyst perspective, or in terms of investors," said Chris Gutek, analyst for the business services sector at Morgan Stanley. "It didn't get as much attention as it would have if it had been a clearer fit for one type of portfolio versus another or one type of analyst versus another."[20]

On the positive side, Gutek pointed out, investors recognized that ARAMARK had "relatively modest economic exposure. It is more of a defensive growth business as opposed to a cyclical growth business. The business also generates a significant amount of money. Back in late 2001, with a weak economic environment, investors' preferences were shifting significantly away from growth companies toward more defensive, revenue-generating companies like ARAMARK."[21]

On July 17, 2001, ARAMARK filed a registration statement with the Securities and Exchange Commission (SEC) for an IPO of ARAMARK common stock to be listed on the NYSE. A few hours later, Neubauer presented the news to 196 members

After ARAMARK purchased the managed services division of ServiceMaster for $800 million, Neubauer met with representatives of both companies to discuss details of the acquisition.

of ARAMARK's Executive Leadership Council who had traveled to Philadelphia from across the United States, Canada, and Europe. Corporate insiders admitted that the announcement was presented in a "dramatic fashion."[22]

In the ballroom of a local hotel, Neubauer stood on stage, positioned in front of a multi-colored backdrop that proclaimed, "Restaging the Dream." As he described ARAMARK's decision to go public, an enthusiastic Neubauer emphasized that this step represented "the next chapter for ARAMARK." He gave full credit to the ARAMARK team:

*Make no mistake about it. You made this possible. All the work, the sacrifice, the sweat, and the tears that you and ARAMARK employees have shed on behalf of our clients, our customers, and our partners, have brought us together today. We built on the dreams and deeds of Davre Davidson and Bill Fishman, and thousands upon thousands of our predecessors. Now, we are beginning the next chapter.*[23]

**Unforeseen Events**

After the July 17th announcement, ARAMARK and its executives went into the "quiet period" required by the SEC after a company announces that it is making a public offering. In the midst of preparing for the IPO, Neubauer accepted a phone call that would dramatically change the company's future.

Neubauer learned that ServiceMaster was selling its managed services division. Jonathan Ward, the new president and CEO of ServiceMaster, wanted to know if ARAMARK was interested. Fred Sutherland could hardly believe the irony of the timing:

> We had conversations with ServiceMaster senior management for a decade about buying their managed services businesses or merging our food business and their managed services business. We got to know them pretty well, but it had never happened. Then they changed the CEO and the new CEO told Joe, "We're going to sell this business. I just wanted you to know. I know you're interested in it." Joe said, "Well, could you wait six months? I'm in the middle of an IPO." They said "No, I don't think so."[24]

After years of courting ServiceMaster, ARAMARK couldn't walk away from the opportunity to buy the company's managed services division. According to Andrew Kerin, then president of ARAMARK Facility Services Group, the acquisition would position ARAMARK as not only one of the world's leading food service companies but also the leading facility services company. The addition of ServiceMaster's 1,400 managed services partnerships under the ARAMARK banner would represent the crowning moment in the company's facility services evolution. The acquisition promised to strengthen ARAMARK's ability to expand to multiple services. "We are accelerating our growth as a managed services company," Kerin said.[25]

According to Neubauer and Sutherland, the chance to acquire the ServiceMaster division surfaced just as ARAMARK was a third of the way into the IPO planning and had already filed a registration statement with the SEC. "We basically accommodated into the process an $800 million acquisition, which had a big impact on the IPO," Sutherland said. "The ServiceMaster acquisition closed two or three weeks before the IPO closed. When we bought it, there was no assurance the IPO would happen. We borrowed the money to finance it under the assumption that the IPO may or may not happen."[26]

Since the Illinois-based company with more than 1,400 clients in the healthcare, education, and business sectors didn't want any stock in the transaction, ARAMARK had to fund the entire deal. Just two days after meeting with long-standing financial partner JPMorgan, Neubauer had a commitment for the financial backing he needed. Both the speed and the size of the deal were staggering. It would be the largest acquisition ARAMARK had ever made, a turn of events that Neubauer called "historic."[27]

As news of the proposed transaction hit the streets, it created an exceptional buzz, not only because it surfaced in the middle of ARAMARK's IPO. The ServiceMaster managed services division was considerably larger than ARAMARK's facility services. According to Lynn McKee, executive vice president of human resources at ARAMARK: "We had a $200 million-plus facilities company, and we were acquiring a billion-dollar facilities company."[28]

**September 11, 2001**

The company's perspective on IPOs and acquisitions changed abruptly on the morning of September 11, 2001, after the horrific terrorist attacks on New York City and Washington, D.C. Dozens of ARAMARK employees found themselves in the middle of the attacks on the World Trade Center and the Pentagon. "Thousands more were nearby," ARAMARK officials wrote. In a move that corporate officials labeled "compassion amidst catastrophe," ARAMARK employees in both cities and in locations up and down the East Coast reached out to others during and after the attacks of September 11 and "stepped up to help."[29] In a special message to his employees, an emotional and deeply moved Neubauer explained what that meant:

> They were risking their lives to save children; they were helping transport people away from danger; they were feeding and clothing

# EXTENDING FACILITIES SERVICES SOLUTIONS

WHEN ARAMARK ACQUIRED THE MANaged services division of ServiceMaster in late 2001, it represented the largest acquisition in the corporation's history. The addition of ServiceMaster's 1,400 managed services partnerships represented a capstone in the company's facilities services evolution. It confirmed that ARAMARK, long renowned as an excellent food service company, could also provide excellent facilities services. For ARAMARK, facilities services include everything from plant operations and energy management to support services for business, education, healthcare, corrections, and recreation clients. The company works closely with clients to efficiently maintain and operate their facilities, lower their operating costs, and provide high-quality support services, allowing companies to focus on managing their core activities.[1]

ARAMARK's facilities services capabilities expanded dramatically in the mid-1990s when it hired Andrew Kerin as senior facilities executive.[2] According to Kerin, the history of ARAMARK's facilities management services began in earnest

with the 1994 acquisition of the Harry M. Stevens Company, a well-known sports entertainment food concessionaire with a lesser-known facilities services component. A year after the Stevens acquisition, ARAMARK entered into a mutual agreement with General Motors (GM) to train GM facilities personnel and manage the staff. ARAMARK eventually bought out GM interests and named the venture ARAMARK Industrial Services. The company also acquired Diversified Facilities Services, a small Atlanta company that provided maintenance and operation services for corrections facilities, a field that would grow from $120 million in 1995 to nearly $500 million by 2005.

In 1998, ARAMARK acquired Facilities Resource Management (FRM), a small business specializing in higher education, with 30 clients and revenues of $25 million. After these four acquisitions, ARAMARK organized an official facilities services division in 1999. Frank Mendicino, who worked for FRM during the ARAMARK acquisition, recalled:

*In the late 1990s, ARAMARK began making facilities commitments. We were on the forefront of the new frontier in facilities services opportunities, and we acquired FRM for its talent, not its market share. It was one of the last small facilities companies with market position and capac-*

Left: ServiceMaster company employees listen as Neubauer describes how the two companies will integrate.

Opposite: Neubauer speaks to a room full of former ServiceMaster employees. He explains how the company's 1,400 managed services partnerships will now operate under the ARAMARK banner.

*ity, and we viewed it as a professional opportunity to take success on a small scale and accelerate it on a much larger scale.*[3]

The ServiceMaster acquisition continued the trend in 2001. According to Kerin, ARAMARK had long wanted to acquire the managed services division of the company. John Babiarz, president of ARAMARK facilities services during the ServiceMaster acquisition, described the transition:

*As an organization, we recognized the importance of capturing the hearts and minds of people by being honest about the differences and similarities and being very methodical. ... We spent time meeting with ServiceMaster managers, both before and after the acquisition. I think the open communication created a knowledge base for the ServiceMaster employees. It*

*also helped us realize who we were, what we believed in, and why we would create a better organization by working together.*[4]

The acquisition and integration of the two companies resulted in facilities services to nearly 2,000 clients under the name ARAMARK ServiceMaster Facilities Services. Mendicino assisted in planning the acquisition. The arrangement succeeded because of ARAMARK's efforts to combine the two companies, as Mendicino explained:

*Many people approached the acquisition with great thoughtfulness and respect for the business culture of ServiceMaster, and for the individuals within both companies. We achieved true integration. ARAMARK did not manage ServiceMaster as a separate entity. The organizations integrated completely with great success. We focused tremendously on making sure that we built trust and credibility with our employees and our clients. Because of our planning and commitment, we lost very few clients and employees during the restructuring. We delivered on our promises. The cultures were different, but there were fundamental similarities in quality of service. That's part of why it has worked so well.*[5]

ARAMARK finalized the ServiceMaster acquisition on November 30, 2001, and the company named Kerin president of the new $1.2 billion division. "This acquisition establishes ARAMARK as a leading provider of support services and enables us to extend our specialized facilities service capabilities in the United States and internationally," explained Joe Neubauer. "In doing so, we strengthen our ability to expand existing partnerships and offer total managed services solutions to our customers in the healthcare, education, and business sectors."[6]

In March 2002, ARAMARK announced that Detroit Public Schools and Pfizer had expanded their long-term food service partnerships to include facilities services. "This is an example of how we can provide broader managed services solutions to long-standing clients," Neubauer said.[7]

Above: During the 9–11 crisis, the cafeteria at St. Vincent's Catholic Medical Center provided free food for staff, patients, and volunteers. The ARAMARK team served three to four times more meals than usual.

Right: ARAMARK donated more than 6,000 meals to support "Remembrance and Reflection," a memorial service held at Jersey City's Liberty Park on September 23, 2001.

Rich Salinardi, general manager of food, beverage, and retail for ARAMARK sports and entertainment services, was among those lost in the tragedy. He and his team worked at the Top of the World restaurant on floor 107 of the World Trade Center, South Tower. On the morning of September 11, they were preparing the restaurant for its normal 9:30 opening. From survivor accounts, Salinardi, Giann Gamboa, Luis Lopez, Victor Barbosa, and Evelyn McKinnedy saw the plane hit the first building and began to work their way down to escape. McKinnedy made it to the first floor and was not seen again. Salinardi, Gamboa, Lopez, and Barbosa were last seen together around the 78th floor. "Rich had an opportunity to get on an elevator at the top," said Joe DeFelice, district manager of sports and entertainment services. "Instead,

rescue workers around-the-clock; they were setting up triage centers for the injured; they were offering food and shelter to hundreds of displaced air passengers in Canada; and they were providing counseling to people who witnessed the attacks.[30]

Soon after the attacks, ARAMARK officials learned some terrible news. While all of their coworkers in Washington were reported safe, seven of their colleagues had been killed in the tragedy in New York City. Their names were Tatyana Bakalinskaya, Victor Barbosa, Mirna Duarte, Giann Gamboa, Luis Lopez, Evelyn McKinnedy, and Richard Salinardi. A special issue of *The Mark*, a publication of news and information for ARAMARK employees, described their stories of heroism, tragedy, and loss:[31]

*he said, 'I'll take the next one. I want to go down with my employees.'"*

*     *     *     *

*Michael Molnar's team was serving breakfast at seven sites in the Pentagon when the plane crashed. "We're located in areas that weren't affected by the blast," said Molnar, general manager of ARAMARK business services. All of Molnar's team, over 180 employees, quickly evacuated to safety. By 7 A.M. the next day, about 65 were back, cleaning up, and preparing for breakfast. Molnar's team offered continental breakfast in the morning, served 5,000 people for lunch, and handled requests for meals to go. "Those 65 people went into a building that was still on fire," said Jay Einspanier, regional vice president of business services. "Think about that."*

*     *     *     *

*Shirley Allen, director of work/life partnerships, oversaw child care at the Pentagon. She heard an explosion and saw smoke rising from the building. "I ran from my office and started the evacuation," she recalled. "The staff did beautifully, and the children were fantastic even though they were rushed out of the center among hundreds of running people. The children were calm because our teachers stayed calm." Once everyone was safely evacuated, Shirley went back in, made sure no one had been left behind, and grabbed emergency paperwork while Assistant Director Seneca Moore managed the evacuation process outside. "The professionalism of Shirley and her team is beyond words," said District Manager Gwen Simmons, who provided counsel and support to Allen by cell phone both during and after the attack. "So many parents have told us how grateful they are."*

*     *     *     *

*By midday on September 11, the ARAMARK refreshment services team at Long Island Market Center determined that two of its employees were missing: Mirna Duarte and Tatyana Bakalinskaya. The next day, despite fear and the harsh reality of personal and professional losses, they returned to work and turned their efforts toward support, heal-*

ARAMARK refreshment services at Long Island Market Center in New York provided supplies for relief workers and clients affected by the tragedies of September 11, 2001.

*ing, and recovery. "Like so many others, our people wanted to do anything they could to assist in the rescue efforts," said Gregg Case, group manager of refreshment services. "The emotional strain of the loss of friends and relatives linked with the logistical challenges of supporting customer needs has made this a very trying time. Our people have found strength in one another and were able to develop a very solid game plan in the face of absolutely tragic events."*

**Returning to Work**

In the aftermath of September 11, Wall Street and all financial markets shut down for four days. The impact of the events on that September day would forever haunt the families of thousands of men and women who lost their lives, and its effects on businesses and the financial markets would linger for a long time. "It wasn't just the four days when the New York Stock Exchange was closed," Sutherland said. "IPOs and the capital markets were in an uproar. There is normally a steady stream of IPOs, and that stream stopped. In fact, we were the first significant IPO after September 11."[32]

# THE AFTERMATH OF TRAGEDY

WITHIN HOURS OF THE SEPTEMBER 11, 2001, terrorist attacks, ARAMARK worked "to gather more information about employees as quickly as possible," according to an e-mail from Chairman and CEO Joe Neubauer. At 6:26 P.M., Neubauer announced that, at the Pentagon, all ARAMARK employees as well as all children at the Children's World Learning Center managed by ARAMARK "had been accounted for and were unharmed."[1]

ARAMARK reported that at the time of the attack on the World Trade Center, approximately 40 sports and entertainment services employees were in the South Tower, and a small number of refreshment services employees were in the

Within days of the tragic events, ARAMARK set up a 9–11 Fund to collect donations for the families of the seven ARAMARK employees who perished on that terrible September day. Pictured are (from left) Leia Latham, Michael Monge, and Maija Bonebrake, students at the Children's World Learning Center in Governor's Ranch, Colorado.

North Tower. Most were accounted for, but ARAMARK continued "seeking information on the others." The husband of an employee was a passenger on one of the planes that crashed in New York City. She was one of several employees who lost a relative that day. As Neubauer stressed in an e-mail update, "our thoughts and prayers go out to her and all employees in this difficult time."

Approximately 30 business services employees were across the street in Building 7 of the World Trade Center, which collapsed during the evening of September 11. All were accounted for and one remained hospitalized. Employees at ARAMARK's other client locations in lower Manhattan were uninjured.[2] As ARAMARK diligently sought information about its missing employees, the company worked around the clock to provide services and compassion in the midst of the catastrophe. ARAMARK employees reached out during and after the attacks of September 11 to help others in this time of crisis.

Two weeks after the attack, seven ARAMARK employees were still missing. On Monday, September 24, 2001, Neubauer issued the following statement:

*No one has been discovered alive in the rubble since September 12, the day after the attacks. Although all hope is not lost for our seven missing men and women, it is severely diminished. That makes this the single most difficult communication I've had to issue in my 18 years as CEO of this company. Not only are these men and women beloved by their families, they are treasured colleagues. They are dreamers and doers like the rest of us.*[3]

Mirna Duarte and Tatyana Bakalinskaya, two of the seven still missing, worked as refreshment services attendants for ARAMARK client Marsh & McLennan, which occupied floors 93 through 100 in the North Tower. The other five— Giann Gamboa, Evelyn McKinnedy, Victor Barbosa, Luis Lopez, and general manager Richard Salinardi—were employees of the sports and entertainment division and worked on the 107th floor of the South Tower at the Top of the World restaurant. They saw the plane hit the North Tower and tried to escape the building. As reported in *The Mark*, McKinnedy made it to the first floor but was never seen again.

Salinardi, Gamboa, Lopez, and Barbosa were last seen together on the 78th floor. ARAMARK employees reported that Salinardi had an opportunity to get on an elevator near the top, but declined. Neubauer observed that Salinardi "sacrificed his own life to ensure as many of his people as possible made it to the elevators. He is every bit as much of a hero as the four courageous men who stormed the cockpit of United Airlines Flight 93."[4]

Within days, ARAMARK set up a September 11 fund to collect donations for the families of the seven ARAMARK employees lost in the tragedy. The company continued to provide assistance to the community during and after the attacks. At Ellis Island, ARAMARK sports and entertainment employees supplied ice, bottled water, sandwiches, and clothing to evacuated employees of the Coast Guard, New York Police Department, Federal Bureau of Investigations, and National Park Service. ARAMARK healthcare support services at St. Vincent's Hospital set up temporary patient treatment areas and worked to ensure adequate food supplies were available.

Employees worked around the clock at New York's Shea Stadium and the Meadowlands Sports Complex to provide breakfast, lunch, and dinner to emergency personnel while the stadiums were used as deployment centers for firefighters and police officers. Galls, Inc., an ARAMARK company, donated public safety supplies and emergency medical equipment to the New York disaster area. ARAMARK work apparel and uniform services donated hard hats, rainwear, and gloves, as well as thousands of other emergency service products, and washed approximately 2,000 pounds of clothing a day for relief workers. The campus services division at New York University, with help from students and volunteers, served dinner for 3,000 at the rescue and recovery site. At the Pentagon, ARAMARK business services and correctional services from the Arlington County Detention Center in Virginia provided thousands of meals for relief workers.[5] "I have always believed our people are at their absolute best when conditions are at their absolute worst," Neubauer said.[6]

Neubauer, surrounded by members of the ARAMARK leadership team, shakes hands with Richard Grasso, chairman and CEO of the NYSE, in celebration of the company's return to the public markets.

In early October, ARAMARK and ServiceMaster announced publicly that they had an acquisition agreement. The deal closed the last day of November, just 11 days before ARAMARK returned to the public equity markets.

Lynn McKee recalled that the process of integrating ServiceMaster and ARAMARK "was an interesting one from the standpoint of two different, very disparate cultures. ... This was an enormous change for that organization."[33] She continued:

*It was different than what usually occurs. You had people in the organization that were focused on, "How are we going to merge these two cultures?" ... They were accustomed to their culture ... and they were the larger of the two facilities businesses. What we had to do very early on was symbolically make some changes there to say, "We like the culture of ARAMARK. We need you to adapt to our culture rather than ARAMARK adapt to your culture."[34]*

Both ServiceMaster employees and long-standing customers felt apprehensive about the ARAMARK purchase. However, John J. Lynch III, who worked for St. Luke's Episcopal Health System in Houston, Texas, when ServiceMaster was acquired, recalled the transition went smoothly and without interruptions. "It was very transparent," Lynch said.[35]

When Lynch later took over as CEO of Main Line HealthCare System based in Philadelphia, he was able to experience ARAMARK's facilities management services and food services firsthand. When the various hospitals in the Main Line HealthCare System competed to see who could throw Lynch the best Texas-style barbeque, he was very impressed with ARAMARK's food service and presence. "They don't flaunt the ARAMARK name," said Lynch. "They flaunt the hospital name that they're associated with. At Bryn Mawr, you think of the Bryn Mawr food service operation, and at Paoli, you think it's Paoli. The consistency of the quality and service was felt across all the institutions."[36]

### ARAMARK Returns to Wall Street

On December 11, 2001, 11 days after the ServiceMaster acquisition, ARAMARK became one of only 83 companies to go public during the slowest year for IPOs since 1990. After 17 years as a private company, ARAMARK was poised to return to the NYSE with a public offering expected to raise more than $650 million. Before ringing the opening bell, Neubauer took the podium with Richard Grasso, chairman and CEO of the NYSE; William Johnston, president and chief operating officer of the NYSE; and Officer AnnMarie Moloney of the New York Police Department. They sang "God Bless America" during a ceremony marking the three-month anniversary of the September 11 terrorist attacks. At 9:30 A.M. a tearful Neubauer, flanked on both sides by his senior managers, rang the opening bell. Moments later, ARAMARK was back on the NYSE, represented by the symbol "RMK."[37]

The RMK stock was initially offered at $23 per share. At 10:01 A.M. it traded for the first time at $26.[38] At the end of the day, the stock closed at $25—about 10 percent above the offering price. The attractive price reflected ARAMARK's extensive marketing of the IPO, including more than 70 meetings with investment firms in 17 cities in the United States and Europe. It was a notable achievement during a time marked by uncertainty in the political system, the events of September 11, a bull market that was quickly losing steam, the warnings of a fast-approaching recession, and what *Forbes* called a "stone-cold IPO market."[39] Sutherland considered the timing of the ARAMARK IPO as prudent:

*We were a very appropriate company to go public because if you look at the years before 9–11, which were dominated by the Internet bubble, we were growing at 6, 7, or 8 percent a year. We weren't worth 150 times last year's losses, and we weren't a seller of airline tickets with a market capitalization greater than every airline in the free world. After 9–11, IPO investors were interested in real companies with real cash flow and real operations. We were perfect. It actually worked out well. I think the SEC pushed us through. It was a large IPO, so we were a good company to go.*[40]

Immediately after the first trade, Neubauer pledged 2,500 ARAMARK shares to Big Brothers Big Sisters of America, one of ARAMARK's Share Opportunity partners—part of ARAMARK's corporate philanthropy focus to help the next generation build their skills through mentoring, literacy, and skills-building.[41]

After a round of media interviews, ARAMARK hosted a recognition luncheon for New York–area employees in honor of their extraordinary service on September 11. By the time the ARAMARK team returned to Philadelphia that evening, more than 400 shareholders and corporate leaders had gathered in the Pennsylvania Convention Center to take part in a "celebration that's been 17 years in the

The Main Line HealthCare System, which is serviced by ARAMARK, includes Bryn Mawr Hospital, a full-service teaching hospital located in the western suburbs of Philadelphia. Bryn Mawr Hospital's state-of-the-art technology and highly trained medical professionals offer both compassion and clinical expertise.

making," said Neubauer. To commemorate the day, ARAMARK managers received reversible bull/bear puppets, which Ray Soria of ARAMARK Healthcare Support Services tucked inside his suit pocket with the bull face looking out for most of the evening. Neubauer spoke to the enthusiastic crowd:

*Now our challenge is to seize our opportunities, to ensure a future that's even greater. It's all out there for us. I can feel it. This day brings us another step closer to our dream of becoming the world leader in managed services.*[42]

The public offering officially closed on December 14, 2001, with ARAMARK selling 34.5 million shares to make the company approximately 20 percent publicly owned. At the time, ARAMARK owner–managers and benefit plan participants held roughly 75 percent of the company's outstanding shares, with stock directly owned by about 6,500 employees and indirectly by another 15,000 employees through retirement plans.[43]

### Familiar Goals

After 17 years as a private company, ARAMARK's first full year as a publicly owned company did not change its philosophy or direction. The corporate staff remained in Philadelphia, while the majority of the company's 200,000 employees worked throughout the world in more than 1,200 business, industry, and government locations;

1,200 hospitals, long-term care facilities, and assisted living communities; 600 Children's World day care centers; 350 college cafeterias; 324 correctional facilities; 200 laundry plants and clothing factories; and 65 public-arena food concessions, convention centers, national and state parks, and leisure attractions.[44] In addition, Neubauer described the acquisition of ServiceMaster Management Services as "transformational," and proudly announced that "our facility services capabilities are now equal to our long-standing competencies in food service."[45]

The company devoted to providing "Unlimited Partnership" continued to advance itself through innovations and acquisitions designed to provide more service solutions for its clients and customers than ever before. Innovations ranged from new contents for vending machines, to increased services for patients, to the opening of a new state-of-the-art industrial plant for processing laundry. One example is "Viva El Sabor" ("The Flavor Lives On"), a new ARAMARK vending program launched in 2001 and expanded in 2002, which provided popular Hispanic foods and beverages for vending machines in areas of the United States with growing Hispanic populations.[46]

In addition, at more than 150 hospitals, ARAMARK Healthcare Support Services introduced a new program called World Class Patient Service that sought to enhance the patient's experience and satisfaction with support services. Another innovation was the ARAMARK Uniform Services $20 million flagship plant in Burbank, California. Labeled "A Plant for the 21st Century" by the media, the new

Left: Neubauer pledges 2,500 shares to Big Brothers Big Sisters of America, one of ARAMARK's Share Opportunity partners. On hand were (left to right) Michael Lewis, vice president of finance and administration for Big Brothers Big Sisters; Brian Scollard, a "big brother" in New York, and his "little brother" Laurence; Jeanette Neubauer, Neubauer's wife; Neubauer; and William Johnston, president and chief operating officer for NYSE.

Opposite: After 17 years as a private company, ARAMARK returned to the public market on December 11, 2001. Neubauer (center) and his senior managers celebrate after ringing the opening bell. *(Photo courtesy of NYSE Media Photo Group.)*

laundry processing and distribution facility includes technology so modern, environmentally sensitive, and employee-friendly that one magazine review noted it "makes you want to drop off your résumé."[47]

Although any acquisition now seemed small compared to the acquisition of ServiceMaster, ARAMARK continued to make acquisitions to build on the company's leadership position in food services, conference center management, and hospital clinical equipment maintenance. In June 2002, ARAMARK bought Harrison Conference Centers for approximately $55 million. The purchase included 14 conference centers and various university hotels from Hilton Hotels Corporation. Renamed ARAMARK Harrison Lodging, the division now managed "anything from a 38-room inn to a 990-room full-fledged conference center and everything in between," said Rory Loberg, former president of Harrison Lodging. He worked for top competitor Marriott Corporation for 18 years before joining ARAMARK. "I would say ARAMARK is much more customized. It really takes a look at each individual piece of business as its own

entity and tries to implement the standards, processes, and systems that best satisfy the customer, client, and users. As we say in our industry, 'we're very non-cookie-cutter oriented.'"[48]

**International Innovation**

With nearly a third of ARAMARK's workforce now based outside the United States, the company worked diligently to provide international innovation as well.[49] With International Food and Support Services operating in 17 countries in 2002, Mike Cronk, executive vice president of the division, noted that "our innovation knows no borders. That is why clients around the world rely on us for solutions that will help them succeed."[50] Some examples of ARAMARK's global entrepreneurial spirit included:

• Food kiosks introduced by ARAMARK Germany in the sports and entertainment market in the mid-1990s, modeled after stadium and arena partnerships in the United

States. An article in *Forbes* noted that "German sports spectators used to wait in long lines at the stadium concession counter. ARAMARK came along, and now Heinrich can get a bratwurst and beer in his seat in stadiums from Hamburg to Nuremberg;"[51]

- "Saborea Tu Mundo" ("Taste Your World") program, serving more than 18,000 children in 90 schools in Spain through ARAMARK Spain's 15 school partnerships;

- AIM Services, ARAMARK's joint venture partner in Japan since 1976, which continued the previous year's launch of a new patient food service management program called SelectService® at the Kitasato Institute Medical Center Hospital in Japan. According to Takeshi Misawa, AIM manager, "It's clear Japanese patients appreciate the right to choose their meals just prior to delivery."

ARAMARK pushed abroad and went head-to-head with its two larger global rivals, Compass Group and Sodexho Alliance. "Three isn't a crowd to ARAMARK in the global race to service just about anything that a company, campus, or event needs to have done," noted *Forbes Global* in 2002, pointing out that only 14 percent of ARAMARK's revenue comes from overseas, an area the company considers ripe for outsourcing growth.[52] While ARAMARK

was No. 3 overseas, business writers in both *Forbes* and *BusinessWeek* consistently pointed out one of the advantages that makes ARAMARK a force to be reckoned with on the international playing field. With revenues approaching $8.8 billion in 2002, a 13 percent increase over 2001 and a 5.5 percent return on assets, ARAMARK "consistently posts higher profit margins than rivals Compass Group and Sodexho Alliance."[53]

While *Forbes Global* cautioned that "a big obstacle for ARAMARK is the lack of partnership and acquisition opportunities in Europe," company officials remained optimistic and globally farsighted. "South America is an area where we will continue to expand our presence very quickly," John Zillmer, ARAMARK's president of food and support services, told *Forbes*. "We're looking for opportunities in emerging markets on a very active basis."[54]

### Accolades and Challenges

As the company moved out of the post-IPO phase and became accustomed to operating as a public company, there were some changes. Chris Malone, hired in 2002 as senior vice president of marketing, noticed right away that ARAMARK "required a complex approach to marketing." He explained:

*The company was in the process of trying to shift toward more balance between decentralization and centralization, and it is going through a real cultural adolescence in that regard. ... There are many practices that are not as well established in our company that you might find at other FORTUNE® 500 companies of a similar size and age.*[55]

ARAMARK's unique public, then private, then back to public business culture did not keep it from being recognized as one of the top companies in the country. In the spring of 2002, *FORTUNE*® magazine ranked ARAMARK among America's 50 Most Admired Companies and proclaimed ARAMARK America's No. 1 Company for Diversified Outsourcing

Martin Spector retired from his position as general counsel, executive vice president, and secretary in 2000 after 33 years with ARAMARK.

# AMERICA'S MOST ADMIRED

IN 2002, ARAMARK ACHIEVED A PRES-tigious milestone. After being rated in the top three every year since 1998, ARAMARK ranked No. 1 for the first time in the outsourcing services category in FORTUNE® magazine's list of America's Most Admired Companies.[1] ARAMARK also ranked in the top 50 on FORTUNE® magazine's overall America's Most Admired Companies list.[2]

"This accomplishment proves that our peers recognize our relentless focus on bringing value to our clients every day," said Joe Neubauer. "It is not only an honor, but a testament to the hard work of everyone at ARAMARK."[3]

Every year FORTUNE® magazine's ranks companies based on eight key attributes: innovation, financial soundness, employee talent, use of corporate assets, long-term investment value, social responsibility, quality of management, and quality of products/services. To determine the score, the magazine asks 10,000 executives, directors, and financial analysts to rate the key attributes of companies in their own industry. In 2002, ARAMARK scored first or second in every category.[4]

"These accomplishments are a direct result of ARAMARK's continued focus on using innovation to deliver measurable results to its clients," said Bill Leonard, president and chief operating officer.

Neubauer agreed. "We are extremely proud of our people and their success in creating measurable economic value for our customers," he said. "We have accomplished this by working to build and expand unlimited partnerships with each of our customers."

ARAMARK has worked hard to maintain its reputation. From 2002 to 2007, ARAMARK has continued to consistently place in the top three in its category.[5]

Services. In newspapers and trade magazines around the country, ARAMARK executives celebrated this accomplishment with full-page advertisements that said "Thank You" to two important groups of people: "We thank the 200,000 ARAMARK men and women who serve our customers around the world. And our customers for putting us on the one Most Admired list that matters most … theirs."[56]

In true ARAMARK fashion, the company did not stop there. Declaring that it was time to "take the next step" and reach for "another mountaintop," Neubauer unveiled a plan designed to make ARAMARK the world leader in managed services.

## Mission One

Long-term ARAMARK employees were already accustomed to exceptionally challenging growth campaigns, recalling past campaigns with names like "Mission 10–5," "Everybody Sells," and "Project Growth." However, Mission One was a strategic initiative that stood out from all the rest of these campaigns by putting forward three individual goals:

1) *One in Organic Growth*: To achieve industry-high client retention in every business; to broaden existing partnerships by providing every client with the full benefit of ARAMARK's services; to win more new business annually to achieve 6 to 8 percent organic growth rates each year.
2) *One ARAMARK*: To attract, retain, and develop a diverse, high-performing workforce and work together as a team across our organization.
3) *One Customer at a Time*: To develop stronger and more enduring partnerships with each client, one at a time.

As an example of the growth, client, and corporate goals of Mission One, ARAMARK pointed to its long-standing relationship with Pfizer Global

# TRUSTED FINANCIAL PARTNERSHIPS

WHEN IT COMES TO FINANCIAL PART-nerships, ARAMARK is never fickle. The company has repeatedly turned to the same trusted financial institutions during ambitious company milestones for more than four decades. ARAMARK has worked closely to ensure its relationships with these institutions remain mutually beneficial. For example:

- The Goldman Sachs Group, Inc. and JPMorgan Chase & Co. facilitated the company's return to the public markets in 2001.
- ARAMARK borrowed $800 million for the ServiceMaster transaction from JPMorgan.
- In 1984, when ARAMARK executives undertook the management buyout, Goldman Sachs served as the primary investment banker and JPMorgan led the bank credit team.[1]
- When Automatic Retailers of America, the forerunner of ARAMARK, acquired Slater System, Inc., a much larger manual food service company, MetLife funded the $14.5 million purchase.

Chairman and CEO Joe Neubauer, in the midst of orchestrating ARAMARK's return to Wall Street at the time, leaned heavily on JPMorgan to help coordinate the ServiceMaster acquisition. Neubauer explained:

*That took 20 years of credibility. Even my son, who is in the financial business, was impressed that we could walk in and, two days later, walk out with a commitment letter for $800 million. We said, "We are going to organize the financial aspects because we do not know whether we will be able to go back to the market or not."*[2]

With the IPO on the horizon, Neubauer felt apprehensive about "how well the markets would receive a company that went private for 17 years."[3] Yet, with Goldman Sachs and JPMorgan by his side, Neubauer remained confident:

*It went off very well. The stock was oversubscribed. Every major investor that we talked to, with a few exceptions, participated in the IPO. It was the same group—Goldman Sachs and JPMorgan, as well as Morgan Stanley and Citicorp. We went back to the same people. Loyalty is very important to us. It is a fantastic group. Our reputation is built by our partners.*[4]

Executive Vice President and Chief Financial Officer Fred Sutherland noted that ARAMARK's long-standing partnerships with financial institutions illustrate "how relationship-oriented we are." Jack Curtin, managing director of investment banking at Goldman Sachs, couldn't agree more. Since participating in the management buyout in 1984, Curtin found it surprising that after more than 20 years, the same "architects" of the buyout, Neubauer and Sutherland, were "still running the show."

"They are definitely partners," he said.[5]

When ARAMARK executives took the company private in 1984, Pieter Fisher worked at Goldman Sachs as ARAMARK's lead partner, and Curtin ran Goldman Sachs' fixed-income syndicate. Curtin became involved with ARAMARK when the parties began to finance the $1.2 billion transaction. He recalled the highly unusual deal:

*We focused on high-grade corporate investment debt, and this was the first time that the firm actually underwrote and distributed a high-yield bond deal. It intimidated everybody. … In the end, they were able to generate enough money by manag-*

An ARAMARK flag hangs outside the NYSE, signifying ARAMARK's initial public offering on December 11, 2001. *(Photo courtesy of ©Candace diCarlo.)*

sold a minority stake of 34.5 million Class B shares at $23 each to Goldman Sachs, JPMorgan, and the brokerage affiliates of Citibank and First Union National Bank. Curtin recalled:

*The IPO had an outstanding order book in terms of investors. ARAMARK had ... a great story to tell. They were going public because they needed capital, both to grow the business, and to provide liquidity for the inside shareholders without straining the balance sheet of the company.*[8]

Since ARAMARK went public soon after the tragic events of September 11, 2001, and directly after an $800 million acquisition, many wondered if the IPO would be effective. Curtin felt certain it would succeed. He explained:

*It never felt like it would be a disaster. It is not the kind of business that would fail at the dot-com level. ... On a relative basis, our stocks are better regarded in the fixed-income mark than the equity markets because ARAMARK is viewed as such a stable, well-managed company.*[9]

ing the business carefully and reducing capital expenditures to reduce debt quickly. It worked out well, and ARAMARK has been a big business for the firm over the years.[6]

"The concept made sense," Curtin explained. "As soon as people met Joe and Fred, they were comfortable that they understood the business."[7]

During the restructuring, ARAMARK again turned to Goldman Sachs. For the IPO, ARAMARK

After 30 years with Goldman Sachs, Curtin is one of the top five senior managing directors of the financial industry giant. "I like working with people like Joe and Fred," he said.[10]

And when Neubauer and his investment associates would take the company private yet again in 2006 and 2007, Goldman Sachs and JPMorgan remained at his side.

Julie Jordan (left), concessions manager, and Judy Moline, suite catering manager for ARAMARK Sports and Entertainment Services, helped open Atlanta's Turner Field in 1997.

Research and Development, a global pharmaceutical company that taps into three areas of ARAMARK expertise for food and beverage services, retail management, and facilities services. ARAMARK first partnered with Pfizer at a Brooklyn manufacturing plant in 1948. The partnership grew to include food, beverage, catering, and refreshment services to more than 6,000 Pfizer employees in more than 80 buildings on the Groton campus.

They also depend on ARAMARK to manage Pfizer's retail store, which offers discounted Pfizer products, clothing, and other convenience items. In February 2002, ARAMARK ServiceMaster Facility Services began providing custodial services for the 137-acre campus, as well as technical cleaning for

laboratories. While adding more services, ARAMARK continued to expand its core food business for Pfizer to include one main cafeteria, an express café, three satellite cafés, a Java City specialty coffee kiosk, and two Java City carts, as well as a Starbucks specialty coffee kiosk. When new locations open, ARAMARK will be there, and ARAMARK's revenues at Pfizer have grown from $2 million annually to $12 million.[57]

"Financial markets ebb and flow, but a company that continues to deliver on its promises to its clients and customers over many decades will succeed," Neubauer and Leonard wrote to ARAMARK shareholders in the 2002 annual report. "Opportunity is calling us, and we intend to answer with Mission One."

By the end of the year, ARAMARK executives were already beginning to see the results they wanted and expected from Mission One. Some of these results even made headlines. "ARAMARK Expands 40-Year Partnership with Ford, Adds Facility Services at New Locations," reported Business Wire on November 5, 2002. As the story pointed out, the new agreement called on ARAMARK to provide facility management services to 13 Ford Motor Company parts distribution centers across the United States, in addition to providing food, refreshment, and uniform services to 50 domestic and international Ford locations. Noted Neubauer in the story, "Our expanded relationship with Ford demonstrates ARAMARK's ability to provide a total solution for a long-term partner that has a wide variety of needs."[58]

According to Neubauer, Mission One may seem simple, but it was not a simple goal to achieve. Still, Neubauer remained optimistic about the future. "We have always been at our best when we are climbing tall mountains," he said.[59]

At the Mission One meeting in Las Vegas in 2003, Chairman and CEO Joe Neubauer challenged more than 5,000 ARAMARK managers to aspire to new heights. It was the largest gathering of ARAMARK managers in the history of the company.

## CHAPTER ELEVEN

# REFINING THE CORE BUSINESSES

## 2003–2006

*There are 240,000 ARAMARK employees who touch [the lives of] millions of people every day all around the world and have the chance to make somebody smile. That is unique.*

—Andrew Kerin, president,
ARAMARK Domestic Food,
Hospitality, and Facility Services

A S ARAMARK GREW, IT ADD-ed more services while continuing to focus on existing relationships. Using its signature systematic and entrepreneurial approach, ARAMARK increased its customer base and provided new programs for specific target groups. By taking advantage of trends in the managed services industry, the company achieved worldwide growth in outsourcing food and facilities management and attracted clients seeking cost-effective solutions for all their outsourcing needs.[1]

ARAMARK executives also continued to focus on new prospects. Concerning the worldwide outsourcing market, Chairman and CEO Joe Neubauer wrote in the 2003 annual report:

*Our analysis and experience show that many market segments are still as much as 75 percent "unpenetrated." The opportunities are enormous. We are proud of the efforts of our team, and we thank them. We are 200,000 strong in 18 countries on five continents. Each day we serve our clients in more than 1,800 colleges and school districts, and 1,500 hospital and health facilities, providing services to more than 11 million students, seven million patients, 200 sports and entertainment venues, and thousands of other business locations.[2]*

By definition, service companies all face the same challenge. Without any product to sell, they are essentially selling something equally important but less tangible—service. Relationships with clients are based on trust and built on the promise that the company can deliver better service, satisfied clients, and happier employees, usually at a lower cost.[3]

In the popular business book, *Built to Last: Successful Habits of Visionary Companies*, authors James C. Collins and Jerry I. Porras suggest that lacking items to sell could contribute to the success of companies like ARAMARK. Collins and Porras argue that companies that endure and prosper over time rarely offer innovative products. Instead, the authors note, in successful companies, "the company itself is the ultimate creation" and the result of strong corporate culture and core ideology.[4] When Neubauer took the stage at the Las Vegas Convention Center on the evening of February 11, 2003, he delivered a memorable challenge to more than 5,000 ARAMARK leaders gathered for

At the Ready, Set, Grow! Expo in Las Vegas, ARAMARK Classic Fare Catering attracted considerable attention.

the company's Mission One meeting, the largest gathering of ARAMARK managers in the history of the company:

> *Each and every one of you has the power to change the way we do business. You can take yourselves and ARAMARK to a whole new level of growth and success. You have the power to accelerate our growth and double the size of this company ... by building on existing clients. We are only scratching the surface in many partnerships. There is much more we can do for our clients. There are more services we can offer and more solutions we can provide. Each time we offer a new service or provide a solution, the results are a happier client, a stronger partnership, and growth for you and for ARAMARK. I have one question for you. Are you ready?*[5]

The managers responded with a resounding "Yes!" as Michael Hoepke, general manager for ARAMARK Sports and Entertainment Services, recalled. "With 5,000 people here, you can really see the power of ARAMARK," he said. "This really builds energy and ignites you to go back to your team and say, 'Let's go out there and make it happen.'"[6]

### Mission One Momentum

During the first full year of the Mission One initiative, the national economy struggled, and ARAMARK stock hit a 52-week low of $18.39 a share in October 2002. However, revenues for 2003 increased by 13 percent to $9.4 billion and the stock rebounded to $23 a share by April 2003. The company realized diluted earnings per share of $1.34, compared to $0.90 in 2001 and $1.25 in 2002. One newspaper called ARAMARK "an industry leader" and reported that "ARAMARK's sales and profits have continued to rise as outsourcing becomes popular as an effective way [for companies to manage costs and receive outstanding service]."[7]

Critical Mission One initiatives included expanding unlimited partnerships by providing more services to existing clients. In some cases, this meant convincing clients to consider outsourcing historically in-house services. Bob Carpenter, president of ARAMARK Healthcare, explained:

> *Part of our challenge at ARAMARK is to continue going after services companies traditionally think of as part of their core business and persuade them that we can help them find better ways to do things.*

**2003**

ARAMARK brings more than 5,000 leaders to the Las Vegas Convention Center for a Mission One conference. It is the largest gathering of ARAMARK leaders in the history of the company.

Mission One initiatives contribute to nearly $850 million in new business.

**2004**

In January, the Board of Directors elects William Leonard as CEO. Later, Leonard steps down and Neubauer returns as CEO of ARAMARK.

ARAMARK serves two million meals at the 2004 Summer Olympic Games in Athens.

**2003**

ARAMARK signs extended contracts with Citigroup and the University of Delaware. The company also signs new contracts with the United Nations, NATO, and the 2004 Summer Olympic Games in Athens, Greece.

**2004**

ARAMARK introduces several new healthy menu items with more nutritional information. The company also launches two campaigns tailored to the lifestyles and eating preferences of children and teenagers.

*The main focus of Mission One is to leverage our home field advantages, including our business relationships, our frontline managers, and our teams. They already understand their business' particular environment. ... There are 10 to 15 different services that these customers outsource every single day, and we normally only have one to three of them at best. We're excited about that as far as the potential of where we can expand our services.*[8]

Bill Leonard, former president and chief operating officer, and John Zillmer, former president of Food and Support Services, credited the ServiceMaster acquisition with generating organic growth from new customers and expanding services to existing customers in both food and facility management. "Buying ServiceMaster made us a world-class facilities management company, and it also gave us many more opportunities to develop the food service business," said Leonard. Zillmer agreed, explaining that the ServiceMaster acquisition "created an organization capable of delivering solutions that are more wide-ranging than those of any of our competitors."[9]

ARAMARK's Mission One campaign focused employees on embracing the company's role as a "solutions" provider, not merely a "service" provider. According to Andrew Kerin, president, ARAMARK Domestic Food, Hospitality, and Facility Services:

*When you are a single service provider, you don't have any peripheral vision because you don't need it. When you try to migrate toward a solutions provider, peripheral vision is everything. You need to anticipate what institutions, clients, and customers need. ... That is part of the evolution of ARAMARK. Mission One is a great approach because it is a manifestation of concrete objectives stating that we are a solutions provider doing a great job.*[10]

Chris Hackem, president, ARAMARK Higher Education, said that all of the company's services on college campuses become a part of the institution: "We are an integral part in delivering the expectations of their institution and a strategic partner and enabler of their vision."[11]

In March 2003, ARAMARK announced it had expanded its 26-year dining services partnership with Barton College to include maintenance, custodial, and groundskeeping services. ARAMARK would provide custodial services for all academic, administrative, and residence buildings at the

**2004**
ARAMARK expands on the international front in the United Kingdom, Chile, Germany, and China, achieving a 28 percent increase in international sales.

**2006**
ARAMARK serves more than three million people at the FIFA World Cup, a four-week international soccer event in Germany.

**2005**
Despite the devastation of Hurricane Katrina, a sagging national economy, and the cancellation of the National Hockey League's 2004–2005 season, ARAMARK exceeds $10 billion in business worldwide, a first for the company.

**2006**
*FORTUNE*® magazine once more ranks ARAMARK No. 1 in its industry.

Wilson, North Carolina, college. The company would also manage all aspects of building maintenance and provide groundskeeping services for Barton's main campus and athletic fields. Additional services included the implementation of a Customer Response Center and a second-shift maintenance crew to alleviate disruptions during classroom and business hours. "We have been extremely pleased with both the corporation and the personnel during our 26-year dining services partnership with ARAMARK," said Gordon Joyner, vice president of administration for Barton College. "We are excited to expand this partnership further."[12]

One of ARAMARK's largest college accounts is the University of Delaware, where the campus services division meets regularly with student represen-

tatives to determine the dining and catering preferences of the university's 20,000 students and 4,000 staff members. "These people have high expectations of the service they receive," said University President David Roselle, PhD, who has worked with ARAMARK since 1989. In addition to demanding good food and a pleasant atmosphere, college residents preferred having food available around the clock. "It was a challenge, and it is one that ARAMARK has met very nicely," Roselle said. "During our relationship with ARAMARK, the company has gone out of its way to make us happy. Any time there have been any questions about the quality of their staff, they have been resolute about having it addressed. There has never been any situation where things were allowed to simmer or were not aggressively addressed. I think that's a hallmark of a good organization."[13]

### Core Business Expansion and Revision

In keeping with its Mission One goals, ARAMARK also signed a new extended contract with Citigroup, a premier financial services company serviced by ARAMARK since 1989.

AIM Services, ARAMARK's joint venture with Mitsui in Japan, specializes in food services, cleaning, and facilities management. It is widely considered one of the most successful joint ventures in Japan between U.S. and Japanese companies. (Photo by LYONS STUDIOS, INC.)

# SUCCESS IN JAPAN

IN 30 YEARS, AIM SERVICES, established in May 1976 as a joint venture between Mitsui & Co. Ltd. and ARAMARK, has grown from a small food service business to a total management services company. Recognized as a leading competitor in Japan's contract food service industry, AIM specializes in food services, cleaning, and facilities management.[1]

Ravi Saligram, president of the international division, considers AIM an incredible achievement for ARAMARK. "For an American and a Japanese company to collaborate and create a company from scratch is an amazing success story," Saligram said. "The relationship between the two companies has endured for a long time, and it keeps getting better and better."

AIM employs 32,000 people and brings in nearly $1.2 billion in revenue each year.[2] "We want AIM to be the No. 1 company in Japan for total management services," said Hisato Ishida, president and CEO of AIM Services. "Each and every employee will take pride in his or her work, and together we will provide services that exceed the expectations of our customers."[3]

Before the AIM Services joint venture, Ishida worked in the food division at Mitsui. He participated in the two-year food service joint venture negotiations between Mitsui and ARAMARK, then known as ARA Services. "I was impressed when Mr. Fishman told us they were pursuing a total management system with their core businesses," said Ishida. "ARAMARK's vision made sense to me. We decided to take ARAMARK's expertise and apply it to the Japanese market."[4]

At first, AIM's territory included China, South Korea, and Taiwan, but the company later pulled back to focus on Japan. From its first project man-

AIM, an important part of ARAMARK's international division, is considered one of the most successful joint ventures in Japan.

aging cafeteria services at Mitsui headquarters in Tokyo, the business grew to embrace food and support services for hospitals, businesses, and schools. AIM also handles total management services for conference facilities, seminar facilities, and company resorts. The company's largest acquisition took place in July 2002 when it purchased one of the largest contract food providers in Japan, Mefos Ltd., for $70 million, or 7.5 billion yen.

Recently, AIM acquired Yamato, an office coffee and tea service company, as part of its efforts to expand its range of services into additional business areas such as corrections services, sports and entertainment, and healthcare management. ARAMARK executives believe AIM has enormous growth potential. "In Japan, food services represent about $35 billion in potential sales," wrote Joe Neubauer in ARAMARK's 2005 annual report.[5]

The joint venture between ARAMARK and Mitsui is widely considered one of the most successful in Japanese history. Hiroshi Ito, Mitsui's senior executive managing officer, explained:

*I think the main factors for our success are ARAMARK's technical and operational expertise in the contract food service industry, along with Mitsui's expertise in Japanese management styles. … I think the specialized functions have been superbly organized. That is why this joint venture has been so successful over such a long period of time.*[6]

"These deep relationships are our main assets," Neubauer said. "Our goal remains to create enduring business partnerships that broaden and deepen over time. Much of our success in 2003 is directly attributed to our Mission One program. ... There are now locations where we provide six, eight, even 10 separate ARAMARK services."[14]

The company achieved a record-high level of nearly $850 million in annualized new business in 2003. During that year, ARAMARK courted some high-profile prospects and won new contracts to serve the United Nations, NATO, and the 2004 Summer Olympic Games in Athens, Greece. ARAMARK expanded faster than ever as it continued to make acquisitions in Europe, Latin America, and Japan as part of its plan to increase its presence in targeted international markets. In September 2003, ARAMARK announced it had acquired Restauracion Colectiva and Rescot, a food service company based in Zaragoza, Spain. The company provided food service to schools, healthcare facilities, and businesses and posted revenues of approximately $25 million in fiscal year 2002.

Left: Hisato Ishida, president and CEO of AIM Services, said, "We intend to be the No. 1 company in Japan for total management services."

Below left: Since 1985, ARAMARK has provided catering and food services to the Philadelphia Flower Show, where viewers are treated to individual exhibits that illustrate outdoor dining, entertaining, and landscaping scenarios. Elaborate outdoor settings, like the one shown here, are a recurring feature of the show.

"This acquisition offers a remarkable opportunity to combine the wealth of knowledge and experience of both companies in the food service sector," said Juan Ameztoy, president, ARAMARK Spain. "We look forward to providing a broader range of managed services to a wider geographic client base."[15]

ARAMARK continued to take advantage of new international and domestic opportunities stemming from two key acquisitions. With Mitsui & Co. Ltd., ARAMARK's joint venture partner in Japan, ARAMARK in 2002 increased its ownership in AIM Services, the No. 2 food service company in the world's second-largest economy. For approximately $37 million in cash, ARAMARK and Mitsui jointly purchased outstanding shares of AIM, which increased each partner's existing ownership interest in AIM to 48.3 percent, for a combined ownership of 96.6 percent. The $800 million acquisition of ServiceMaster in 2001 also provided ARAMARK with many opportunities to expand their service offerings.

In an effort to continue focusing on its core businesses, ARAMARK executives decided that educational and child care services no longer fit in with its mission to become the world leader in food and facilities management, uniforms, and career apparel. In May 2003, the company sold ARAMARK Educational Resources (AER) for $225 million to Knowledge Learning Corporation, one of the largest child care providers in the United States. "This move will enable us to focus on our food and support services as well as our uniform and career apparel business segments," Neubauer said. "We have proven we can build long-term relationships and expand opportunities for growth with each of our clients in these segments. AER can better realize its growth potential by aligning with a company focused exclusively on early education and child care."[16]

**Investing in ARAMARK Employees**

ARAMARK continued its tradition of investing in its employees by providing initiatives such as the Executive Leadership Institute, the Executive Leadership Conference, and the Kaleidoscope Program. In 2003, ARAMARK again invested in its workforce by introducing a unique training program for employees in the Refreshment Services division. The company designed the new program, called ServiceStars, to elevate the role of the company's frontline service providers by shifting focus from sales and operations to sales and services. The program was designed for service technicians, who stock beverage and snack machines and provide coffee and break room supplies for 60,000 businesses worldwide. It focused on customer service skills, such as listening and problem-solving, and it resulted in improved client retention and decreased employee attrition. Richard Wyckoff, former president of ARAMARK Refreshment Services, called it "one of the most important strategic initiatives we've ever implemented."[17]

One consistent element recognized throughout ARAMARK is its ability to select employees who are client-focused. John Babiarz, group president, ARAMARK Healthcare, noted that when ARAMARK turned a 20-year relationship with Evanston Northwestern Healthcare into a comprehensive service contract in early 2004, 600 employees transitioned from the hospital's payroll to that of ARAMARK. "The integration went seamlessly," recalled Babiarz. "Not just for the client, but for their former employees as well. Not one person left."

Babiarz and Evanston Northwestern Chief Operating Officer Jeffrey Hillebrand credited this client-focused approach as the reason all 600 employees at the Chicago-area health system remained. "At a time that could have been filled with stress and uncertainty, those employees knew that ARAMARK wanted them to help that hospital fulfill its mission," said Babiarz. "They felt welcomed. That mattered to them, and it made a real difference to the client. And that is why we strive to be a company where the best people want to work."[18]

ARAMARK's efforts to provide exceptional service and a unique work environment were not going unnoticed. In 2003, *FORTUNE* magazine once again named ARAMARK the No. 1 Most Admired Diversified Outsourcing Services Company. ARAMARK achieved its highest score ever, moving to No. 10 in *FORTUNE* magazine's overall list of Most Admired Companies. ARAMARK also improved in every attribute measured by *FORTUNE* and earned its highest ratings ever in each area. According to surveys, ARAMARK demon-

ARAMARK's presence on British Petroleum's North Sea Strategic Performance Unit has grown from a massive housekeeping program to a complete facilities management service provider, including services for the heli-deck landing crew.

# ARAMARK's 24 Hours

THE ARAMARK EXPERIENCE COMPRISES a wide spectrum of services. The essence of the company is not found in a signature product or process. It is defined by its dedication to clients' missions. A comprehensive consideration of the full spectrum of ARAMARK's professional services in hospitality, food, facilities, and uniforms covers the entire day and night, every day of the week, every week of the year, around the world, at every stage of a person's life.

Andrew Kerin, executive vice president and president of Domestic Food, Hospitality, and Facility Services, takes the long view.

"When you're born in the hospital, we're there, managing many of the non-clinical functions," he said. "You grow and go to elementary school, and we're there doing the grounds, maintaining the facilities, and providing you a nutritious lunch. It's the same with high school and college. Then, when you go into business, we're there as well. If you are admitted into the hospital, or go off the path and end up in a correctional facility, we're there. If you want to go to a convention center, a concert, a ballgame, or a national park, we're in all those places. And when you're ready for a senior living center, we're there as well."[1]

For example, the coffee is already brewing when a baby is born at Evanston Hospital in Illinois, where ARAMARK maintains buildings, transports patients, keeps the operating rooms clean, brews coffee, and serves a meal to the baby's mother as soon as she is rested. On the East Coast, before classes start at the University of Hartford, any number of the Connecticut institution's 7,000 students stop by one of ARAMARK's 12 food service locations or the 3,500-square-foot convenience center for a taste of ARAMARK's branded "Real Food on Campus" concept and that bottomless cup of freshly brewed coffee. In the Midwest, at Kellogg Company in Battle Creek, Michigan, an electrician gears up for another day of production wearing one of ARAMARK's fire-resistant uniforms and protective gear, just one of 20,000 clean uniforms ARAMARK provides every week for Kellogg employees at 11 production sites around the United States. And even though the baseball game is not until that evening, by midday ARAMARK executives at Atlanta's Turner Field are already monitoring the company's innovative Internet ordering system for client suites, just one of the services at nearly 200 facilities managed by ARAMARK Sport and Entertainment Services for nearly 100 million people every year.[2]

### A Snapshot of 2004

Throughout Belgium and Luxembourg, ARAMARK provides coffee, cappuccino, espresso, hot chocolate, tea, and even soup at every Shell Oil gas station. At the British Petroleum (BP) Grangemouth Petrochemical Complex in Grangemouth, Scotland, word of ARAMARK's new portfolio of U.K. food brands—called "Fresh!"—creates a dramatic increase in sales among employees who told ARAMARK they wanted fresher, healthier, more diverse foods.

strated improvements in innovation, employee talent, use of corporate assets, social responsibility, quality of management, financial soundness, long-term investment value, and quality of products and services. "We are extremely proud of the dedication and commitment of our employees and their success in creating greater value for our clients year after year," Neubauer said. "We will build on this achievement and continue to be No. 1 as we work to expand even more opportunities for growth with each of our clients."[19]

### Executive Restructuring

After being courted aggressively by both Delaware and New Jersey officials, ARAMARK decided in December 2003 to remain at 1101 Market Street in

ARAMARK's success at The Concordia, the Washington, D.C., hotel of the International Monetary Fund (IMF), not only introduced guests to such international cuisine as Thai chicken with basil but also led to an expanded ARAMARK partnership that included all dining services at IMF properties.

By mid-afternoon in the Pacific Northwest, a visitor at Olympic National Park in Washington has just finished hiking in the rainforest, one of 14 national and state parks and forests served by ARAMARK for tourists and vacationers across the United States. At the Wharton Executive Education Conference Center, ARAMARK employees have just finished setting up afternoon coffee, tea, and an assortment of still-warm cookies on tables outside the packed conference room, where a panel discussion on business opportunities in Latin America is coming to a close at the University of Pennsylvania.

At Duval County Public Schools in Jacksonville, Florida, ARAMARK ensures that the students in America's 20th-largest school system have great food and well-managed facilities until the bell rings to dismiss the day. The physicians at Mount Sinai Hospital in New York continue to focus on the more than 50,000 patients a year who come here for inpatient treatment, leaving ARAMARK to take care of all environmental services, centralized patient transportation, a centralized call center, laundry cleaning and distribution, and all patient food and retail food operations. And just as the day's last visitors begin to leave Ellis Island in New York Harbor, ARAMARK staff begin to prepare for a special evening event in the Registry Room.

As the lights begin to glow at Oriole Park at Camden Yards, Baltimore, teams of ARAMARK employees prepare for another evening of hungry and thirsty baseball fans, while the KPMG project team in Silicon Valley prepares for a long night of a different sort: a grueling 18-hour day to meet an important deadline, fueled by a critical delivery of fresh coffee, sandwiches, fruit, and desserts from ARAMARK Refreshment Services. Another successful ARAMARK meal service at the Hamilton County Justice Complex in Ohio helps keep inmates fed for another day, a critical factor in running criminal justice, inmate, and rehabilitation facilities. And at one of its 26 elder care centers across the United Kingdom, BetterCare relies on ARAMARK to help create warm, comfortable environments for nearly 2,000 elderly residents, including preparing meals, serving mid-morning coffee and afternoon tea, maintaining the residents' rooms, and delivering laundry.

And although the day is technically over in some parts of the world, ARAMARK's work never really stops. Throughout the night, there are schools, hospitals, airports, conference centers, and peanut-littered stadiums that require cleaning. There are uniforms to wash, press, and deliver for clients as diverse as Wendy's, Goodyear, PepsiCo, and Toyota. There are catering assignments to plan for from Ireland to Chile to Japan, and school lunches to prepare for millions of children and 80 percent of America's top colleges. There are corporate dining rooms to ready for the next day's important meetings. And rest assured there is always an important meeting because ARAMARK's 240,000 employees serve customers in 20 countries, including 40 of the 50 Most Admired Companies as defined by *FORTUNE*® magazine.

As ARAMARK management and employees like to say, "We're here." And they don't just say it. They live it.

Philadelphia, signing a 15-year lease on its 32-story Center City tower. However, while the address at headquarters remained the same, some of the key executives within would change positions.[20]

In January 2004, Neubauer became executive chairman, while President and Chief Operating Officer Bill Leonard became the company's new CEO, a position held by Neubauer since 1984.

Leonard faced the challenge of absorbing several unprofitable business contracts signed in 2003.[21] The company's bottom line suffered in 2004, as reported operating income and net income dropped significantly below 2003 levels.[22]

In September 2004, the ARAMARK Board of Directors named then-Executive Chairman Joe Neubauer as Chairman and CEO, a role he had relinquished in January. The change resulted in a one-time charge that reduced the company's fourth-quarter earnings by approximately $6 million. Leonard stepped down as president and CEO and resigned from the Board of Directors. The company issued a statement explaining the change and thanking Leonard for his 20 years of service. Neubauer, who rarely spoke publicly about the transition, recalled:

*The Board asked me to come back, and I agreed. I remained Executive Chairman because I had a significant investment in ARAMARK. It is more than a financial investment to me. I also have a big emotional investment in the company. I had responsibilities and a sense of duty. Bill is a good man, and the parting was very amicable.*[23]

To many employees, Neubauer's return proved he had remained firmly involved with the company during the transition. "While his role may have changed, from my perspective, Joe's influence never changed," said Frank Mendicino, president, Strategic Assets, Domestic Food, Hospitality, and Facility Services. "The leadership restructuring did not create a disturbance. Joe has such credibility that his transition back was nearly instantaneous."[24]

### High-Profile Progress

ARAMARK provided exceptional food and facility services for several high-profile events in 2004. In Houston, ARAMARK served 3,000 rib eye steaks, 500 pounds of crab cakes, and 9,000 gallons of soda during the Super Bowl at Reliant Park. At the 80th birthday party for former President George H. W. Bush at Minute Maid Park, also in Houston, 5,000 invited guests dined on six buffets represent-

---

Worldwide, ARAMARK's facilities management employees manage 1.8 billion square feet of space, including hospitals, schools, universities, production and office facilities, and sports stadiums.

Left: ARAMARK's innovations in vending technology include single-serve coffee dispensers and cashless vending machines.

Right: Twenty-five ARAMARK chefs prepared special menus for former President George H. W. Bush's 80th birthday celebration at Minute Maid Park in Houston. More than 5,000 invited guests dined on selections from six buffets representing the various stages of Bush's life.

ing various stages of President Bush's life. At the baseball All-Star Game at the same location, a multiple-day event in which the company invited its "All-Star Vendors" to serve the crowd, ARAMARK employees provided 5,400 bags of peanuts to tens of thousands of fans and spent 100 hours cleaning up the peanut shells.

That August, ARAMARK's own Olympic team traveled to Athens, Greece, for the 2004 Summer Olympic Games. "I think this is a once-in-a-lifetime opportunity," said Matt Brown, an ARAMARK food service director at United Health Group. "I mean, this is the Olympics!" Brown served as one of the three executive chefs in the 147,700-square-foot Olympic Village Dining Hall and Kitchen in Athens, the world's largest freestanding temporary food service facility. ARAMARK served two million meals for 24,000 athletes, coaches, officials, and staff.[25]

The 2004 Summer Games, ARAMARK's 13th trip to the Olympic Games, was considered the largest catering deal in Europe, according to the Olympic Organizing Committee.[26] To help win the Athens bid, ARAMARK partnered with Daskalantonakis Group, a local concessionaire, to form ARAMARK Dasko. The well-researched menus reflected the diverse cultures of the athletes attending the games and were sure to feature Greek favorites. Recipes included Senegalese *yassa* (chicken), *moussaka* (eggplant), and *skordalia* (garlic-based dip).[27]

Meanwhile, guided by extensive research into customer preferences, ARAMARK introduced several new offerings designed to meet customer demands in other lines of business:[28]

- ARAMARK created Just4U™, a dining program featuring hundreds of new, healthier menu items with easy-to-understand nutritional information and menu identifiers. Just4U™ helped customers distinguish among low-carb, low-calorie, low-fat, heart-healthy, vegetarian, and vegan dining options. *Food Management* magazine recognized the innovative approach and rewarded it with a "Best Concepts Award."
- In the K–12 sector, ARAMARK studied the nutritional preferences of middle and high school students by surveying 700 families across the country. Based on the results, the company launched two new brands tailored to their lifestyles: the 12 Spot™ for middle school students and the U.B.U. Lounge™ for high school students.
- For uniform clients, ARAMARK identified a growing demand for workplace safety gear and responded with new products like enhanced-visibility vests, fire-resistant uniforms, and steel-toed shoes.

Because they were generated by research and increased knowledge about client needs, ARAMARK's new services, products, and uniform features were well received. Increased customer knowledge contributed to more than just improved services. According to Neubauer, if ARAMARK possessed more client insights than its competitors, then ARAMARK provided an incalculable value to customers and clients. In the 2005 annual report, Neubauer wrote:

*We have a clearer picture of our clients' and customers' needs than at any time in our history. Over the past two years, we have surveyed more than one million customers to better understand their expectations. As a result, our solutions are more robust than ever before. ... Our ability to execute our ideas and deliver measurable value helps us build strong trust relationships with our clients.*[29]

ARAMARK's clients agreed. "The key is that they are proactive," said Zelda Casanova, senior commodity manager for American Airlines. "They don't just wait for us to make requests. Typically, they are ahead of our thinking, and they bring many new ideas to the table. They like to serve, they are easy to work with, and they are very calm. They remain profitable, yet they have helped reduce our costs. They have been a true partner, and they always come up with creative ways to do things."[30]

In the Refreshment Services division, technology innovations created key changes for small-office refreshment solutions. Thanks to the single-cup brewing systems now available, ARAMARK "can bring a very high-quality product to employers that may have small groups of employees in a particular place," said Jack Donovan, former president, Business, Sports, and Entertainment.[31]

Single-cup brewing was the fastest-growing segment in refreshment services in 2005, accounting for 40 percent of coffee sales.

With more than 100,000 points of distribution, ARAMARK-serviced vending machines changed very little over the years. However, after recognizing that many college students rely on credit cards instead of cash, ARAMARK created cashless vending devices.

ARAMARK also helped develop specialty systems at James Madison University and the University of Virginia that allowed students to use their credit

# KEEPING STUDENTS HEALTHY

ARAMARK PROVIDES K–12 STUDENTS IN 420 school districts across the country with 1.7 million meals per day, or 350 million meals per year. After studying the nutritional preferences of "tweens" in grades six through eight and teenagers in grades nine through 12 by surveying 700 families across the country, ARAMARK launched the 12 Spot™ for middle school students and the U.B.U. Lounge™ for high school students in 2005. Both feature new menu items, sophisticated lighting and furniture, and music in a relaxed atmosphere.[1]

Beyond K–12, ARAMARK also offers nutrition education and healthy product promotions—part of the company's "Fresh & Healthy" campaign—at more than 2,000 businesses, college and university campuses, and hospitals where ARAMARK manages food services. The popular program, which is updated quarterly and reviewed by the American Dietetic Association, includes healthier menu promotions, table tents, and a newsletter that educates consumers on a variety of healthy living tips, from the benefits of vitamin-packed autumn vegetables to nutritious make-at-home recipes and heart health. In addition, ARAMARK's award-winning healthier menu program, Just4U™—Food That Fits Your Life!, continues to expand.

In 2006, ARAMARK introduced SnackFactor, a healthy snack program for middle and high school students. SnackFactor offers students more than 150 healthy snack options, including mainstream and organic versions of low-fat granola bars, cereal bars, baked goods, animal and graham crackers, yogurt, water, 100 percent juice and smoothie beverages, fresh fruits, and vegetables.[2]

cards or meal plan cards at a Starbucks machine. Richard Wyckoff explained:

*Students can get a cup of Starbucks coffee while they are in the library or their dorm room working late at night. It is entrepreneurial. This project resulted from our performance and relationships. We succeed at ARAMARK because we are good at fostering relationships and teamwork within the organization and with our customers.[32]*

### International Milestones

Several milestones achieved in the International division in 2004—acquisitions and expansions in the United Kingdom, Chile, Germany, and Japan, and expansion into China—inspired ARAMARK executives to rethink their position on international business. Neubauer noted that International Food and Support Services generated $1.8 billion in sales; ARAMARK managed closer to $3 billion in overseas business when the sales of AIM Services were included, which were not included in ARAMARK's sales.

The opportunity to grow ARAMARK's international business attracted Ravi Saligram to ARAMARK in 2003, when he accepted the position of president of the International division. Formerly chief marketing officer for InterContinental, Saligram decided to take the job after examining ARAMARK's inherent growth opportunities, the integrity of the company, and Neubauer's personality. "I think Joe never takes 'no' for an answer," Saligram said. He continued:

*I felt that the opportunity for ARAMARK to take its best practices and move them to different parts of the world had significant prospects. It is not just an issue of getting to more countries. We've collectively embarked on a path to transform this company from being an American company, to an international company, and to finally becoming a truly global company. Global doesn't mean that you need a presence in 90 countries. You can be global by thriving in 20 countries. Being global is an attitude and a philosophy, and it affects how we approach the world.[33]*

---

"ARAMARK understands that good nutrition is essential for sound academic performance, and it impacts the health and success of our nation's children," said Jeff Wheatley, former executive vice president of operations, ARAMARK Education. "Everybody has heard about childhood obesity. It has become an incredibly important issue, and it is essential to us that we deliver nutritious meals in an economically efficient way that also provides nutritional awareness and education programs for children and their families." Wheatley noted that there are tremendous growth opportunities in the educational food services segment because nearly 75 percent of public school district lunchrooms in the United States are still self-operated.[3]

In an effort to communicate the importance of adopting healthy lifestyles to students and their parents, ARAMARK constantly works to develop nutrition-related educational tools. "This is a culture with a passion to serve," Wheatley said. "The people here, above all, have a passion to help clients, customers, children, and teachers. I have never experienced that in any of the other industries I have worked in."[4]

---

ARAMARK's new trademark services for middle school students recognize that "tweens," shown here at the 12 Spot™, love to socialize and have a place to communicate with their friends during their lunch period.

Above: The highly advanced online menu selection system allowed chefs at the 2004 Summer Olympic Games in Athens to manage recipes; food production, ordering, and stocking needs; and nutritional properties of meals, all from a computer terminal in the back of the dining hall.

Left: Neubauer celebrates ARAMARK's 13th Olympic experience alongside ARAMARK executives and chefs in Athens, Greece.

ARAMARK appointed 11-year company veteran Andrew W. Main to aggressively address challenges in the United Kingdom ranging from stiff competition to the valuation of the dollar. As the new president of ARAMARK UK, Main described the division as "a microcosm of the entire ARAMARK operation."

"There are multiple lines of business and sectors that we serve in the United Kingdom," he explained. "It is not just one single strategy, it is multiple strategies that we work with for each of the specific sectors that ARAMARK serves."

He recognized that operating in the United States is very different from operating in the United Kingdom. In Europe, ARAMARK faces stiffer competition from Compass Group and Sodexho than in the United States. Main expects emerging growth opportunities in both the military markets and the educational food outsourcing markets. "The common thread is ARAMARK's core values, our business philosophy, and what we stand for as an organization," Main said.[34]

With sales in the international segment of food and support services clearly driving corporate sales in 2004, ARAMARK experienced growth in country-to-country and client-to-client international business. For instance, ARAMARK has provided food service since 1983 at the European Patent Office in Munich. The number of European patent applications is expected to reach 256,000 applications by 2010 (versus 30,000 applications in 1985), according to Thomas Michel, the principal director. Because of the increase, the office has grown from one building in Munich to five, with additional offices in the Netherlands. ARAMARK has consistently expanded its food services to meet the growing needs of the office, its employees, and the nearby European School, an educational facility for the children of employees of European organizations. ARAMARK introduced an innovative cashless payment system at the facility and currently operates four restaurants for the office. "I am totally happy with ARAMARK in all of our buildings," said Michel. "I think the attitude of ARAMARK to solving problems is very customer-oriented and very helpful."[35]

At the 2006 FIFA World Cup in Germany, ARAMARK Germany was named Master Concessionaire and oversaw concessions at the 12 stadiums in the tournament. Nearly three million soccer fans attended the games at stadiums such as Commerzbank Arena in Frankfurt, shown here in a match between Argentina and the Netherlands.

**Time to Focus**

Guided by the goals of Mission One, ARAMARK succeeded during a period that Neubauer called an "economy that would not get better in a hurry." ARAMARK faced rising energy prices and a drop in sales caused in part by the cancellation of the 2004–2005 National Hockey League season. Yet the company ended the year on a positive note, and Neubauer declared it "one of our most successful years ever."[36] For the first time in the company's history, sales exceeded $10 billion worldwide, up from $5 billion a decade earlier. ARAMARK achieved more than $800 million in annualized new businesses, with more than 242,000 ARAMARK employees serving millions of customers in 19 countries. Neubauer

sensed, however, that the company's leadership and its employees were relatively anxious about the possibility of continual and unexpected change at the company. With that in mind, Neubauer promised two things for ARAMARK in 2005: less change and more time to focus.[37]

Neubauer and his leadership team remained in place during 2005, backed by a Board of Directors that continued to reflect the company's exemplary professional standards. ARAMARK made relatively few acquisitions during the year, including expanding its ownership in Ireland's Campbell Catering from 45 percent to 90 percent and completing the acquisition of L&N Uniform Supply, a Southern California–based industrial uniform business.

By applying the strategic growth goals of Mission One, the company acquired new business at record rates. In the first half of the year, new business rose 15 percent over the previous year. Cross-selling opportunities and a new lead-sharing program encouraged managers and employees to exchange ideas about increased client services. The company announced that "Mission One sales accounted for about one-third of new business during the second quarter." ARAMARK also celebrated major wins by securing contracts with the U.K. Ministry of Defence, Grupo Allianza in Spain, Roosevelt University in Illinois, and Bayfront Medical Center in Florida. In addition, the company served at the largest international soccer event of 2005, the FIFA Confederations Cup in Germany.[38]

During a comprehensive overview of the company in May 2005, Neubauer reported to investors that by focusing on existing business opportunities,

---

ARAMARK pulled together an estimated 500 food service employees, 250 facilities management employees, and 50 managers from ARAMARK accounts throughout the south Texas region to care for nearly 25,000 displaced victims of Hurricane Katrina.

"we are solidly on our way to achieving our objectives for fiscal year 2005."[39]

### Helping Hurricane Victims

ARAMARK continued to stay focused in the wake of Hurricane Katrina, which devastated New Orleans, Biloxi, Mobile, and other coastal areas. The storm hit Louisiana on August 31, 2005. The next day, ARAMARK executives worked around the clock to ensure the safety of all employees and families in the affected areas. Galls, the public safety division of ARAMARK Uniform and Career Apparel, donated more than $100,000 worth of safety equipment and supplies to help with relief efforts. The company also provided food service for thousands of victims evacuated to the Astrodome in Houston and worked to help clients in every way possible, coordinating financial contributions to help with the long recovery process. "When this is all over, I want people to say 'ARAMARK went in there and did what needed to be done,'" said Gloria Speaker, head supervisor for facility services at the Astrodome.[40]

An estimated 500 food service employees, 250 facilities management employees, and 50 managers from ARAMARK accounts throughout the south

Texas region prepared and served more than 75,000 meals a day to evacuees in the Astrodome. "All of us have seen the horrific devastation," said Joe Glynn, district manager for Sports and Entertainment in Houston. "We have an opportunity to make things better, and we are blessed with the chance to do something to help."[41]

It was an extraordinary response to a true disaster, but it was not out of character for ARAMARK or its employees. Through the years, thousands of ARAMARK employees have made valuable daily contributions, positively affecting the lives of millions. The company has a long tradition of community service, and employees have given generously of their own time in thousands of cities, towns, and neighborhoods around the world. They serve in soup kitchens, raise money for medical research, build houses, and teach schoolchildren by volunteering

Left: Victims of Hurricane Katrina kept hope alive after the tragedy. "We have to take care of these people the same way they would take care of us if our city was under water," said Gloria Speaker, head supervisor for ARAMARK Facility Services at the Astrodome.

Below: As many as 13,000 children were displaced by Hurricane Katrina, and ARAMARK food and facility teams worked hard to provide them with food and services.

their time to organizations in their communities. At work, they have consistently provided financial support to nonprofit organizations and volunteered during times of crisis.

"There are 240,000 ARAMARK employees that touch [the lives of] millions of people every day all around the world and have the chance to make somebody smile," said Andrew Kerin. "That is unique."[42]

### Growth Potential

At the end of 2005, Neubauer reported record sales of $11 billion, an 8 percent increase over 2004. Net income rose a record 10 percent to $288 million, and diluted earnings per share increased 13 percent to $1.53. He concluded that ARAMARK's core sectors contained more than "$700 billion in potential sales ... more than half a trillion dollars of which remains untapped by us or three of our largest competitors."[43]

Former Board member Ron Davenport, chairman of Sheridan Broadcasting Company in Pittsburgh, explained:

> With the outsourcing of food service, we have demonstrated the ability to do things in an efficient and fair way that protects the reputations of the institution and its employees. ... The record demonstrates quite clearly that we are very efficient in terms of delivery of service. Our growth is exponential, and we have only scratched the surface.[44]

### Transition to Truly Global

In 2006, ARAMARK once more reached the top of *Fortune®* magazine's list of America's Most Admired Companies. Having placed in the top three in its category each year since 1998, ARAMARK was ranked first in its industry. The company won top honors in the Diversified Outsourcing category, which studies businesses that offer a range of value-added professional services.

"I am proud of all of our employees for making our company one of the most respected in the business," said Chairman and CEO Joe Neubauer. "We are honored by this recognition of our excellence in our ability to provide world-class experiences for our clients and customers and of the role we play in helping clients realize their core mission through the

Left: The ARAMARK Education team from Houston Community College in Houston, Texas, recently joined forces to work with Habitat for Humanity® to build a home in Houston.

Below: ARAMARK serves nearly 70 million sports fans worldwide at more than 60 major and minor league venues.

# A HISTORY WITH BOEING

THE BOEING COMPANY IS KNOWN AS the world's leading aerospace company and the largest manufacturer of commercial jetliners and military aircraft. But to this day, ARAMARK executives view Boeing as much more than a global aerospace company and a valued, long-term customer. Boeing is considered ARAMARK's first industrial customer, dating back to 1937 when founder Davre Davidson signed a contract to place vending machines in a location for Douglas Aircraft, the forerunner to Boeing. Davidson always credited this first industrial account with helping him launch his new vending business.

Today, Boeing employs more than 153,000 people in more than 67 countries and continues to turn to ARAMARK for an array of managed services at 41 separate Boeing locations throughout the United States, providing everything from dining and coffee services to uniform rental and uniform purchase services, to specialized products for security guards and customized building cleaning services.

"ARAMARK has been able to provide us with superior service," said Laurel Lutz, manager of business services at Boeing, based in St. Louis. "I think ARAMARK has shown us that growth is a business process, and it begins from listening to their customer. That growth has endured because they keep their customers happy. They gear their food service program toward our employees' needs by offering different foods in different areas."[1]

Lutz points out that ARAMARK is "very supportive of our wellness and our health awareness campaigns. If they can help our employees make healthy choices, it's just good business sense, and they're so proactive about their wellness programs."[2]

In 2002, ARAMARK and Boeing jointly announced the signing of a 10-year contract for food service, vending, and coffee services.[3] The contract covered five Boeing facilities in Southern California, as well as in Mesa, Arizona;

The Boeing Company recently asked ARAMARK to plan and execute a complete renovation of its food service area at Boeing's Integrated Defense Systems headquarters in St. Louis. Shown here, the new corporate eating area resembles a casual restaurant more than a corporate setting, appointed in modern designs and arranged to provide both group and individual dining options.

Philadelphia; and the Boeing World Headquarters in St. Louis. Later, the contract grew to include Boeing's Chicago headquarters. In total, the relationship now has an annual value of more than $40 million.[4]

In St. Louis, Lutz recalled the remarkable transformation and success of an ARAMARK renovation project that created in record time a brand-new food service operation at Boeing's Integrated Defense Systems headquarters. In just six weeks, from Thanksgiving to after the Christmas holiday, ARAMARK "brought all of their resources together, including their design team and food service experts from Philadelphia. They met with us constantly."

When the new food court opened after the Christmas break, Lutz remembered, "It was beautiful. People were just shocked and amazed. … The cafeteria was absolutely phenomenal. ARAMARK was able to do so much in such a short period of time."[5]

services we provide. We feel our leadership on this list is a testament to our ability to create long-term value for our stakeholders, delivering sustainable, profitable growth in a global company built on pride, integrity, and respect." [45]

While many in the industry recognized ARAMARK's steady global efforts, the strategic push to transform the company as a global entity continued in 2006. As Ravi Saligram, president of ARAMARK International, explained, "One of the most significant changes at ARAMARK today is that we're transforming it from a U.S.-centric company to a truly global company. We're seeing that in so many ways." [46]

Right: While baseball fans may still find the traditional peanuts and hot dogs at the various baseball stadiums where ARAMARK manages food service, ballpark menus have come of age to reflect today's fans' diverse tastes.

Below: Every day, ARAMARK provides an array of services to dozens of correctional institutions throughout the United States, including food and maintenance services. This particular segment offers tremendous growth opportunities for the company, because there are about 1,200 state correctional facilities in the country, and about 80 percent still operate their own dining services.

The transition, Saligram noted, represents much more than simply increasing the company's market share and expanding into new countries. Transforming ARAMARK into a global company would require strategic growth, including a change of mindset and attitude. [47]

With several distinct ways to expand in international markets, opportunities have been plentiful. For example, ARAMARK has had the chance to expand geographically within a country where it already has a strong base and then offer additional services.

"We have the opportunity to expand into facilities services in some countries, leveraging our food operations," Saligram said. "Everywhere you look, there is opportunity." [48]

According to the international division's Marty Welch, senior vice president, Finance, who has also been an ARAMARK employee for nearly 25 years, there are more similarities than differences between ARAMARK's international and U.S.–based businesses. As a result, the company has started to encourage a cultural shift from independence to intradependence, sharing best practices across the globe. "We are working as a team," said Welch. "The opportunity internationally is tremendous." [49]

## Strength in Partnerships

ARAMARK entered China for the first time in 2004 when it purchased Bright China Service Industry (BCSI). "We used the acquisition as a launch model into the country," said Saligram. Often, though, the company will enter a country through a joint venture. This approach emphasizes a smooth integration of the local culture with corporate cus-

tom. When ARAMARK entered Chile, it participated in a joint venture with Central Restaurantes; when the company entered Ireland, it formulated a joint venture with Campbell Catering.[50]

Nowhere has the joint venture been more successful for ARAMARK than in the case of AIM Services, a 30-year collaboration with Japanese industrial giant Mitsui. In 2006, AIM Services produced $1.2 billion in revenue. According to Saligram:

*Thirty years for an American and Japanese company to work together is extraordinary. ... Because of the stability of top management at ARAMARK, we have a long-term view, just like our Japanese partners. Together, we seek ways to make AIM the best in the food service business, the best in the healthcare industry, the best in educational services, and the best in business services. ... The key*

ARAMARK's Board of Directors in 2005 (sitting, front row, left to right): Karl M. von der Heyden; Patricia C. Barron; Joe Neubauer; James E. Ksansnak; Ronald R. Davenport; and Thomas H. Kean. Back row, left to right: Lawrence T. Babbio, Jr.; James E. Preston; Leonard S. Coleman, Jr.; Ronald L. Sargent; and Robert J. Callander.

# A PARTNERSHIP WITH BANCO SANTANDER

ARAMARK DOES BUSINESS IN CHILE AS Central Restaurantes, a company with a long history of client relationships. For more than 25 years, Central Restaurantes has served Banco Santander in Santiago, Chile, the No. 1 bank in a country located in one of ARAMARK's key regions for international business growth. When Central Restaurantes first formed this partnership in 1981, the bank was called Santiago Bank, a name that was eventually changed to Banco Santander when the organization merged with Santander Bank.[1]

As of 2006, Central Restaurantes manages four employee restaurants and two executive restaurants for Banco Santander, serving more than 3,200 bank employees and executives.

Central Restaurantes' award-winning employee dining and executive fine-dining options include breakfast, lunch, box lunches, coffee and refreshment services, cocktail receptions, and catering for special events. Although the options seem standard today, Central Restaurantes' food service seemed revolutionary when Banco Santander became the first canteen in the country to offer banking employees multiple food options, a fresh salad bar, and soft drinks (they were free).

Alfonso Palavecino, the human resources manager for Banco Santander and a banking employee for more than 15 years, believes that the successful relationship between the two institutions is due to Central Restaurantes' focus on the actual needs of its clients through a profes-

---

*has been combining Mitsui's strength in understanding Japan, its stature in the country, and its access to great clients, along with our own strength of understanding the business of food and facilities management around the world.*[51]

ARAMARK views all of its international endeavors as partnerships. Longtime client British Petroleum (BP) has been a partner since 1977. In 1999, BP chose ARAMARK to manage all of its offshore accounts under one single contract. Today, this contract covers 13 BP installations and approximately 2,000 BP personnel, with ARAMARK's services including offshore hotel services, catering, housekeeping, laundry, electrical, and domestic maintenance to refurbishment, architectural design, and heli-deck administration.

"We were their lead contractor for providing people such as medics, radio operators, and heli-deck landing crew," said Andrew Main, president, ARAMARK UK. "We capitalized on the management talent we already had to become the lead contractor on the platform." ARAMARK also took a leadership

role in aligning with BP's safety goals, and the client has been impressed.[52]

When ARAMARK received BP's safety performance award, David Blackwood, director of BP's North Sea Strategic Performance Unit, said, "We don't draw any demarcation lines [between employees and service providers]. We capture the statistics of everyone on the facilities offshore. [We recognize] when somebody is exceptional or has a sustained track record of excellent safety performance. In ARAMARK's case, it was more about consistently turning in an impressive safety performance across all the installations over a period of time."[53]

Whether it's Ravi Saligram's push for "intradependence" or a global approach, ARAMARK is forging a worldwide identity as a partner that clients can rely on to help them realize their core mission. And often, the bigger the stage, the more impressive the success, including the 13 Olympic Games that ARAMARK has served.

In 2006 that big stage was the FIFA World Cup, and ARAMARK Germany was one of the stars. "We had a lot of great success stories in Germany, but

sional and close-knit management team. "They are respectful of acquired commitments and provide an excellent level of service," he said. "Our company has given them the Suppliers of Excellence award for the past three years."[2]

To illustrate his point, Palavecino related three crises in which Central Restaurantes went beyond the call of duty to help Banco Santander. First, in June 1992, Chile was affected by cholera, an intestinal bacterial illness. "The situation required changes to certain foods that contained vegetables, as per instructions from the Chilean government," he said. "Central Restaurantes reacted quickly, in fact in less than 24 hours, and modified its preparations and suppliers."[3]

Second, in 1993, a mudslide in the city of Santiago contaminated the drinking water supply in company cafeterias. "However, Central Restaurantes continued to provide food service in our cafeterias, with no alterations of any kind," explained Palavecino.[4]

And third, in April 2005, as Palavecino recalled, "There was an emergency at one of our cafeterias. Central Restaurantes responded immediately with their epidemic procedures program."[5]

Although Banco Santander appreciates Central Restaurantes' international reputation and believes that its passion for service fits well with the bank's corporate values and business principles, banking executives also welcome the fact that ARAMARK's Chile operation has kept "local professional management" and maintained its ability to be "agile and flexible" when it comes to making decisions and understanding the client's needs.

Palavecino believes Central Restaurantes will continue as one of the best service suppliers to Banco Santander for many more years. "We know they will remain innovative in food delivery through the large variety and high standards of quality that we have learned to expect from Central Restaurantes. They will continue to offer a broad range of services that allow us to cover other needs at competitive prices but with high standards of quality."[6]

the highlight was certainly the FIFA World Cup," said Udo Luerssen, president, ARAMARK Germany. "As Master Concessionaire, we were responsible for catering to about three million fans over a four-week period, which included 64 games in 12 arenas and involved 4,000 employees."[54]

ARAMARK was selected to serve at international soccer's main event for several reasons, including how the company has revolutionized concessions and service in German stadiums. "We already operate half of the stadiums in the First German Federal League," said Luerssen, "which makes us the leader. ARAMARK's many years of experience as caterer at the Olympic Games was especially helpful."[55]

The previous year under Luerssen's leadership, ARAMARK Germany had become the first international division awarded the Davidson Cup, named for Davre Davidson. It is the corporation's highest honor for the ARAMARK business unit that most embodies Davidson's spirit of entrepreneurship and risk-taking. Analyzing ARAMARK's coup in landing arguably the world's highest-profile sporting event, Saligram said:

*ARAMARK helped stage a championship in Germany for international soccer, a sport that is No. 1 everywhere in the world except in the United States. So why would FIFA trust us with this? Because when FIFA looks at ARAMARK, they don't see an American company. They see a global network of passionate service associates who collaborate and innovate across borders, breaking down cultural barriers and building on commonality as one global team.*[56]

**Poised for the Future**

ARAMARK's diverse businesses continued to serve as a positive factor for the company's future in 2005 and 2006. Efforts to realign ARAMARK's divisions created increased value for its people, clients, customers, and communities. In speeches around the company, Chairman and CEO Joe Neubauer consistently reported that ARAMARK's key sectors in food, facility management, and uniform services offer "$700 billion in potential sales," much of which is currently untapped by the company or its largest competitors.[57]

Chief Financial Officer Fred Sutherland said the growth opportunities lie in several areas: "We don't rely on one or two specific constituents. We don't rely only on healthcare workers and sports fans, but also on business workers and school-children and college students."[58]

John Babiarz, group president of ARAMARK Healthcare, predicts that acute care hospitals and senior living services represent exceptional growth opportunities for ARAMARK. "I believe that with the existing clients we serve, which include 1,000 acute care hospitals, we have something under 10 percent of the potential business within our existing client base if we get them to do all the things we do. From an opportunity point of view, it's staggering, though it's not without competition."[59]

Liza Cartmell, group president of Sports and Entertainment, believes that similar opportunities exist for providing services at stadiums and arenas, in expanding concessions, retail, and facilities management. "In facilities, we've only scratched the surface," Cartmell said. "We only have six of the more than 120 major league accounts for facilities cleaning, preventive maintenance, and others. So there

is huge opportunity from a facilities standpoint, especially packaging all that together."[60]

"Opportunity" was the rallying cry for the organization in 2005 and 2006. At regional Star Team meetings across the country, on the cover of the 2005 annual report, in executive speeches, training sessions, and elsewhere, ARAMARK leadership announced its focus on a largely untapped opportunity.

In preparation to meet the opportunity, identify the levers for success, and organize its people, ARAMARK underwent an "evolution," which took place in three steps. The first was a codification of the company's new way of thinking, referred to as the "Business Purpose," which included a few short

Thousands of managers across the United States and Canada met at regional Star Team meetings in 2006, exchanging ideas and learning about the company through the "ARAMARK Experience." This interactive display shows the many ways ARAMARK delivers experiences, environments, and outcomes.

statements that outlined the company's mission. The Business Purpose emphasized phrases such as "professional services," "experiences, environments, and outcomes," and the clients' "core mission." This first step was a way to organize the company's thinking and provide a foundation for the second step, which was just around the corner.

### Realignment and Structure

In the spring of 2006, ARAMARK began a series of realignments throughout the organization. As the company was organized, there were eight domestic businesses, namely, Business Services, Refreshment Services, Corrections, Sports and Entertainment, Campus Services, Education Facilities, School Support Services, and Healthcare, working from different business, technology, and personnel platforms. To work in a more cohesive, consistent, and coordinated fashion, and to better pursue opportunities across the domestic food and facilities businesses served, these disparate organizations were realigned into one organization. In April, two of ARAMARK's domestic groups—Business, Sports, and Entertainment; and Healthcare, Facilities, and Education—were united under the leadership of Andrew Kerin as Domestic Food, Hospitality, and Facility Services. In his announcement at the time, Neubauer said, "By aligning ourselves with more clarity, we will better position our great people and our enormous capabilities against each of our opportunities. We will enable our people to better share best practices, exchange business insights and consumer research quickly and efficiently, leverage core platforms, all while ensuring a consistent, common approach."[61]

More realignments followed. In July 2006, Education began rolling out a new structure. In August, Business Services, Refreshment Services, and Business and Industry–Facility Services joined to form the Business and Industry Group. ARAMARK Uniform Services followed that same month, realigning into four areas: customer services, sales, operations support, and field operations. And in October, Corrections welcomed Correctional Facilities into its group.

While ARAMARK has grown steadily over the years and undergone realignments as necessary, the company's governance structure has remained relatively the same. The corporate leadership team has for years numbered around 200 people, with an emphasis on "autonomous, independent, business leadership, which has worked for us," said Lynn McKee, executive vice president, Human Resources. "I think the constant over the last 25 years has clearly been Joe [Neubauer]'s leadership," she continued. Neubauer, whom Goldman Sachs' Jack Curtin noted for his "sharp mind, his incredible work ethic, his dedication to the culture of building the organization, and his loyalty to his people," was about to shake things up again.[62]

"Joe is a person of great personal integrity, and big companies don't have long-term success unless they have CEOs who have great personal integrity," said Drayton McLane, Jr., owner of the Houston Astros and Board chairman of Scott and White Hospital and Clinic, as well as former chairman and current Board member of Baylor University, both ARAMARK clients.[63]

In 2006, ARAMARK was successful, and it was stable. The first step in the company's evolution, the "Business Purpose," was completed. The second step was on its way to completion, but the third step of the transformation was yet to come. ARAMARK was about to embark on another journey. Neubauer had been thinking hard about long-term success in 2005 and 2006. He was growing increasingly dissatisfied with the company's performance in the public markets. Something had to change.

After five years of trading on the public market, ARAMARK went private again in 2007. In that five-year period, sales, earnings, and earnings per share had increased considerably, while the stock price remained relatively flat. "That just didn't seem fair to our shareholders," said Chairman and CEO Joe Neubauer. *(Image courtesy of* The Philadelphia Inquirer.*)*

## CHAPTER TWELVE

# LOOKING TO THE FUTURE

## 2007 AND BEYOND

*The reality is, we outperformed the broader market and all of our chief competitors. But ... from an absolute perspective, the mediocre returns in the stock certainly were underwhelming versus the strong financial performance of the company.*

—Chris Holland, ARAMARK senior vice president and treasurer

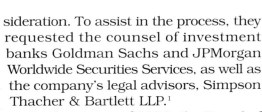

ON MAY 1, 2006, CHAIRMAN AND CEO Joe Neubauer announced that he and a group of investors had decided to take the company private once again. It was a stunning announcement. The $11 billion company had been public for less than five years, and buying it would be a huge undertaking. Huge, but not impossible. As one of the chief architects of the management buyout (MBO) in 1984, having headed the IPO and stood on the floor of the New York Stock Exchange (NYSE) when ARAMARK went public again in 2001, Neubauer had led the company through transformations before. The idea of making ARAMARK a privately held company again was a bold decision, but not a rash one. It had been under considerable study for more than six months.

### A New Blueprint

In December 2005, Joe Neubauer and Fred Sutherland, executive vice president and chief financial officer, presented several options to the Board of Directors, such as strategic alternatives for ensuring the company's continuing profitable growth. The options were as follows: maintaining the status quo; disposing of assets; strategic combinations; and acquiring the company, that is, going private. Each option seemed perfectly valid, and management took all of them into consideration. To assist in the process, they requested the counsel of investment banks Goldman Sachs and JPMorgan Worldwide Securities Services, as well as the company's legal advisors, Simpson Thacher & Bartlett LLP.[1]

In the spring of 2006, the Board of Directors held two milestone meetings:

- On March 22, Neubauer and Sutherland reported to the Board of Directors on the ongoing examination of the company's options, followed by a discussion of the alternatives. The possible "going-private transaction" remained central to the discussion.[2]
- On April 28, Neubauer and Sutherland met with the Board to discuss management's continued exploration of strategic alternatives, including potential combinations with strategic partners. One of the central discussions, as a buyout became a subject of increasing focus, was the fundamental feasibility of going private.[3]

A key feature of the management buyout was a deep ownership pool. Shown above is the subscription package that invited the initial management group to buy into the company. Since the buyout, the ownership group has grown even larger.

ARAMARK Chairman and CEO Joe Neubauer.

Three days after the April 28 meeting, on May 1, Neubauer announced his plans in a proposal letter to the Board of Directors to lead an investment group that was prepared to offer $32 per share to every stockholder to purchase the company and place it in private hands. In addition to Neubauer, who pledged to make a "significant investment" in the deal, investment sponsors included Goldman Sachs Capital Partners; JPMorgan Partners, LLC; Thomas H. Lee Partners; and Warburg Pincus, LLC. According to Neubauer, he and several members of the ARAMARK senior management team would finance the buyout bid with equity investment and "through a combination of equity from investment funds managed by the four sponsors."[4]

The months that followed the May 1 announcement would be fraught with negotiations between the investment group and the Board. The public courtship had begun, but this latest bold move—for a company that has had several—had been germinating as a private idea for a while.

**December 6, 2005**
Joe Neubauer and Chief Financial Officer Fred Sutherland begin a series of meetings with ARAMARK's Board of Directors to consider possibilities for enhancing shareholder value, including the option of going private.

**May 1, 2006**
Neubauer announces that he plans to take ARAMARK private, with an offer of nearly $5.8 billion, worth $32 per share to every stockholder.

**2006**
ARAMARK explores opportunity for growth in all areas: facilities management, food services, and uniform services. Neubauer believes that ARAMARK's core services still offer billions of dollars in potential sales opportunities.

John Lafferty (left), senior vice president, controller, and chief accounting officer, shares a celebratory moment with Fred Sutherland, executive vice president and chief financial officer.

### The Germ of an Idea

When Neubauer returned as CEO in 2004, he publicly committed to remain as the chief executive until at least 2007. Now and again, Neubauer would comment that running a public company in the current business climate was more challenging than at any time in the company's history. As many close to him already knew, Neubauer was especially frustrated with what he perceived as Wall Street's preoccupation with short-term financial results. From the date of the IPO in December 2001, the company had performed well. Sales, earnings, and earnings per share had all increased at healthy rates. All the right indicators were present, but the stock price had not followed suit. The longer the stock price of ARAMARK remained relatively flat, the more apparent it became that the public market was not assigning it an accurate or fair value and that it did not know how to properly evaluate the company. Neubauer especially disliked the distraction generated by quarterly earnings volatility and issuing dividends that emphasized short-term gains, all factors that took away corporate and public incentives to keep an eye on the long-term goals of the company.[5]

In the end, the decision to buy out the company hinged on the stark contrast between ARAMARK's

**August 7, 2006**
The investor group, headed by Neubauer, offers $33.60 per share; the special committee counters with $33.80, just shy of its request for $34 per share. Late that evening, the investor group agrees to a transaction price of $33.80, 5.6 percent more for the shareholders than the original offer of $32 per share.

**June 28, 2006**
A special committee of the ARAMARK Board is appointed by the Directors to review the offer. The committee works with outside financial analysts and determines that the $32 per share offer is not a good value for the stockholders. Negotiations begin for the two sides to agree on a fair price.

**August 8, 2006**
ARAMARK issues a press release announcing the $8.3 billion MBO, subject to final approval from the SEC and shareholders.

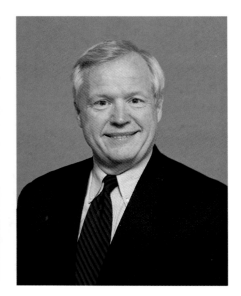

Above left: Chris Holland, ARAMARK senior vice president and treasurer.

Above center: Ravi Saligram, executive vice president, ARAMARK Corporation, and president, ARAMARK International.

Above right: John Babiarz, group president, ARAMARK Healthcare.

Below: A small string band plays at the February 1, 2007, party celebrating ARAMARK's completion of the leveraged buyout transaction.

actual performance and its undervalued stock price. As Chris Holland, ARAMARK senior vice president and treasurer, said:

> We spent a ton of time looking at our performance versus other companies' performance and versus the market's performance since we went public in 2001. The reality is, we outperformed the broader market and all of our chief competitors. So from a relative perspective, we've performed well and have nothing to feel bad about. But we asked ourselves, "Are you an absolute investor or a relative investor?" From an absolute perspective, the mediocre returns in the stock certainly were underwhelming versus the strong financial performance of the company.[6]

Sales were up 40 percent over the five-year period that ARAMARK had been a public company. Earnings had increased 45 percent over that same period, and earnings per share were up 70 percent. But the stock price had increased only 20 percent, from $23 to $28 per share. "That just didn't seem fair to our shareholders in general," said Neubauer, "and in particular, it didn't provide a lot of incentive to the management team here."[7]

### Negotiations

ARAMARK would also receive approximately $6.25 billion of debt financing from two of its long-standing financial partners, Goldman Sachs Credit

Partners LP and JPMorgan Worldwide Securities Services. "Our proposal would provide a substantial premium for all of the company's public stockholders," said Neubauer, "I would continue as chairman and CEO following the transaction and would expect that our senior leadership team would continue to lead the company into the future with me."[8]

The Friday before the Monday, May 1, announcement, ARAMARK stock sold for $28.11 per share. After the proposal was made public on May 1, shares of ARAMARK surged as high as $34.95, settling at $33.90 by the end of the day. Some shareholders felt the $32 per share price offered by ARAMARK insiders might be too low and quickly began pushing for a higher offer.[9]

ARAMARK's Board of Directors formed a committee of independent directors to review the bid.[42] The special committee of five, chaired by Board member Ronald Davenport, soon hired its own team

of lawyers and retained Credit Suisse Securities LLC as its financial advisor, charged with reviewing the offer to determine its fairness to the stockholders. As the merger process wore on into the summer of 2006, members of the special committee were not allowed to communicate or share information with other Board members. In contrast to the company's first leveraged buyout in 1984, described by Davenport as a defensive measure designed primarily to thwart a hostile takeover, "this LBO was an offensive measure and a recognition that the stock had not performed well, even though we had hit all the performance marks."[10]

On June 28, 2006, members of the special committee had a telephone conference with representatives of Credit Suisse. Following the call, the committee announced that it "would not be prepared to pursue a proposal at $32 per share," but it would entertain an offer at a higher price. In short,

# THE IMPORTANCE OF ETHICS

AT A TIME WHEN IMPROPER AND UNETHical accounting practices exposed one corporate scandal after another, Chairman and CEO Joe Neubauer's insistence on exceptional corporate governance standards ensured ethical responsibility at ARAMARK during the volatile post-Enron era. "Doing the right thing is not complicated," Neubauer said. "You do not have to know many rules and regulations."[1]

In publications and on its corporate Web site, ARAMARK repeatedly emphasizes that it is "committed to conducting its business with the utmost integrity and according to the highest ethical standards." The 10-member Board of Directors adopted governance principles and committee charters in an effort to serve the best interests of ARAMARK and its shareholders.[2]

When corporate institutions like Enron and WorldCom became synonymous with corporate greed in the early years of the new millennium, Neubauer and ARAMARK remained associated with exceptional business leadership and ethical

practices. *Fortune*® magazine consistently placed ARAMARK at the top of its category in its annual Most Admired Companies list, *BusinessWeek* named Neubauer "The Straight Shooter" in a 2002 article on outstanding CEOs, and the Outstanding Directors Institute named Neubauer an Outstanding Director in 2005. Congress passed the Sarbanes–Oxley Act in 2002, a new law requiring executives and auditors to evaluate internal financial controls and hold themselves accountable for financial statements. ARAMARK, in its efforts to remain ethical, had complied with many of their requirements even before the law passed.[3]

According to former New Jersey Governor Tom Kean, an ARAMARK director: "Joe assembled a top-notch Board at ARAMARK while it was still a private company. They were people of real independence and integrity. We had a Board of Directors for 10 years before going public. We also had an audit committee at the time, and we did not release any numbers until the audit committee signed off."[4]

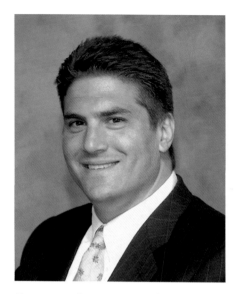

the special committee had determined that the proposed stock price of $32 from Neubauer and the investor group could be improved upon.[11]

And so negotiations over the offer price began in earnest between the special committee and the investor group. On July 13, the investor group increased its offer to $32.75, "subject to negotiation of an acceptable merger agreement with no condition that a majority of the unaffiliated stockholders approve the transaction." Before the day was over, the special committee responded that "it did not view a $32.75 per share price favorably." On July 20, the investor group increased its offer to $33.50 per share; the special committee responded on July 25

that the offer was still not sufficient. At times, the negotiations resembled a financial chess game, and at other times, a standoff. Two days later, Neubauer said that "any possible proposal by the investor group beyond $33.50 per share would be no more than a nickel and a few pennies." In the two weeks that followed, no more offers were put on the table.[12]

"It was an interesting experience, but not pleasant," said Davenport.[13] Neubauer referred to the process as "very difficult and frustrating." He explained: "You know that everybody was reading a script prescribed by their primary legal and financial advisors, and not to have an open dialogue with people whom I have known and worked with for more than 20 years felt artificial."[14]

While the special committee continued to perform its due diligence, the four financial players for the MBO worked to structure what would soon become an $8.3 billion transaction. In contrast to the tension surrounding negotiations for a fair buyout stock price, Goldman Sachs' Jack Curtin noted that because so many of the financial players knew each other and had worked together on previous ARAMARK deals, it was almost like working for one firm on this transaction. "You don't see it that often," said Curtin. "We

Above left: Andrew Kerin, executive vice president, ARAMARK Corporation; and president, Domestic Food, Hospitality, and Facility Services.

Above center: Liza Cartmell, group president, Sports and Entertainment.

Above right: Bart J. Colli, executive vice president, general counsel, and secretary.

Right: Thomas J. Vozzo, executive vice president, ARAMARK Corporation; and president, ARAMARK Uniform and Career Apparel.

would probably put this transaction in the first quartile in terms of relative ease."[15]

Jamie Grant and Barrett Pickett of JPMorgan agreed. "The biggest challenge was getting the Board to understand that some of the factors that were preventing ARAMARK's stock price from performing [at its peak] were real and persistent, and to persuade them that ARAMARK belonged as a private company," said Pickett. According to Grant, the only so-called nail-biting period that investors experienced occurred not while working to structure the deal, but while the special committee considered the offer. "It was a deafening silence, for periods of time," he said.[16]

Looming in the background of every attempted buyout is the specter of some other party swooping in with a higher offer. Any company "in play" will receive a good deal of attention. A few other groups thought ARAMARK was worth considering, and during the course of the negotiations, members of the special committee met with representatives from two other companies in the professional services industry and two additional private equity firms. They all had expressed interest in pursuing transactions to acquire the company, but after more than a month of discussions, confidentiality agreements, countless phone calls and meetings, all four parties dropped out without making a single formal offer. "Any time you make a public offer, you're never 100 percent sure that someone you didn't think about may put in a higher offer," said Grant. "Given the homework that we had done, we didn't think that this would be the case. And, indeed, we were right."[17]

In late July, negotiations between the investor group and the special committee continued. The offer remained $33.50 per share. An intense week and a half of frequent meetings and contentious reviews of ARAMARK financial data came to a critical juncture on August 7, 2006. That morning, the special committee told the investor group that it would consider a proposal at $34 per share. The investor group quickly countered with a proposal of $33.60 per share, an increase of 10 cents per share and included in the

Valerie Wandler, senior vice president, Human Resources, and Alan Griffith, senior vice president, Finance and Planning.

offer an important consideration. In a move to ease any possible shareholder worries, Neubauer agreed to reduce his shareholder votes from 33 percent to less than 5 percent. For purposes of obtaining shareholder approval, each share owned by Neubauer "would have only one vote, rather than the 10 votes to which each such share is otherwise entitled."[18]

The special committee requested a personal meeting with Neubauer, its members clearly worried that they would not be able to reach an agreement on a per-share price. Neubauer stood firm, reiterating his view that the "investor group's proposal was more favorable to the company's stockholders than any alternative available to the company."[19]

Following this meeting, the special committee convened in an executive session with the other outside directors to review the status of the negotiations. They considered Credit Suisse's financial analysis, the draft merger agreement, and all related documents. Hanging over the discussion remained the obstinate 40-cent gap between the request and the offer. "We had to think about what would happen if the deal didn't go through," said Davenport, "what effect that would have on the company, on the morale of the employees. We had to consider what

Fred Sutherland (left) and Ravi Saligram discuss Sutherland's "Cash is King" button, a holdover from the 1984 MBO that Sutherland and Neubauer helped design.

that would mean to the shareholders, too." The special committee felt that the offer had to be better, and decided to see if they could simply split the difference with the investor group. The special committee announced it was willing to consider a proposal by the investor group at $33.80 per share.[20]

Later in the evening of what had become a very long day—it was, incredibly, still August 7—the investor group informed the special committee "that it was willing to enter into the transaction at a price of $33.80 per share," an offer that represented 20 percent more for the shareholders than the $28.11 per share the stock was trading at on April 28. And with that agreement, the negotiations came to a close. "It was after 10 P.M. that night," said Davenport. "Maybe it was 11, but it was late. We were relieved that we had finally come to an agreement that served the interests of the shareholders and protected them."[21]

The following day, prior to the opening of trading on the NYSE, ARAMARK issued a press release announcing the $8.3 billion MBO. Subject to final approval of the shareholders, who would vote on it at a late December meeting, ARAMARK would soon become a private company once again.

**Reaction to the Management Buyout**

When word of the revised MBO hit the streets, there was "no sign of the kind of shareholder rancor that greeted a 'too low' buyout bid in May," according to media reports. Financial analysts, who had criticized the initial $32 bid as inadequate, applauded the sweetened offer of $33.80 per share as "more than fair" and "a good deal" for the shareholders and the company.[22] In negotiating the MBO, ARAMARK joined a growing list of nearly 100 public companies since the beginning of 2005 whose top-level executives had participated in MBOs and acquired their company through the use of private

equity—companies like HCA, Inc., the hospital chain acquired for $31.6 billion, and Harrah's Entertainment, acquired for $25.7 billion.[23]

ARAMARK's $8.3 billion deal would include the assumption of approximately $2 billion in debt. Neubauer, estimated to hold nearly $800 million worth of ARAMARK stock, had agreed to contribute up to $250 million toward the buyout, with the balance coming from the four investment fund partners and an MBO contribution that included about 250 employee shareholders from ARAMARK's Executive Leadership Council (ELC). At a specially convened ELC meeting in Philadelphia on September 18 and 19, Neubauer explained the transaction and investment opportunities to the top leaders of the organization. The level of excitement in the room was palpable.

These insider shareholders, as Neubauer liked to call them, would have the chance to own up to 15 percent of the company starting out, with the possibility of another 15 percent in stock options. "We have the opportunity to own about a third of the company," said Neubauer, acknowledging the powerful incentive that ownership provides for management to work hard and perform. "That's precisely why we're doing this. It is about growth and service. The whole premise of this management buyout hinges on the growth prospects for our company. We happen to be in the right place at the right time with the right people, and that is why it's going to work," Neubauer said.[24]

Below left: Ira Cohn, president, Business and Industry Group.

Below center: Lynn B. McKee, executive vice president, Human Resources.

Below right: Fred Sutherland, executive vice president and chief financial officer.

*Davre J. Davidson*

*1911 – 1995*

*Were a star quenched on high,*

*for ages would its light,*

*still traveling downward from the sky,*

*shine on our mortal sight.*

*So when a great man dies,*

*for years beyond our ken,*

*the light he leaves behind him lies*

*upon the paths of men.*

*-Henry Wadsworth Longfellow*

*The ARAMARK men and women who trod the path*

*lit by Davre Davidson,*

*our great founder and friend,*

*mourn our loss even as we celebrate his extraordinary life*

*and enduring memory.*

ARAMARK

Three months after the ELC meeting, the shareholders convened to discuss the proposal at the Marriott Hotel just a block from the ARAMARK Tower, at 11th and Market Streets in Philadelphia. Nearly 100 people were in the Liberty Ballroom when the meeting got under way at 9 A.M., December 20, 2006. Presided over by Joe Neubauer—who was joined on the dais by Bart J. Colli, executive vice president, general counsel, and secretary—the meeting was attended by members of the local business community, members of ARAMARK's Management Committee, bankers, Board members, shareholders, and former employees. No one expected any surprises. Proceedings took seven minutes, and then the proposed buyout was put to a vote. It passed overwhelmingly, 97 percent of the votes cast in favor.

"Our business began in the 1930s, with a few vending machines in Southern California," Neubauer said in his remarks. He continued:

> *Ever since, ARAMARK has been in a constant state of change, as each generation of leaders has taken advantage of new growth opportunities and better ways to serve our clients and customers around the world. Our predictability, stability, and historically strong cash flows provide us options— options we are willing to examine, explore, and execute. As a private company, we believe ARAMARK's economic value will be more directly aligned with our performance.[25]*

The shareholders had spoken, the proposal had been ratified, and the deal was allowed to move forward. The meeting was over in less than an hour.

### The Future

A little more than a month later, on January 26, 2007, the deal officially closed. ARAMARK was a private company again.

"The depth of ownership that we're providing to our people is extraordinary, and we're proud of that,"

As ARAMARK returns to private ownership, the company founded by Davre J. Davidson continues to follow his entrepreneurial ways, more than a decade after his death.

said Lynn B. McKee, executive vice president, Human Resources. "It's a bigger group right from the start than it was when we went private in 1984, and if we can, we intend to expand the ownership even deeper." Indeed, in spring 2007, just months after the transaction closed, the company granted stock options to additional management-level employees.[26]

Since part of ARAMARK's debt would be publicly traded, the company would be required to continue filings with the SEC. But acquiring billions of dollars in debt did not seem like a predicament to ARAMARK. "The amount of debt relative to our cash flow is typical in private transactions," explained Sutherland. "We plan to start paying off the debt in the ordinary course, but at the same time and more important, we will continue to reinvest in the business in the form of capital expenditures and selective acquisitions. We certainly don't want to starve the business for capital at the altar of debt payoff."[27]

Alan Griffith, senior vice president, Finance and Planning, is looking forward to the excitement created when a company goes private:

*If you look at the original buyout [in 1984], I think people had a good sense of being in this together and pulling on the same oar to move things along. I'm hoping that we get more of that back in terms of saying, "Okay, we're working for ourselves again." … I think people will get excited that we can grow the company and create value, and that we're going to directly participate in that value creation.*[28]

According to Sutherland, the private ARAMARK will not be markedly different from the company that was public not so long ago. "We want to make sure that all of our employees understand that it is very much business as usual," he said. No matter what the future holds for ARAMARK, Sutherland believes that the essence of the company will always remain grounded in one aspect:

*This is a company that has always tried, generally successfully, to accomplish goals the right way with a high sense of integrity and a strong moral compass. It has a strong obligation to and a sense of relationship with its customers and clients. It is a long-term, relationship-oriented company as opposed to a transaction company. The success of ARAMARK is built on the strength of the management and the employees, who are its single biggest resource.*[29]

When it comes to ARAMARK and the company's future, perhaps Neubauer has always said it best. In one of his most memorable speeches, he delivered a message that would ring true time and again in the company's history. Exhibiting his trademark confidence and intensely focused composure, the long-term CEO reminded his employees that "this company has always been about dreamers and doers. We are at our best when we're dreaming big and doing bold things. That will be the blueprint for our future as, together, we write the next chapter for ARAMARK."[30]

# NOTES TO SOURCES

## Chapter One

1. Harold Davidson, interview by Jeffrey L. Rodengen, digital recording, 20 April 2005, Write Stuff Enterprises, Inc.
2. "From Penny Peanuts to Industry Leader ... a Uniquely American Success Story," ARA Services, Inc., 28 December 1981.
3. G. R. Schreiber, *A Concise History of Vending in the USA* (Lake Bluff, Illinois: Sunrise Books, 1961).
4. Alexander McQueen, "Thank the Silent Barber," *VEND*, November 1953.
5. Schreiber, *A Concise History of Vending in the USA*.
6. Ibid.
7. Ibid.
8. The Automat History, http://www.theautomat.com/inside/history/history.html/.
9. Schreiber, *A Concise History of Vending in the USA*.
10. Harold Davidson, interview.
11. Davre Davidson, interview by Brian Gail, Beverly Hills, California, 8 August 1994.
12. Ibid.
13. Sidney Furst and Milton Sherman, eds., *Business Decisions That Changed Our Lives* (New York: Random House, 1964).
14. "From Penny Peanuts to Industry Leader ... a Uniquely American Success Story."
15. Ibid.
16. Ibid.
17. Harold Davidson, "Charlotte Davidson Eulogy," 21 March 1999.
18. Jim Hodgson, interview by Jeffrey L. Rodengen, digital recording, 24 March 2005, Write Stuff Enterprises, Inc.
19. Furst and Sherman, *Business Decisions That Changed Our Lives*.
20. Davre Davidson, interview.
21. "From Penny Peanuts to Industry Leader ... a Uniquely American Success Story."
22. Ibid.
23. Davre Davidson, interview.
24. "Conversations with the Chairman of the Board of ARA Services, William S. Fishman," Knipes–Cohen Associates.

## Chapter One Sidebar: Davre Davidson

1. Davre Davidson, interview by Brian Gail, Beverly Hills, California, 8 August 1994.
2. Ibid.
3. Harold Davidson, interview by Jeffrey L. Rodengen, digital recording, 20 April 2005, Write Stuff Enterprises, Inc.

## Chapter One Sidebar: Charlotte Davidson

1. Harold Davidson, interview by Jeffrey L. Rodengen, digital recording, 20 April 2005, Write Stuff Enterprises, Inc.
2. *Dreamers and Doers*, ARAMARK Frontline Managers Meeting, 19 September 1994.

## Chapter One Sidebar: Bill Fishman

1. "Conversations with the Chairman of the Board of ARA Services, William S. Fishman," Knipes–Cohen Associates.
2. Harold Davidson, interview by Jeffrey L. Rodengen, digital recording, 20 April 2005, Write Stuff Enterprises, Inc.
3. Ron Davenport, interview by Jeffrey L. Rodengen, digital recording, 9 March 2005, Write Stuff Enterprises, Inc.
4. "From Penny Peanuts to Industry Leader ... a Uniquely American Success Story," ARA Services, Inc., 28 December 1981.
5. "Conversations with the Chairman of the Board of ARA Services, William S. Fishman."

## Chapter Two

1. William Hammack, "The Greatest Discovery Since Fire," *Invention and Technology*, http://www.AmericanHeritage.com/.
2. Timeline of SRI International Innovations: 1946–1960, http://www.sri.com/about/timeline/.
3. Gerson Miller, interview by Jeffrey L. Rodengen, digital recording, 10 August 2005, Write Stuff Enterprises, Inc.
4. "Conversations with the Chairman of the Board of ARA Services, William S. Fishman," Knipes–Cohen Associates.
5. Ibid.
6. Ibid.
7. Ibid.
8. Ibid.
9. Ibid.
10. Davre Davidson, interview by Brian Gail, Beverly Hills, California, 8 August 1994.
11. Harold Davidson, interview by Jeffrey L. Rodengen, digital recording, 20 April 2005, Write Stuff Enterprises, Inc.
12. Jim Hodgson, interview by Jeffrey L. Rodengen, digital recording, 24 March 2005, Write Stuff Enterprises, Inc.
13. Davre Davidson, interview.

## Chapter Three

1. "Conversations with the Chairman of the Board of ARA Services, William S. Fishman," Knipes–Cohen Associates.
2. Jim Hodgson, interview by Jeffrey L. Rodengen, digital recording, 24 March 2005, Write Stuff Enterprises, Inc.
3. Gerson Miller, interview by Jeffrey L. Rodengen, digital recording, 10 August 2005, Write Stuff Enterprises, Inc.
4. Harold Davidson, interview by Jeffrey L. Rodengen, digital recording, 20 April 2005, Write Stuff Enterprises, Inc.
5. Martin Spector, interview by Jeffrey L. Rodengen, digital recording, 29 March 2005, Write Stuff Enterprises, Inc.
6. "From Penny Peanuts to Industry Leader … a Uniquely American Success Story," ARA Services, Inc., 28 December 1981.
7. Lee Driscoll, interview by Jeffrey L. Rodengen, digital recording, 10 March 2005, Write Stuff Enterprises, Inc.
8. *ARA and America's Service Industry: 25 Years at the Cutting Edge of Change* (Philadelphia: ARA Services, Inc., 1984).
9. "20th ARA Anniversary 1959/1979," *ARA Services News*, ARA Services, Inc., Spring 1979.
10. "Conversations with the Chairman of the Board of ARA Services, William S. Fishman."
11. Ibid.
12. Ibid.
13. John H. Slater, "Of Food and Feathers," *Pennsylvania Gazette*, 1977.
14. Harold Davidson, interview by GailForce Communications, Inc., 28 February 2000.
15. Driscoll, interview.
16. Ibid.
17. Ibid.
18. "From Penny Peanuts to Industry Leader … a Uniquely American Success Story."
19. "Conversations with the Chairman of the Board of ARA Services, William S. Fishman."
20. Ibid.
21. Davidson, interview.
22. Ibid.
23. Ibid.
24. Driscoll, interview.
25. Annual report, ARA Services, Inc., 1962.

## Chapter Three Sidebar: ARA Conference

1. *ARA Services News*, ARA Services, Inc., December 1963.
2. Ibid.
3. Ibid.
4. Ibid.

## Chapter Three Sidebar: Slater System

1. Joan Voli, interview by Jeffrey L. Rodengen, digital recording, 9 August 2005, Write Stuff Enterprises, Inc.
2. John H. Slater, "Of Food and Feathers," *Pennsylvania Gazette*, 1977.

## Chapter Three Sidebar: Project Cafeteria Freeman

1. "20th ARA Anniversary 1959/1979," *ARA Services News*, ARA Services, Inc., Spring 1979.

## Chapter Three Sidebar: Notable Stadiums and Arenas

1. Sean Rooney, interview by Jeffrey L. Rodengen, digital recording, 29 June 2005, Write Stuff Enterprises, Inc.

## Chapter Three Sidebar: The Olympic Games

1. "Types of Foods Served," *ARA Services News*, ARA Services, Inc., 1968.
2. Matthew Robb and Nancy C. Robb, "Feeding Olympian Appetites," *Today's Dietitian*, Volume 7, No. 1.

## Chapter Four

1. Harry Belinger, interview by Jeffrey L. Rodengen, digital recording, 30 March 2005, Write Stuff Enterprises, Inc.
2. Ibid.

3. "Unsung Success Story," *Forbes*, 18 September 1978.
4. Ibid.
5. Gerson Miller, interview by Jeffrey L. Rodengen, digital recording, 10 August 2005, Write Stuff Enterprises, Inc.
6. "Unsung Success Story."
7. Davre Davidson, "Farewell Message to Employees," ARA Services, Inc., 15 July 1977.
8. Joan Voli, interview by Jeffrey L. Rodengen, digital recording, 9 August 2005, Write Stuff Enterprises, Inc.
9. William Fishman, taped interview, tape 9.
10. Martin Spector, interview by Jeffrey L. Rodengen, digital recording, 29 March 2005, Write Stuff Enterprises, Inc.
11. *ARA Services News*, April 1978.
12. *ARA Services News*, March 1977.
13. Davre Davidson, 80th birthday remarks, October 1991.
14. "Farewell Message to Employees."
15. "Work Wear Rental Services in U.S. Merges with ARA," *The ARA Management Review*, ARA Services, Inc., July 1977.
16. *ARA Services News*, March 1979.
17. William S. Fishman, "Developing a New Industry: Service Management," The Newcomen Society in North America, 20 January 1977.

**Chapter Four Sidebar:**
**From Work Wear to ARATEX**

1. Miles Corwin, "Legendary Laundry Still Growing," *San Jose Mercury*, 17 January 1980.

**Chapter Four Sidebar:**
**The 1970s Economy and ARA Services**

1. Annual report, ARA Services, Inc., 1975.

2. Annual report, ARA Services, Inc., 1979.

**Chapter Four Sidebar:**
**Developing a New Industry:**
**Service Management**

1. William S. Fishman, "Developing a New Industry: Service Management," The Newcomen Society in North America, 20 January 1977.

**Chapter Five**

1. Joe Neubauer, interview by Jeffrey L. Rodengen, digital recording, 11 March 2005, Write Stuff Enterprises, Inc.
2. Neubauer, interview.
3. Ibid.
4. Ibid.
5. Ibid.
6. Chris Hackem, interview by Jeffrey L. Rodengen, digital recording, 23 March 2005, Write Stuff Enterprises, Inc.
7. Annual report, ARA Services, Inc., 1981.
8. Harry Belinger, interview by Jeffrey L. Rodengen, digital recording, 30 March 2005, Write Stuff Enterprises, Inc.
9. Neubauer, interview.
10. Lee Driscoll, interview by Jeffrey L. Rodengen, digital recording, 10 March 2005, Write Stuff Enterprises, Inc.
11. Jim Hodgson, interview by Jeffrey L. Rodengen, digital recording, 24 March 2005, Write Stuff Enterprises, Inc.
12. Lynn McKee, interview by Jeffrey L. Rodengen, digital recording, 19 April 2005, Write Stuff Enterprises, Inc.
13. Driscoll, interview.
14. Neubauer, interview.
15. Martin Spector, interview by Jeffrey L. Rodengen, digital recording, 29 March 2005, Write Stuff Enterprises, Inc.
16. McKee, interview.
17. Ron Davenport, interview by Jeffrey L. Rodengen, digital

recording, 9 March 2005, Write Stuff Enterprises, Inc.
18. Neubauer, interview.
19. Annual report, ARA Services, Inc., 1981.
20. Spector, interview.
21. Ibid.
22. Fred Sutherland, interview by Jeffrey L. Rodengen, digital recording, 10 March 2005, Write Stuff Enterprises, Inc.
23. Hodgson, interview.
24. "Unsung Success Story," *Forbes*, 18 September 1978.
25. Joe Neubauer, "The Service Industry: Maintaining the Competitive Edge," Town Hall of California, Los Angeles, 16 March 1982.
26. Ibid.

**Chapter Five Sidebar:**
**Joe Neubauer**

1. *Only in America: Opportunity Still Knocks* (Alexandria, Virginia: Horatio Alger Association of Distinguished Americans, 1994).
2. Ibid.
3. Ibid.
4. Ibid.
5. Ibid.

**Chapter Six**

1. Management Information Bulletin, ARA Services, Inc.
2. *ARA Services News*, ARA Services, Inc., June 1994.
3. *Barron's Investment News and Views*, 10 January 1983.
4. Joe Neubauer, interview by Jeffrey L. Rodengen, digital recording, 11 March 2005, Write Stuff Enterprises, Inc.
5. Jim Hodgson, interview by Jeffrey L. Rodengen, digital recording, 24 March 2005, Write Stuff Enterprises, Inc.
6. *ARA Services News*, September 1983.

7. Press release, ARA Services, Inc., 1983.
8. *The ARA Management Review*, ARA Services, Inc., January 1984.
9. *ARA Services News*, May 1984.
10. Daniel P. Puzo, "Feeding the Olympic Flame Entourage," *Los Angeles Times*, 19 July 1984.
11. *The ARA Management Review*, ARA Services, Inc., October 1983.
12. "ARA Goes for the Gold," *Focus*, 9 May 1984.
13. *ARA Services News Special Report*, ARA Services, Inc., September 1984.
14. "ARA Goes for the Gold."
15. Ibid.
16. *ARA Services News*, Special Report.
17. Ira Cohn, interview by Jeffrey L. Rodengen, digital recording, 18 April 2005, Write Stuff Enterprises, Inc.
18. News Release, ARA Services, Inc., 29 September 1983.
19. Ellen Kurtz, "Help!! ... How Am I Supposed to Get to 26 Events in This Mess?" *SportsNow*, July 1984.
20. "ARA Goes for the Gold."
21. Ibid.
22. Annual report, ARA Services, Inc., 1983.
23. Annual report, 1984.
24. Terry Bivens, "ARA's Olympian Operations," *The Philadelphia Inquirer*, 16 January 1984.
25. Neubauer, interview.
26. Ibid.
27. Ibid.
28. Phyllis Berman with John Gorham, "Sweaty Equity," *Forbes*, 1 December 1997.
29. Neubauer, interview.
30. Ibid.
31. Hodgson, interview.
32. Martin Spector, interview by Jeffrey L. Rodengen, digital recording, 29 March 2005, Write Stuff Enterprises, Inc.

33. Charles Bernstein, "How ARA's LBO Overcame the Odds: Chemistry, Integrity, Employee Equity," *Nation's Restaurant News*, Volume 24, No. 60.
34. Fred Sutherland, interview by Jeffrey L. Rodengen, digital recording, 10 March 2005, Write Stuff Enterprises, Inc.
35. Neubauer, interview.
36. Spector, interview.
37. Neubauer, interview.
38. Lee Driscoll, interview by Jeffrey L. Rodengen, digital recording, 10 March 2005, Write Stuff Enterprises, Inc.
39. "How ARA's LBO Overcame the Odds: Chemistry, Integrity, Employee Equity."
40. Ibid.
41. Sutherland, interview.
42. Annual report, ARA Services, Inc., 1983.
43. Lynn McKee, interview by Jeffrey L. Rodengen, digital recording, 19 April 2005, Write Stuff Enterprises, Inc.
44. Harold Davidson, "Eulogy for Davre J. Davidson," 22 May 1995.
45. Ron Davenport, interview by Jeffrey L. Rodengen, digital recording, 9 March 2005, Write Stuff Enterprises, Inc.
46. Neubauer, interview.
47. Ibid.
48. Harry Belinger, interview by Jeffrey L. Rodengen, digital recording, 30 March 2005, Write Stuff Enterprises, Inc.
49. McKee, interview.
50. "Sweaty Equity."
51. Hodgson, interview.
52. Neubauer, interview.
53. Spector, interview.
54. Fred Sutherland, interview with *Cash Flow* magazine, September 1987.
55. Neubauer, interview.
56. "ARA Services: Brainy and Brawny and on the March," *Nation's Restaurant News*, December 1990.

57. "How ARA's LBO Overcame the Odds: Chemistry, Integrity, Employee Equity."
58. Davenport, interview.
59. "How ARA's LBO Overcame the Odds: Chemistry, Integrity, Employee Equity."
60. "ARA Services: Brainy and Brawny and on the March."

**Chapter Six Sidebar:
1984 Olympic Games**

1. Robert Ajemian, "Master of the Games," *Time*, 7 January 1985.
2. Ibid.
3. Ibid.

**Chapter Six Sidebar:
America's Hostile
Environment in the 1980s**

1. Charles V. Bagli, "The Civilized Hostile Takeover: New Breed of Wolf at Corporate Door," *The New York Times*, 19 March 1997.
2. *Dreamers and Doers*, ARAMARK Frontline Managers Meeting, 19 September 1994.
3. Fred Sutherland, interview by Jeffrey L. Rodengen, digital recording, 10 March 2005, Write Stuff Enterprises, Inc.
4. Jim Hodgson, interview by Jeffrey L. Rodengen, digital recording, 24 March 2005, Write Stuff Enterprises, Inc.

**Chapter Six Sidebar:
Management Buyouts**

1. James Cook, "A Buyout That Worked," *Forbes*, 23 July 1990.
2. Ibid.
3. American Capital. "Management Buyouts— Basics," http:// www.americancapital.com/.

**Chapter Six Sidebar:**
**ARA's Streetwise Leaders**

1. Robert J. Callander, interview by Jeffrey L. Rodengen, digital recording, 21 March 2005, Write Stuff Enterprises, Inc.

**Chapter Seven**

1. "From the Chairman's Desk," *The ARA Management Review*, January 1989.
2. Terry Bivens, "Buyout Is Just the Latest Landmark in the Odyssey of ARA's Savvy Chief," *The Philadelphia Inquirer*, 7 January 1985.
3. Joe Neubauer, interview by Jeffrey L. Rodengen, digital recording, 20 October 2005, Write Stuff Enterprises, Inc.
4. Joe Neubauer, Oral History Project interview, 1990, ARA Services, Inc.
5. Terry Bivens, "A Private ARA Gears Up for Competition," *The Philadelphia Inquirer*, 8 December 1986.
6. Fred Sutherland, interview by Jeffrey L. Rodengen, digital recording, 10 March 2005, Write Stuff Enterprises, Inc.
7. "ARA Is Running Strong, Paying Debt and Turning a Profit Since Buyout," *The Wall Street Journal*, 26 June 1986.
8. Ibid.
9. "A Private ARA Gears Up for Competition."
10. Joe Neubauer, "ARA's Post-LBO Strategy: Why a Giant Company Pushed Growth after Going Private," case study, *Mergers & Acquisitions*, November/December 1987.
11. Sutherland, interview.
12. Davre Davidson, speech before ARA Services Executive Corps, 21 October 1991, Dallas, Texas.
13. Neubauer, interview.
14. James Cook, "A Buyout That Worked," *Forbes*, 23 July 1990.
15. "A Private ARA Gears Up for Competition."
16. "ARA's Post-LBO Strategy: Why a Giant Company Pushed Growth after Going Private."
17. "A Private ARA Gears Up for Competition."
18. "A Buyout That Worked."
19. "A Private ARA Gears Up for Competition."
20. "ARA's Post-LBO Strategy: Why a Giant Company Pushed Growth after Going Private."
21. "A Private ARA Gears Up for Competition."
22. Ron Davenport, interview by Jeffrey L. Rodengen, digital recording, 9 March 2005, Write Stuff Enterprises, Inc.
23. Robert J. Callander, interview by Jeffrey L. Rodengen, digital recording, 21 March 2005, Write Stuff Enterprises, Inc.
24. "From the Chairman's Desk," *The ARA Management Review*, April 1987.
25. "From the Chairman's Desk," *The ARA Management Review*, October 1986.
26. "From the Chairman's Desk," *The ARA Management Review*, May 1988.
27. Ibid.
28. Report to employees, ARA Services, Inc., 1986.
29. Report to employees, ARA Services, Inc., 1987.
30. Ibid.
31. Report to employees, ARA Services, Inc., 1988.
32. Report to employees, ARA Services, Inc., 1989.
33. Ibid.
34. Proxy Statement, proposed Stockholder Enhancement Plan, ARA Holding Company, 11 March 1988.
35. "From the Chairman's Desk," *The ARA Management Review*, May 1988.
36. Phyllis Berman with John Gorham, "Sweaty Equity," *Forbes*, 1 December 1997.
37. Frank Allen, "ARA, Betting on Pride, Approves Plan to Give Its Managers Voting Control," *The Wall Street Journal*, 16 March 1988.
38. Ibid.
39. "From the Chairman's Desk," *The ARA Management Review*, May 1988.
40. Report to employees, ARA Services, Inc., 1987.
41. "Sweaty Equity."
42. Neubauer, interview.
43. "A Buyout That Worked."
44. "ARA's Post-LBO Strategy, Why a Giant Company Pushed Growth after Going Private."
45. "A Buyout That Worked."
46. Report to employees, 1988.
47. "From the Chairman's Desk," *The ARA Management Review*, December 1987.
48. Report to employees, 1989.
49. ARA Information Brief, ARA Services, Inc., 1989.
50. "A Buyout That Worked."
51. Ibid.
52. *The ARA Management Review*, July 1987.
53. "A Buyout That Worked."
54. Jack Donovan, interview by Jeffrey L. Rodengen, digital recording, 29 March 2005, Write Stuff Enterprises, Inc.
55. Chris Malone, interview by Jeffrey L. Rodengen, digital recording, 8 August 2005, Write Stuff Enterprises, Inc.
56. "Celebrating 30 Years of Services Innovation: 1959–1989," *ARA Services Times*, 1989.
57. "Working for Customers: A Strategy for Quality in Services," speech by Joe Neubauer, delivered to the American Productivity Center Executive Conference, Dallas, Texas, 1990.
58. Ira R. Cohn, interview by Jeffrey L. Rodengen, digital recording, 18 April 2005, Write Stuff Enterprises, Inc.

59. "From the Chairman's Desk," *The ARA Management Review*, January 1989.

**Chapter Seven Sidebar: Strategic Acquisitions**

1. Report to employees, ARA Services, Inc., 1985.
2. File on ARA Milestone Acquisitions, ARA Services, Inc., 1984–1994.
3. Ibid.
4. Ibid.
5. Ibid.
6. Ibid.
7. Ibid.

**Chapter Seven Sidebar: "Everybody Sells"**

1. Report to employees, ARA Services, Inc., 1987.
2. Ibid.
3. Ibid.

**Chapter Seven Sidebar: "Goodbye One Reading; Hello ARA Tower"**

1. Gary Thompson, "Goodbye 1 Reading, Hello ARA Tower," *Philadelphia Daily News*, 14 December 1984.
2. *Tower Talk*, ARA Services Bulletin, July 1985.
3. *Tower Talk*, ARA Services Bulletin, January 1986.

**Chapter Eight**

1. Joe Neubauer, interview by Jeffrey L. Rodengen, digital recording, 20 October 2005, Write Stuff Enterprises, Inc.
2. "Neubauer Q&A: What makes ARA tick?" *Nation's Restaurant News*, 17 December 1990.
3. *Update*, ARA Services, Inc., May 1991.
4. Steve Duffy, interview by Jeffrey L. Rodengen, digital recording, 3 March 2006, Write Stuff Enterprises, Inc.

5. Ibid.
6. Terry Bivens, "ARA Is Riding the Crest of a Buyout That Paid Off," *The Philadelphia Inquirer*, 29 April 1991.
7. Ibid.
8. "Business Dining: ARA Aims for Small-business Accounts," *Nation's Restaurant News*, 17 December 1990.
9. "School Nutrition Services Wins Accounts with Educational Efforts," *Nation's Restaurant News*, 17 December 1990.
10. "Ellis Island Opens Door to Tourists, Contract Feeding," *Nation's Restaurant News*, 17 December 1990.
11. "From the Chairman's Desk," *Update*, ARA Services, Inc., January 1991.
12. "The Soul of the Machine," *Nation's Restaurant News*, 17 December 1990.
13. Neubauer, interview.
14. John Orobono, interview by Jeffrey L. Rodengen, digital recording, 10 March 2005, Write Stuff Enterprises, Inc.
15. "Farquharson Named Operator of the Year," *Nation's Restaurant News*, 15 October 1990.
16. "Neubauer Q&A: What makes ARA tick?"
17. *Update*, ARA Services, Inc., July 1991.
18. Ibid.
19. Report to employees, ARA Services, Inc., 1991.
20. Report to employees, ARA Services, Inc., 1992.
21. ARA Information Briefs, 1991 and 1993.
22. Tom Vozzo, interview by Jeffrey L. Rodengen, digital recording, 9 March 2005, Write Stuff Enterprises, Inc.
23. Report to employees, 1992.
24. *ARA Inside Report*, April 1993.
25. *Update*, ARA Services, Inc., July/August 1992.

26. *Update*, ARA Services, Inc., May/June 1992.
27. Ibid.
28. *Update*, ARA Services, Inc., July/August 1992.
29. Sean Rooney, interview by Jeffrey L. Rodengen, digital recording, 29 June 2005, Write Stuff Enterprises, Inc.
30. "From the Chairman's Desk," *Update*, ARA Services, Inc., May/June 1992.
31. Report to employees, 1992.
32. *Update*, ARA Services, Inc., July 1994.
33. Ibid.
34. *Update*, ARA Services, Inc., October/November 1994.
35. *Update*, ARA Services, Inc., January/February 1993.
36. Ibid.
37. *Update*, ARA Services, Inc., November 1993.
38. "ARA Services Is Leading Corporation in Global Service Management Marketplace," PR Newswire Association, Inc., 16 July 1993.
39. *Update*, ARA Services, Inc., November 1993.
40. Steve Duffy, interview by Jeffrey L. Rodengen, digital recording, 3 March 2006, Write Stuff Enterprises, Inc.
41. "From the Chairman's Desk," *Update*, ARA Services, Inc., January/February 1993.
42. Rooney, interview.
43. Dan Jameson, interview by Jeffrey L. Rodengen, digital recording, 12 August 2005, Write Stuff Enterprises, Inc.
44. Report to employees, ARA Services, Inc., 1994.
45. *Update*, ARA Services, Inc., November 1993.
46. Report to employees, 1994.
47. *ARA Inside Report*, ARA Services, Inc., February 1994.
48. Report to employees, 1994.
49. *ARA Inside Report*, February 1994.

50. "ARA Services Is at Forefront of Emerging School Food Service Trends in 90s," PR Newswire Association, Inc., 9 September 1993.
51. "National Parks Are on Itinerary of Summer Vacationers," PR Newswire Association, Inc., 29 April 1994.
52. "ARA Named New Food Service Manager at Dodger Stadium," PR Newswire Association, Inc., 7 June 1994.
53. "Food Distribution Firm Will Close," *The Philadelphia Inquirer*, 25 June 1994.
54. Fred Sutherland, interview by Jeffrey L. Rodengen, digital recording, 10 March 2005, Write Stuff Enterprises, Inc.
55. *Update*, ARA Services, Inc., October/November 1994.
56. Ibid.
57. "ARAMARK Swallows Harry M. Stevens Like a Slice of Personal Pizza," Snowden Publications, Inc., Business Dateline, 11 January 1995.
58. "ARAMARK Buys Longtime Vendor Harry M. Stevens," *The Philadelphia Inquirer*, 13 December 1994.
59. *Update*, ARA Services, Inc., July 1994.
60. *Update*, ARA Services, Inc., October/November 1994.
61. Ibid.
62. "ARA Switches Names to ARAMARK," *The Denver Post*, 11 October 1994.
63. Report to employees, 1994.

**Chapter Eight Sidebar:
An Intellectual Visionary:
William S. Fishman**

1. *Update*, ARA Services, Inc., July 1991.
2. Joan Voli, interview by Jeffrey L. Rodengen, digital recording, 9 August 2005, Write Stuff Enterprises, Inc.

**Chapter Eight Sidebar:
Olympic and Ballpark Food
over the Years**

1. *Update*, ARA Services, Inc., July 1990.
2. Marco R. della Cava, "Ballpark Food Is Haute Stuff," *USA Today*, 4 April 2003.
3. *Update*, ARA Services, Inc., March 1994.
4. *Update*, ARA Services, Inc., July 1990.
5. Ibid.
6. "ARAMARK Awaits Hungry, Thirsty Fans at Cavs Home Opener at Gund Arena," PR Newswire Association, Inc., 7 November 1994.
7. Report to employees, ARA Services, Inc., 1992.
8. *Update*, ARA Services, Inc., July/August, 1992.
9. *Update*, March 1994.
10. Ibid.
11. Jack Donovan, interview by Jeffrey L. Rodengen, digital recording, 29 March 2005, Write Stuff Enterprises, Inc.

**Chapter Nine**

1. *Update*, ARAMARK, February 1995.
2. "Jambalaya, Gumbo and Alligator Sausage: ARAMARK Prepares for 1995 Sugar Bowl," PR Newswire Association, Inc., 30 December 1994.
3. "ACOG Selects Nine-time Olympic Veteran ARAMARK as Food Service Manager," Business Wire, Inc., 1 March 1995.
4. "ARAMARK Fuses Domestic, International Operations into Global Division," *Nation's Restaurant News*, 6 March 1995.
5. *The Mark*, ARAMARK, May 1995.
6. "ARAMARK Named to Disney Cast in Orlando," Business Wire, Inc., 16 March 1995.

7. Joe Neubauer, keynote speech at the Wharton School leadership conference, 13 May 1999.
8. *Update*, ARA Services, Inc., October/November 1994.
9. Phyllis Berman with John Gorham, "Sweaty Equity," *Forbes*, 1 December 1997.
10. Neubauer, keynote speech.
11. "On the Mark," *Human Resource Executive Magazine*, May 1996.
12. Ibid.
13. Ibid.
14. All statistics from 1995–1996 reports to employees, *Update*, and *The Mark*.
15. *The Mark*, ARAMARK, December 1995.
16. *The Mark*, ARAMARK, August 1995.
17. Ibid.
18. Tom Vozzo, interview by Jeffrey L. Rodengen, digital recording, 9 March 2005, Write Stuff Enterprises, Inc.
19. *The Mark*, ARAMARK, August 1995.
20. James E. Preston, interview by Jeffrey L. Rodengen, digital recording, 19 April 2005, Write Stuff Enterprises, Inc.
21. *The Mark*, December 1995.
22. Ibid.
23. Ibid.
24. Ibid.
25. Report to employees, ARAMARK, 1995.
26. Report to employees, ARAMARK, 1996.
27. *The Mark*, ARAMARK, September 1996.
28. "ARAMARK to Be Food Provider for New Sprint Headquarters," *Nation's Restaurant News*, 15 June 1998.
29. "Neubauer Q&A: What makes ARA tick," *Nation's Restaurant News*, 17 December 1990.
30. "Sweaty Equity."
31. Report to employees, ARAMARK, 1997.

32. Report to employees, 1996.
33. Report to employees, ARAMARK, 1998.
34. Phyllis Berman with John Gorham, "Sweaty Equity," *Forbes*, 1 December 1997.
35. "Sweaty Equity."
36. Ibid.
37. Report to employees, 1998.
38. "Sweaty Equity."
39. Joe Neubauer, interview by Jeffrey L. Rodengen, digital recording, 20 October 2005, Write Stuff Enterprises, Inc.
40. "ARAMARK Hits the Mark with Latest Goldman, Sachs Cafeteria," *Nation's Restaurant News*, 10 August 1998; "ARAMARK Renovates Ops at University of Tennessee, Del. Accounts," *Nation's Restaurant News*, 14 September 1998.
41. *The Mark*, ARAMARK, May/June 1998.
42. "Sweaty Equity."
43. Lynn McKee, interview by Jeffrey L. Rodengen, digital recording, 19 April 2005, Write Stuff Enterprises, Inc.
44. Ibid.
45. Report to employees, ARAMARK, 1999.
46. Ibid.
47. *The Mark*, ARAMARK, August 1999.
48. "ARAMARK Acquires Most of Restaura," *Automatic Merchandizer*, 1 February 1999.
49. Joe Neubauer, prepared speech, Human Resources Conference, 27 September 1999.
50. *The Mark*, ARAMARK, December 1999.
51. Ibid.
52. Ibid.
53. Ibid.
54. Ibid.
55. Ibid.
56. Ibid.
57. Ibid.
58. Ibid.
59. McKee, interview.

**Chapter Nine Sidebar:
Reinventing the Uniform Business**

1. Report to employees, ARA Services, Inc., 1991.
2. Tom Vozzo, interview by Jeffrey L. Rodengen, digital recording, 9 March 2005, Write Stuff Enterprises, Inc.
3. *The Mark*, ARAMARK, March 1996.
4. Samuel Coxs, interview by Jeffrey L. Rodengen, digital recording, 2 March 2006, Write Stuff Enterprises, Inc.
5. Report to employees, ARAMARK, 1996.
6. Vozzo, interview.
7. *The Mark*, ARAMARK, May/June 1999.

**Chapter Nine Sidebar:
Davre Davidson**

1. *Update*, ARA Services, Inc., November/December 1991.
2. *The Mark*, ARAMARK, August 1995.
3. Ibid.
4. Harold Davidson, "Charlotte Davidson Eulogy," 21 March 1999.
5. Press release, ARAMARK, 19 May 1995.
6. "Charlotte Davidson Eulogy."
7. *Inside Report*, special issue, ARAMARK, June 1995.
8. *The Mark*, ARAMARK, February 1998.

**Chapter Nine Sidebar:
Managing the 1996 Summer Olympic Games**

1. "Biggest Olympic Grocery List Ever," Business Wire, Inc., 1 March 1995.
2. *The Mark*, ARAMARK, September 1996.
3. "A Look Behind the Scenes: ARAMARK's Olympic Diary," *Nation's Restaurant News*, 29 July 1996.
4. "A Look Behind the Scenes: ARAMARK's Olympic Diary."

5. *The Mark*, ARAMARK, September 1996.
6. Ibid.

**Chapter Ten**

1. Report to employees, ARAMARK, 2000.
2. "Nowhere But Up For ARAMARK," *The Food Institute Report*, 20 May 2002.
3. "ARAMARK Gets Ogden Food Units," *The Philadelphia Inquirer*, 31 March 2000.
4. "ARAMARK Acquires CFM," *Food Management*, 1 January 2001.
5. Report to employees, 2000.
6. Ibid.
7. "Gourmet Coffee: The New Employee Perk," PR Newswire Association, Inc., 30 June 2000.
8. Report to employees, 2000.
9. "ARAMARK Lands Boeing," *The Mark*, ARAMARK, July 2000.
10. "ARAMARK Wins World's Largest Foodservice Contract in Deal with Boeing," Business Wire, Inc., 20 June 2000.
11. Report to employees, 2000.
12. Ibid.
13. Ibid.
14. Ibid.
15. "ARAMARK Uniform Services Acquires Sunshine Uniform Rental in Orlando," Business Wire, Inc., 15 February 2000.
16. "ARAMARK Uniform Services Acquires Crescent," Business Wire, Inc., 16 May 2000.
17. Joe Neubauer, interview by Jeffrey L. Rodengen, digital recording, 11 March 2005, Write Stuff Enterprises, Inc.
18. Fred Sutherland, interview by Jeffrey L. Rodengen, digital recording, 10 March 2005, Write Stuff Enterprises, Inc.
19. Neubauer, interview.
20. Chris Gutek, interview by Jeffrey L. Rodengen, digital

recording, 19 August 2005, Write Stuff Enterprises, Inc.
21. Ibid.
22. "ARAMARK Announcement Begins a New Chapter," *The Mark*, ARAMARK, November 2001.
23. Ibid.
24. Sutherland, interview.
25. "ARAMARK Signs Agreement to Acquire Managed Services Division of ServiceMaster," *The Mark*, ARAMARK, November 2001.
26. Sutherland, interview.
27. Annual report, ARAMARK, 2001.
28. Lynn McKee, interview by Jeffrey L. Rodengen, digital recording, 19 April 2005, Write Stuff Enterprises, Inc.
29. *The Mark*, special issue, ARAMARK, October 2001.
30. Ibid.
31. Ibid.
32. Sutherland, interview.
33. McKee, interview.
34. Ibid.
35. John J. Lynch, III, interview by Jeffrey L. Rodengen, digital recording, 7 March 2006, Write Stuff Enterprises, Inc.
36. Ibid.
37. Neubauer, interview.
38. "ARAMARK Returns," *The Mark*, special issue, ARAMARK, January 2002.
39. Alexandra Kirkman, "ARAMARK's Entrée," *Forbes Global*, 27 May 2002.
40. Sutherland, interview.
41. "ARAMARK Returns."
42. Ibid.
43. Ibid.
44. Annual report, ARAMARK, 2002.
45. Ibid.
46. *The Mark*, ARAMARK September 2002.
47. "A Plant for the 21st Century," *Textile Rental Magazine*, April 2001.
48. Rory Loberg, interview by Jeffrey L. Rodengen, digital recording, 10 March 2005,

Write Stuff Enterprises, Inc.
49. "ARAMARK Finds a Welcome Return at NYSE," *The Philadelphia Inquirer*, 12 December 2001.
50. *The Mark*, ARAMARK, July 2001.
51. "ARAMARK's Entrée."
52. Ibid.
53. Nanette Byrnes, "The Good CEO," *BusinessWeek*, 23 September 2002.
54. "ARAMARK's Entrée."
55. Chris Malone, interview by Jeffrey L. Rodengen, digital recording, 8 August 2005, Write Stuff Enterprises, Inc.
56. ARAMARK copy of *FORTUNE*® magazine, America's Most Admired Companies, 15 April to 31 May 2002.
57. *The Mark*, ARAMARK, May 2002.
58. "ARAMARK Expands 40-Year Partnership with Ford," Business Wire, Inc., 5 November 2002.
59. *The Mark*, ARAMARK, May 2002.

**Chapter Ten Sidebar:
Extending Facilities Services
Solutions**

1. Annual report, ARAMARK, 2001.
2. Andrew Kerin, interview by Jeffrey L. Rodengen, digital recording, 10 March 2005, Write Stuff Enterprises, Inc.
3. Frank Mendicino, interview by Jeffrey L. Rodengen, digital recording, 10 March 2005, Write Stuff Enterprises, Inc.
4. John Babiarz, interview by Jeffrey L. Rodengen, digital recording, 30 March 2005, Write Stuff Enterprises, Inc.
5. Mendicino, interview.
6. "ARAMARK Completes Acquisition of Facility Services Business from ServiceMaster," Business Wire, Inc., 30 November 2001.

7. ARAMARK and Pfizer Build on 40-Year Partnership with New Facility Services Contract," Business Wire, Inc., 19 March 2002.

**Chapter 10 Sidebar:
The Aftermath of Tragedy**

1. Corporate e-mail, ARAMARK, 11 September 2001.
2. Ibid.
3. Corporate e-mail, ARAMARK, 24 September 2001.
4. *The Mark*, special issue, ARAMARK, October 2001.
5. Ibid.
6. Ibid.

**Chapter Ten Sidebar:
America's Most Admired**

1. Press release, ARAMARK, 21 February 2006.
2. "ARAMARK Reaches Top 50 on *FORTUNE*® Most Admired Companies List," *The Mark*, ARAMARK, May 2002.
3. Ibid.
4. Ibid.
5. Press release, 21 February 2006.

**Chapter Ten Sidebar:
Trusted Financial Partnerships**

1. Fred Sutherland, interview by Jeffrey L. Rodengen, digital recording, 10 March 2005, Write Stuff Enterprises, Inc.
2. Joe Neubauer, interview by Jeffrey L. Rodengen, digital recording, 11 March 2005, Write Stuff Enterprises, Inc.
3. Ibid.
4. Ibid.
5. Jack Curtin, interview by Jeffrey L. Rodengen, digital recording, 7 March 2006, Write Stuff Enterprises, Inc.
6. Ibid.
7. Ibid.
8. Ibid.
9. Ibid.
10. Ibid.

### Chapter Eleven

1. Annual report, ARAMARK, 2003.
2. Ibid.
3. Tim Cost, interview by Jeffrey L. Rodengen, digital recording, 11 March 2005, Write Stuff Enterprises, Inc.
4. James C. Collins and Jerry I. Porras, *Built to Last: Successful Habits of Visionary Companies* (New York: HarperCollins Publishers, 1997).
5. "ARAMARK Managers Energized, Ready to Double Company Sales," *The Mark*, ARAMARK, March 2003.
6. Ibid.
7. "At Your Service: ARAMARK Has Thrived Providing Services to Diverse Companies," *The Post-Standard*, 21 April 2003.
8. Bob Carpenter, interview by Jeffrey L. Rodengen, digital recording, 10 March 2005, Write Stuff Enterprises, Inc.
9. "ARAMARK: On-Site Company Targets Partnerships with Clients and Vendors in Attempt to Hit Financial Bull's-eye," *Nation's Restaurant News*, 18 August 2003.
10. Andrew Kerin, interview by Jeffrey L. Rodengen, digital recording, 10 March 2005, Write Stuff Enterprises, Inc.
11. Chris M. Hackem, interview by Jeffrey L. Rodengen, digital recording, 23 March 2005, Write Stuff Enterprises, Inc.
12. "ARAMARK Expands Long-Term Partnership with Barton College," Business Wire, Inc., 27 February 2003.
13. David Roselle, interview by Jeffrey L. Rodengen, digital recording, 3 March 2006, Write Stuff Enterprises, Inc.
14. Annual report, ARAMARK, 2003.
15. "ARAMARK Expands in Europe with Acquisition of Food Service Company in Spain," Business Wire, Inc., 19 September 2003.
16. "ARAMARK to Sell Child Care Group," *The Daily Deal*, 5 March 2003.
17. "ARAMARK Introduces Unique Training Program for Frontline Service Employees," PR Newswire Association, Inc., 14 May 2003.
18. John Babiarz, interview by Jeffrey L. Rodengen, digital recording, 30 March 2005, Write Stuff Enterprises, Inc.
19. "ARAMARK Named Most Admired Outsourcing Company in New *FORTUNE*® Ranking," Business Wire, Inc., 24 February 2003.
20. "ARAMARK to Remain for at Least 15 Years," *The Philadelphia Inquirer*, 17 December 2003.
21. Chris Gutek, interview by Jeffrey L. Rodengen, digital recording, 19 August 2005, Write Stuff Enterprises, Inc.
22. Annual report, 2004.
23. Joe Neubauer, interview by Jeffrey L. Rodengen, digital recording, 20 October 2005, Write Stuff Enterprises, Inc.
24. Frank Mendicino, interview by Jeffrey L. Rodengen, digital recording, 10 March 2005, Write Stuff Enterprises, Inc.
25. "Olympic Chef Brown Takes Cooking Skills to Athens," High Point Enterprise, 25 June 2004.
26. "Supersized Summer Olympics in Athens," Associated Press, 18 July 2004.
27. "ARAMARK Goes for Gold as Olympics Foodservice Provider," *Nation's Restaurant News*, 7 July 2004.
28. Annual report, ARAMARK, 2004.
29. Annual report, ARAMARK, 2005.
30. Zelda Casanova, interview by Jeffrey L. Rodengen, digital recording, 27 January 2006, Write Stuff Enterprises, Inc.
31. Jack Donovan, interview by Jeffrey L. Rodengen, digital recording, 29 March 2005, Write Stuff Enterprises, Inc.
32. Richard Wyckoff, interview by Jeffrey L. Rodengen, digital recording, 4 May 2006, Write Stuff Enterprises, Inc.
33. Ravi Saligram, interview by Jeffrey L. Rodengen, digital recording, 9 March 2005, Write Stuff Enterprises, Inc.
34. Andrew Main, interview by Jeffrey L. Rodengen, digital recording, 29 March 2005, Write Stuff Enterprises, Inc.
35. Thomas Michel, interview by Jeffrey L. Rodengen, digital recording, 19 May 2006, Write Stuff Enterprises, Inc.
36. Keynote speech, Joe Neubauer, ARAMARK Executive Leadership Conference, 15 November 2004.
37. Ibid.
38. "Message from the CEO: Sales Strong, Margins Improve," *The Mark Online*, 16 May 2005.
39. Annual report, 2004.
40. *The Mark Online*, ARAMARK, 1 September 2005.
41. Ibid.
42. Andrew Kerin, interview by Jeffrey L. Rodengen, digital recording, 10 March 2005, Write Stuff Enterprises, Inc.
43. Annual report, ARAMARK, 2005.
44. Ron Davenport, interview by Jeffrey L. Rodengen, digital recording, 9 March 2005, Write Stuff Enterprises, Inc.
45. Press release, ARAMARK, 2006, http://www.aramark.com/.
46. Saligram, interview.

47. Ibid.
48. Ibid.
49. Marty Welch, interview by Jeffrey L. Rodengen, digital recording, 1 June 2006, Write Stuff Enterprises, Inc.
50. Saligram, interview.
51. Ibid.
52. Main, interview.
53. David Blackwood, interview by Jeffrey L. Rodengen, digital recording, 1 June 2006, Write Stuff Enterprises, Inc.
54. Udo Luerssen, interview by Jeffrey L. Rodengen, e-mail, 16 June 2006, Write Stuff Enterprises, Inc.
55. Ibid.
56. Saligram, interview.
57. Annual report, 2005.
58. Fred Sutherland, interview by Jeffrey L. Rodengen, digital recording, 10 March 2005, Write Stuff Enterprises, Inc.
59. John Babiarz, interview by Jeffrey L. Rodengen, digital recording, 30 March 2005, Write Stuff Enterprises, Inc.
60. Norman Miller, interview by Jeffrey L. Rodengen, digital recording, 26 May 2005, Write Stuff Enterprises, Inc.
61. Press release, ARAMARK, 2006.
62. Lynn McKee, interview by Jeffrey L. Rodengen, digital recording, 19 April 2005, Write Stuff Enterprises, Inc.
63. Press release, ARAMARK, 2006.

**Chapter Eleven Sidebar:
Success in Japan**

1. AIM Services Co. Ltd., brochure and Web site, 2005, http://www.AIMservices.co.jp/english/.
2. Hisato Ishida, interview by Jeffrey L. Rodengen, digital recording, 16 May 2006, Write Stuff Enterprises, Inc.
3. AIM Services Co. Ltd., brochure and Web site.
4. Ishida, interview.
5. Annual report, ARAMARK, 2005.
6. Hiroshi Ito, interview by Jeffrey L. Rodengen, digital recording, 6 June 2006, Write Stuff Enterprises, Inc.

**Chapter Eleven Sidebar:
ARAMARK's 24 Hours**

1. Andrew Kerin, interview by Jeffrey L. Rodengen, digital recording, 10 March 2005, Write Stuff Enterprises, Inc.
2. Annual reports, ARAMARK, 2000 to 2005.

**Chapter Eleven Sidebar:
Keeping Students Healthy**

1. Annual report, ARAMARK, 2005.
2. "ARAMARK Launches Innovative Program," press release, ARAMARK, 5 April 2005.
3. Jeff Wheatley, interview by Jeffrey L. Rodengen, digital recording, 10 March 2005, Write Stuff Enterprises, Inc.
4. Ibid.

**Chapter Eleven Sidebar:
A History with Boeing**

1. Laurel Lutz, interview by Jeffrey L. Rodengen, digital recording, 22 February 2006, Write Stuff Enterprises, Inc.
2. Ibid.
3. "ARAMARK Reports $700M Boeing Pact Is Biggest of Its Kind," *Philadelphia Business Journal*, 20 June 2000.
4. "ARAMARK Loses Boeing Food Services Deal," *Seattle Post–Intelligencer*, 17 May 2002.
5. Lutz, interview.

**Chapter Eleven Sidebar:
A Partnership with Banco Santander**

1. Alfonso Palavencio, e-mail interview, 19 June 2006, Write Stuff Enterprises, Inc.
2. Ibid.
3. Ibid.
4. Ibid.
5. Ibid.
6. Ibid.

**Chapter Twelve**

1. Proxy Statement, ARAMARK, United States Security and Exchange Commission, 2006.
2. Ibid.
3. Ibid.
4. "ARAMARK Announces Receipt of 'Going Private' Proposal at $32 Per Share," press release, ARAMARK, 2006.
5. Joe Neubauer, interview by Jeffrey L. Rodengen, digital recording, 18 September 2006, Write Stuff Enterprises, Inc.
6. Chris Holland, interview by Jeffrey L. Rodengen, digital recording, 27 September 2006, Write Stuff Enterprises, Inc.
7. Neubauer, interview.
8. "ARAMARK Announces Receipt of 'Going Private' Proposal at $32 Per Share."
9. "Hot Dog Deal—Chairman Relishes Ballpark Food Big on the Cheap," *The New York Post*, 2 May 2006.
10. Ron Davenport, interview by Jeffrey L. Rodengen, digital recording, 11 September 2006, Write Stuff Enterprises, Inc.
11. Proxy Statement, 2006.
12. Ibid.
13. Davenport, interview.
14. Neubauer, interview.
15. Jack Curtin, interview by Jeffrey L. Rodengen, digital recording, 26 September

2006, Write Stuff Enterprises, Inc.

16. Jamie Grant and Barrett Pickett, interviews by Jeffrey L. Rodengen, digital recording, 20 September 2006, Write Stuff Enterprises, Inc.

17. Ibid.

18. Proxy Statement, 2006.

19. Ibid.

20. Davenport, interview.

21. Ibid.

22. "ARAMARK to Go Private in $8.3 Billion Deal; Board OKs CEO-led Group's Sweetened Offer, 3 Months after a Lower Bid," *Nation's Restaurant News*, 21 August 2006.

23. "The Financial Page—Private Lies," *The New Yorker*, 28 August 2006.

24. Neubauer, interview.

25. Press release, ARAMARK, 2006.

26. Lynn McKee, interview by Jeffrey L. Rodengen, digital recording, 20 September 2006, Write Stuff Enterprises, Inc.

27. Fred Sutherland, interview by Jeffrey L. Rodengen, digital recording, 12 September 2006, Write Stuff Enterprises, Inc.

28. Alan Griffith, interview by Jeffrey L. Rodengen, digital recording, 18 September 2006, Write Stuff Enterprises, Inc.

29. Sutherland, interview.

30. "ARAMARK Announcement Begins a New Chapter," *The Mark*, ARAMARK, November 2001.

**Chapter Twelve Sidebar: The Importance of Ethics**

1. Karen Murray, "Boardroom Bulldog," *Outstanding Directors*, 2005.

2. "Corporate Governance," http://www.aramark.com/.

3. "Boardroom Bulldog."

4. Ibid.

# INDEX

*Page numbers in italics indicate photographs*